RETURNING TO THE FATHER

RETURNING
TO THE
FATHER

Dr. William Gaultiere

MOODY PRESS
CHICAGO

*To the Father
and to those who have revealed Him to me
in ways small and big
in my own journey to the Father:
Dad, Grandpas B. and G., Steve, Dave, Wayne, Fred, and Ike.*

*Also to the other prodigals,
who are returning to Father's house,
and to the elders,
who still need to begin.*

Contents

Gifts of Grace and Steps of Faith

Father's Gifts of Grace	Prodigal's Steps of Faith
1. Free choice	Humility
2. Patience	Accurate perceptions of God and self
3. Seeking love	Trust
4. Compassion	Self-examination
5. Forgiveness	Confession of sin
6. Affection	Reconciliation
7. Robe	Boundaries
8. Ring	Accountability
9. Sandals	Responsible adulthood
10. Feast	Celebration of faith
11. Forgiveness	Forgiving others
12. Purpose	Ministry

Preface

Setting the Stage

Jesus is travelling down a dusty desert road that leads to Jerusalem. Following Him is a mixed crowd. Zealous disciples who have much to learn from Him. Evil-eyed Pharisees and teachers of the law looking to find a "lawful" reason to have Him killed. Despised "sinners" wondering if this man really can set them free from condemnation. And many curious common folk sitting on the fence, not sure about this man who calls God "Father."

The snobbish religious elite can be heard muttering, "This man welcomes sinners and eats with them."

Jesus tells a story.

This story is for the religious leaders and everyone else in the crowd. This story is for you and me.

Like no other story ever told, this story dramatically portrays the Father God's love for us who are lost.

Hurting in our hearts, we need healing. Longing for a father's love, we need to be filled. Caught in a web of sin, we need to be set free. Overwhelmed by problems, we need help. Burdened with responsibilities, we need rest. Bored with life, we need to be revived.

Whatever your need, read this story and you'll find that your loving Father in heaven is looking to find you and to change your life.

But this story isn't only for those who know they need help. It's also for those who don't think that they are the ones who are lost. They focus on the needs and problems of others, sometimes to the neglect of themselves. If this is you, then keep reading, because Jesus' story has something to say to you, too.

What is this story? It's known as "The Parable of the Prodigal Son." Some have called it the greatest short story ever told. It is certainly the most widely read. And everyone who reads it—young and old, religious and secular, scholars and uneducated—all seem to love it.

Yet few who read Jesus' story of the prodigal son really understand its depth. They fail to see clearly themselves and the Father in this story; they don't step inside the drama and encounter Father God's amazing love for themselves; they neglect to follow in the prodigal son's steps as he returns to the father; they, like the elder son, miss out on the celebration of their heavenly Father's love for them.

You needn't be like those who have seen without seeing and heard without hearing. Don't stand off in the distance, casually listening to what Jesus has to say. Don't miss the Father's love.

Instead, leave behind the skeptical folk sitting on the fence in the background. Walk past the hostile Pharisees. Nudge your way through the crowd of tax collectors, prostitutes, beggars, and drunkards, and stand with the eager disciples. Look Jesus in the eye. Open your ears and your heart to His beloved parable. You'll encounter your Father's love for you in a new way.

To be sure, seeing and hearing what the crowd following Jesus saw and heard is no small task. We need to go back in time two thousand years. We need to understand an Eastern culture that is very different from our Western culture. We need to study the meanings of the words, idioms, and phrases that Jesus uses.

Also, we need to appreciate the historical background of this story. Many young Jewish men did just what Prodigal did in the beginning of Jesus' story. They gathered all of their money (though rarely an inheritance), left their family and their village, traveled far away to a big city, chased their dreams, and came to ruin. Prodigal's actions are not out of the ordinary. But the rest of Jesus' story is wholly unexpected and powerfully dramatic.

And perhaps the hardest and yet most important task for us in reading the parable of the prodigal son is to see and hear what Jesus is trying to communicate from His heart. To grasp His message we need to take some time with this story. We need to read between the lines. We need to let Jesus speak to our imaginations and to our hearts.

Let's enter into this amazing story. Pull up a chair and sit at the dinner table. Prodigal, his older brother, and his father are already there. Phillip, the family servant, is serving the food.

Listen and (with the rest of the family) you'll be shocked by Prodigal's cold and callous death wish to his father: "Give me my share of the property which falls to me."

Watch as the starry-eyed Prodigal gallops out of town on a black horse. He's heading far north to the big city of Antioch. He's chasing fleeting fantasies: fortune, fame, fun. And for a moment he has them all. Then he runs out of money and a famine strikes the country. Suddenly the rich nobleman becomes a forgotten beggar. He hits bottom in a smelly pigsty, his stomach knotted in hunger.

Imagine his nightmares of returning home as a beggar to the family and village that he has brought shame upon.

Then learn the lesson he learned in the pigsty. Model his humble courage. Follow him in his journey home across the desert. Return to his Father. You'll be amazed, for his Father will greet you in the same warm way, with grace and love. You'll want to make his Father your Father!

Look and you will see the Father running to you, not with a fist but with arms outstretched. Not with a frown but with tears of compassion in his eyes. Not with anger but with forgiveness filling his heart.

And the Father brings gifts to Prodigal: a hug and a kiss, a robe, a ring, and a pair of sandals. He even hosts a party for his once wayward son! These fatherly gifts change Prodigal's life. Indeed, they are the things that every son or daughter yearns for from a father. The gifts bring with them fatherly blessings of affection, approval, encouragement, affirmation, and honor. Did you receive these gifts from your father? If not, read this parable and learn how your heavenly Father desires to give you these life-changing gifts.

What about Elder, Prodigal's older brother? Where has he been all this time? He's out working in the fields, and he becomes quite angry when he hears the music and dancing and smells the fatted calf—all in honor of this spoiled brother of his whom he hates. But Father will go out to Elder and offer him his sacrificial love just as he did to Prodigal.

Jesus' story ends somehat abruptly; He leaves us in suspense by not telling us how Father's love ultimately affected Prodigal and Elder. However, many weeks after He told the story, Jesus would display the power of the Father's love and forgiveness through Jesus' sacrificial death and eventual resurrection. Thus history reveals the final application of the parable: some countrymen would embrace the Father's love, others would reject it as not acceptable according to the law of Moses. So what about the responses of Prodigal and Elder? We explore their potential responses with a new, quite probable ending to the parable.

What a story this is! To help you step into it and to appreciate its meaning and application to your life, here is a thirteen-part dramatic interpretation of the parable of the prodigal son. I wrote this story after much study and prayer. I think you'll find the narrative to be true to the spirit of Jesus' parable and the teachings of the Bible.

Fifty-two weekly devotional readings will help you understand the powerful truths that come out of the parable of the prodigal son. At the end of each reading are some personal questions, "Footsteps of Faith," that you can follow. These are designed to help you apply Jesus' message to your life and to take the steps you need to take in order to progress on the path to healing and growth that God has for you. You may not want to follow the suggested weekly format exactly, and that's OK. The important thing is that you take the time you need to work through each step.

The parable contains twelve steps of faith that can bring all of us back to a loving relationship with the Father and make us willing sons and daughters. From humility to ministry, these twelves steps are part of the healing journey that can make us strong in a broken, hurting world. The fifty-two devotional readings are divided among the twelve steps of faith the prodigal—and we—must learn in our return to the Father. Put together, the twelve elements of faith form an inspiring and healing journey.

A companion volume to _A Walk with Your Shepherd_ (Moody), _Returning to the Father_ leads you on another journey to wholeness in God. Join me on this journey. Let's follow in the steps of the prodigal son; let's return to the Father.

Acknowledgments

Behind the Scenes

Y ou are about to begin an inspiring journey of drama and healing, as you follow in the footsteps of the prodigal son. The following story should speak to your personal hurts and needs and draw you to the Father's love. Before I raise the curtain, though, let me take you backstage to introduce you to the people and preparations that made this project a reality.

The real inspiration for this book is Jesus. He spoke this incredible parable two thousand years ago in order to describe the Father and to explain how we could return to Him. Not only is He a marvelous storyteller, but Jesus is the Savior and Lord of all who would put faith in Him.

I first read the parable not long after I became a Christian twenty-five years ago, and I loved it. Since then I've reread the story hundreds of times. Each time I meditate on it I learn something new about myself and my Father. Each time, as I pray about its message, I change a little. When I've explained the parable to groups, people have encountered and understood themselves and their Father in new ways. These are the reasons I wrote this book.

In writing this book, I have used many Bible commentaries, handbooks, and other books to gain insight into the background, meaning, and application of Jesus' famous parable. One book—probably the smallest and simplest of all I read—helped me more than any other to grasp the spiritual meaning and dramatic impact the parable had upon its original hearers. That book is *The Cross and the Prodigal* (Concordia), by Kenneth Bailey.

The prodigal's journey home to his Father is one we all need to take; it a journey I am taking. I'm thankful to the people who have influenced my own journey to the Father, especially the Fatherlike men to whom I dedicate this book. I am also thankful to my clients, who have sought my help in their own journeys to the Father. My hours with these courageous people have taught me much about the benefit of healing wounds, changing destructive behaviors, encountering the Father's love, and growing in character.

Publishing a book is a big process, and I'm grateful to the fine people at Moody Press who put this project into print, especially Greg Thornton for believing in me, Jim Bell and Jim Vincent for their editorial expertise, and Bill Thrasher, Sandy Smith, and Heather Rowley for their marketing help. Many thanks also to Rick Christian for his help in developing this project and in handling the business side of things.

Finally, this book would have been much harder to write if it were not for the support of two people. My wife, Kristi, has given me steady support, heartfelt encouragement, and helpful feedback. My son, David, has given me a wonderful inspiration and helped to shape a father's heart in me.

Jesus continued: "There was a man who had two sons. The younger one said to his father, 'Father, give me my share of the estate.' So he divided his property between them.

"Not long after that, the younger son got together all he had [and] set off for a distant country."

*Luke 15:11-13*a

Introduction

Take the Money and Run!

Prodigal was sitting underneath a shady sycamore tree and sucking on a long blade of grass. Surrounding him this late winter afternoon were the calm farmland and rolling green hills of the Galilean countryside. It had been an unusually warm and dry winter. Above him, in the sycamore tree, two birds flitted about from branch to branch as if engaged in a game of tag. They chirped wildly, but Prodigal didn't hear their songs or watch their little game. He was lost in thought.

And Prodigal was wasting the day away, though he would not admit it. He was supposed to be at the market in the nearby village of Nain buying seeds for the planting season, feed for the livestock, and a whole list of food supplies for the family.

Phillip, the head servant for the family, had been preparing one of the fields for the planting of beans. Wondering what was taking Prodigal so long, he went looking for him. '

He found Prodigal sitting underneath the shade tree. Phillip stood in front of him, thrust his hands upon his hips, and said in exasperation, "It's almost sundown! Where's the seed? I have the field all prepared. I've been waiting for you for hours! If I don't plant the beans right away I'll have to wait until tomorrow. And tomorrow I have to plant the cucumbers."

"I didn't go into the village today."

"What do you mean? Why not?" Phillip insisted.

"What's the use? Why plant seed when we've had hardly a drop of rain all season?"

"Prodigal, where's your faith in God? The early rains will come. We just have to be patient. Besides, that's no excuse. Why don't you go into the village like you were supposed to?"

Prodigal's head dropped as he mumbled, "I've been thinking, Phillip."

"Thinking! About what?"

"I don't want to work here on the farm anymore."

"That's obvious!" Phillip laughed.

"No. You don't understand. I'm leaving home. I'm going to ask Father for my inheritance and go up north to Antioch."

"What? You'd waste the family inheritance with foolish living in the big city, a *Gentile* city no less!"

"No, it won't be all fun and games. I'm going to make my fortune and live on my own!"

"Prodigal! Get hold of your mind! This request is a death wish to your father, an insult to him, to the family, to the entire village!"

"I want my inheritance, Phillip!"

"You don't want the responsibility of managing your father's hard-earned estate. You want to do as you please!"

"Yes! Freedom at last!"

"Freedom? Freedom is not in escaping from responsibility and indulging yourself in pleasure. Freedom is in being who you are. Being loved and loving. Living in a way that is right and good, not bound by obligations nor enslaved to selfish impulses."

"Nice philosophy, Phillip. But I want to make something of myself."

"You want to rebel against your father!"

"Elder will be glad to have me gone anyway."

"If you would respect Elder maybe he would treat you better."

"Enough, Phillip! I've heard enough about all that I should do. You're just a servant anyway. What do you know about responsibility and freedom? And how do you know how my father will feel about this?"

Just then Elder strutted up and stood next to Phillip. "Sitting down on the job again, eh, Prodigal? Living up to your name and wasting the day away are you? Well, I ran out of feed for the chickens and the cattle. I've been waiting for you to bring me more. But no, I had to come to you to get it. Where is it?"

There was a long pause; all eyes were on the gnawed blade of grass that Prodigal was spinning around in his fingers. Finally, Phillip spoke and answered, "We'll have to wait until tomorrow, Elder."

"Oh! Not again!" Elder moaned as he threw his arms in the air and then walked away, shaking his head in disgust.

Prodigal looked up at Phillip, "See? That is why I'm leaving."

An hour or so later, after walking back to the house and washing up, Prodigal joined Elder at the dinner table. Phillip was making preparations.

"What a glorious sunset," Father said as he entered the dining area. "Look, sons! God has revealed His beauty to us again, hasn't He?" Then turning around he called, "Say, Phillip, we're ready for dinner." Turning back to Prodigal he said, "Dear son, why do you look so gloomy this evening? You haven't taken in the sunset or—"

Elder interrupted. "Well, Father, I'll tell why we're sharing our meal with a 'Sullen Sour Puss' this evening! While I was working all day harvesting the winter figs Prodigal did nothing!"

"That's not true!" Prodigal defended himself. "Didn't you notice when you were in the barn that I cleaned up the chicken coops. Or that I gave the cattle fresh water. Or—"

Elder interrupted again. "All I know is that you didn't go to the village market like you were supposed to. Instead you were lying under the sycamore tree daydreaming again!"

"Who made you the boss over me, anyway?" Prodigal retorted.

"I'm Elder!"

"Sons! Sons!" Father exclaimed. "How I long for the sun to go down with the two of you at peace! Elder, please mind your own business this evening. Besides, you ought to sit under the sycamore tree yourself now and again instead of working so hard all the time."

"But, Father," Elder replied, "I *must* work for you!"

With a look of disappointment Father corrected Elder. "No, son, that is where you're wrong. For work to be good it must spring forth from love, not obligation. But enough of this now."

Then Father turned his attention back to Prodigal and said, "Son, I'm concerned about you. Why didn't you do your work today? What troubles you?"

Prodigal's face had dropped as he sadly mumbled, "I don't belong here anymore, Father."

"What do you mean, son?" Father replied.

"I—"

Suddenly Phillip interrupted, clearing his throat quite loudly. Prodigal sat up straight and looked over at Phillip. The servant was shaking his head back and forth desperately. Prodigal turned and looked at Father, and then he looked away. Finally he blurted out, "Father, give me the share of the property that falls to me!"

"What did you say?" Elder shouted.

Phillip rushed to Father's side, "Please sir, don't listen to him. He doesn't mean it. He just—."

Prodigal cut him off. "Be quiet, Phillip! I know exactly what it is that I'm saying." Prodigal turned and looked at his brother and continued, "It's the law of Moses! I am due a third of the family estate. I want my share to do with as I please."

"Father!" Elder pleaded. "Listen to this selfish, wicked son of yours! He hasn't worked an honest day in his life and now he wants your money! You can't let him get away with asking such a thing." Turning to Prodigal, Elder glared at him and blurted, "Why don't you just say it! You wish Father was dead!"

"No," Prodigal clarified. "I just want my freedom."

"Freedom! Freedom! Some of us have to work for our living. Don't you realize how hard I've worked to benefit our farm? Now you want to throw it all away! What will the neighbors and the people in the village say? I'll tell you. They'll say that the brother of Elder destroyed the honor of Father's household and that of the whole village of Nain! The men at the market will frown at me. The boys in the street will mock me."

Prodigal replied to Elder, "Listen to you. You're the one thinking of yourself."

"That's it! I can't take this anymore!" Elder screamed. He stood up and shoved his chair back so hard that it crashed to the floor. Then he leaned over the table and pounded it with his fist so that the table shook.

With quick reflexes, Phillip grabbed the teetering pitcher of wine with one hand and the rolling loaf of bread with his other hand. Elder glared across the table at Prodigal. Through clenched teeth he challenged, "We'll see who the real man around here is!" And he shoved Prodigal, who was still sitting in his chair.

Prodigal fell backwards onto the floor. He quickly recovered and stood up, his face reddening. Prodigal took a lunging swing at Elder and missed. But before either could throw another punch their father stepped between them and with strong arms held them apart. "Enough! How it breaks my heart to see the two of you fight! You both are boys, not men! Neither of you acts like a son of mine. Now go to your quarters!"

"But Father," Elder repeated. "We can't let him talk like this. You're not going to give him our property, are you?"

"Enough! I said enough! Go to your quarters for the evening."

Phillip, still holding the bread and the wine, began to apologize to Father, "Sir, I tried to tell Prodigal that this was not a good—"

"Please clean up the table now, Phillip. None of us shall eat tonight." Father went off alone to the family altar where the candelabra was lit. He got onto his knees to pray.

Much later that night, Father went to his desk and wrote out two documents. On one he assigned two-thirds of the inheritance to Elder; on the other he assigned the remaining third to Prodigal. He signed each with the seal of his signet ring. Finally he lay down to sleep. He tossed and turned throughout the night.

The next morning Prodigal was out walking in the vineyard, and Elder was in the village buying all the things that Prodigal had neglected to purchase the day before. Father put Elder's document on Elder's mattress. He put Prodigal's document in a large pouch on his mattress. He also dropped into the pouch a flat, smooth rock. Later that afternoon Prodigal came into the house and walked past Father without looking at him. Then he saw the rolled-up document in the pouch and exclaimed, "Yes! Yes! It's mine! I'm free at last!"

Hastily he tossed a few items of clothing into a sack, grabbed the pouch, and headed for the front door. On the way out he looked at his father, who was sitting on his chair. Their eyes met. He opened his mouth to say, "Thank you," but the words wouldn't come. He saw tears forming in his father's eyes. He started to feel a lump form in his own throat, and he quickly turned to run out the door. Prodigal was bound for the village of Nain.

Returning from the village with a cart full of supplies, Elder saw his younger brother in the distance, running and carrying a sack. Putting two and two together, Elder ran up to the house. There was his father sitting in his chair and looking sad. Elder began to open his mouth to ask what was going on when his father pointed toward the corner of the room where Elder's mattress lay rolled up.

Elder rushed over. He saw the rolled up document. He grabbed it and quickly pulled it open. He couldn't believe his eyes! *This is too good to be true! This grants me the rights to two-thirds of the family estate! And it means that Prodigal took his third and left. He's gone! The 'Lazy Lunk' is gone! And I'm in charge of everything that's left!* He kissed the document and then held it up to his heart and smiled as he walked back outside. He didn't say a word to Father. Not even "Thank you."

Meanwhile, Prodigal had reached the village, but it was sundown and all the shops were closed, so he rented a room for the night. Early the next morning before the sunrise Prodigal awoke suddenly. He was so anxious to begin his new life that he had hardly slept. Prodigal rushed out of his room and headed over to the office of Timothy, one of the town merchants he knew. When he arrived he saw that the light was out in the office and no one was there, so he walked around back and pounded on the back door where Timothy and his family lived.

"Timothy! Timothy! Quickly, come to the door!" he shouted as he pounded and pounded, waking up anyone who was within earshot.

"Prodigal? Well, good morning to you, too!" Timothy responded sarcastically. "Now that you've woken up the neighborhood, tell me why you couldn't have waited until my shop opens in another hour."

"Timothy, I have property to sell. Fifty acres of olive groves, orchards, vineyards, and farm land. And also one barn full of chickens and twenty cattle."

"Your father wouldn't sell all that!" Timothy replied. "That land was settled by his great grandfather. That property is your livelihood. And why would you sell all that to me? I'm not the only merchant in this town. Tell me, what are you talking about, son?"

Prodigal was insistent. "Look here, Timothy. See Father's seal from his signet ring? This property is mine! Now hurry up and give me your price!"

There was a glimmer in the town merchant's eyes as he looked over the document and thought about this opportunity. "I'll give you two hundred denari," he answered finally.

"What?! The cattle alone is worth that much!"

"Well, that's my offer." There was a long silence. Timothy knew how to negotiate, but soon he began feeling guilty about taking advantage of an impulsive adolescent. Finally he said to Prodigal, "Look, I must have my breakfast with my family before I open up shop. Maybe you ought to talk this over with your father anyway. You don't want to . . ."

"OK, OK," Prodigal interrupted. "It's a deal if you'll also give your black horse in the stable."

"Shadow? That's my beloved horse! I can't . . ." Timothy paused to scratch his head, "Well, if you must have him, he'll cost you twenty denari."

"Twenty denari! You shyster!" Prodigal was irate, but he had no time for bargaining. He wanted his money! He looked

Timothy in the eye with cold determination, "Just give me my 180 denari and the horse, and I'll be on my way!"

Prodigal opened his pouch wide and smiled as he listened to the sound of the clanking gold coins. He tied up his pouch, handed Timothy the paper with the property rights, and saddled up his new black horse. Within seconds, Shadow trotted briskly off into the distance, carrying Prodigal north. Far north. The sun was just coming over the horizon behind him, but it was blocked by dark clouds.

Where are you in this story? This parable, like all parables that Jesus tells, is a mirror for you to look into. You need to read it carefully and thoughtfully in order to see yourself clearly.

I remember the first time my son, David, saw himself in the mirror. He was about five months old. I had shown him his reflection in various mirrors in our house many times before, but it wasn't until this particular time that he saw that it was truly himself he was seeing. His eyes lit up with a sparkle, he smiled big, and he pointed at himself. Then he looked at me, giggled, and exclaimed, "Eeel-go-gee-ga-ga-daaaa!"

I knew exactly what he was saying. "Daddy, I see myself over there!"

You may not be able to see it yet, but in this story you are the prodigal son. So am I. He is a young man who is anxious to get the most out of life. He is in search of the things he wants. Self-rule. Self-gratification. Self-advancement. Self-recognition. We may be more polite, more discrete than Prodigal, but the motives are the same.

Prodigal, like us at times, breaks his father's heart and leaves home in order to live out his fantasies. In different ways, we too have walked away from God's management of our lives and said, "I'm going to do it my way!" We too have impulsively indulged ourselves in sinful pleasures. We too have stepped on other people to further our own success. We too have sought to impress other people with ourselves. And we did these things even though it meant walking away from our heavenly Father's love.

As you'll see when we continue our story, high living in the far country eventually leads us to "hit bottom" in a pigsty of despair. Stay with Prodigal, though, and you'll soon be following his courageous steps of faith across the desert and toward home. You'll find yourself on a journey of spiritual regeneration, emotional healing, and personal reconciliation to Prodigal's father and our Father. In some ways this will be a difficult journey, but it will also be one that surprises you with one heavenly blessing after another.

Perhaps you don't think that you're like Prodigal. Along with Elder you've been working hard in Father's fields while your lazy and spoiled brother (or sister) has been doing as he pleases. You're righteous; you'd never indulge in sinful pleasures. You're responsible; you'd never chase after foolish fantasies. You're successful; you'd never fall on your face and give up. You're dignified; you'd never get so desperate as to feed pigs!

To be sure, on the outside, people like Elder do look very different from people like Prodigal. But are they really? If you identify with Elder, keep reading; by the end of this story you'll see that you and Elder are no better than Prodigal. At that point you may be able to take the step that Elder refused to take, and you will model Prodigal's faith and join the joyous celebration of forgiveness and new life.

There will be other characters in our story for you to learn from. For instance, maybe you'll find that in some ways you are similar to Phillip, the family's faithful servant. He serves the interests of others and seeks to please them whenever he can. He is quick to get into a mediator role and to speak for people in order to smooth out the conflicts that make him so anxious. But watch him in our story, for his character will strengthen and become more secure. He'll go from being "The Dodger of Disagreements" to being "The Bearer of Blessings" when he discovers that Father loves him with the same love he shows to Prodigal.

In fact, Father's display of forgiving love to Prodigal will affect the entire cast of characters from the village. Timothy, the selfish businessman; Joshua, the hard-line village mayor; Rabbi Benjamin, the soft-hearted but pious priest; Sarah, the gossiping neighbor; and the gang of hostile boys will also encounter Father's love. And so will you.

This Father is truly amazing. In fact, he is the hero of the parable. This is "The Parable of the Prodigal Father"![1] Yes, Father is the real prodigal! Prodigal means lavish spendthrift, extravagant, wasteful. And Father is that. He lavishly—even wastefully—pours out his extravagant love to all who will open their hearts to him.

Of course, the father represents our heavenly Father. You will see God to be a model father, one for all fathers to emulate, one for all adult children to compare against their own fathers in order to see what they needed as children and what they still long for today as adults. He is the one Father you will never outgrow your need for. Through Him we can learn how to forgive our earthly fathers, who generally were imperfect in their representation of our heavenly Father.

Let's return to our story now. Where were we? Oh, yes, riding to the big city on a black horse. The rising sun is covered by dark clouds and behind our backs . . .

NOTE

1. Pastor Lloyd John Ogilvie describes the parable this way in *Autobiography of God* (Regal).

"The younger son . . . squandered his wealth in wild living. After he had spent everything, there was a severe famine in that whole country, and he began to be in need. So he went and hired himself out to a citizen of that country, who sent him to his fields to feed pigs. He longed to fill his stomach with the pods that the pigs were eating, but no one gave him anything."

Luke 15:13–16

STEP 1

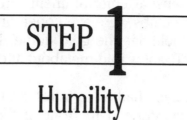

Humility

Hitting Bottom in a Pigsty

Look, Shadow, the city lights! Wow! It's Antioch! The third largest city in the Roman empire! The city of pleasure. C'mon, giddy-up! We're almost there, ol' boy."

Shadow was dragging. It had been a long three-hundred-mile journey in the hot sun. Three twelve-hour days of riding and Shadow was tired and thirsty.

"Don't worry, Shadow, it'll be worth it. I'll get you a stall of your own with fresh grain and cool water. I'll clean you up and get you a new and more comfortable saddle. First, though, we'll ride through town and see what's here."

When they reached Antioch, a tired Shadow trudged down the four-mile-long main street. It was lined with magnificent mansions. And the businesses in town offered a variety of goods, from imported clothes made of dyed silk to shocking and sensual entertainment. Prodigal soon would discover that the clubs were even open on the Sabbath.

"Shadow, look! See the gold dome? It must be the Purple Palace that Timothy told me about after that business trip he took."

Prodigal urged Shadow to a trot, and they proceeded to the palace. They stopped in front of the double door entrance. The doors, twelve feet tall, were made of cedar wood imported from Lebanon and framed in pure gold. Standing also near the doors and close to Prodigal and his horse was a young Greek man about Prodigal's age. He was as wide-eyed with wonder as Prodigal was, but by his dress it was obvious he was just a peasant.

"I wish I could go inside there!" the young man said out loud, knowing that a well-to-do man on horseback was listening. "Oh! It delights the senses! To touch the purple silk furniture and curtains! To smell the fragrant incense at the altar to the goddess Diana! To taste the delicious foods, rich pastries, and strong wine! To see the all-night entertainment! Beautiful women dancing to live music! A dramatic play portraying the grand lives of the rich! To listen to the lewdest and most hilariously funny comedian in town! To play at the casino table! Ah, the Purple Palace is what makes Antioch 'the City of Pleasure.'"

Prodigal jumped down from his horse. His buttocks and back were quite sore, though, and he winced in pain. He wasn't used to such long horse rides. After tying up his horse, Prodigal turned to the young man. "What's your name?"

"Alex, sir."

Prodigal pulled out his fancy, plush pouch full of gold coins and said, "C'mon, Alex, let's go inside and have some fun!" Alex was elated. That evening Alex became quite impressed with Prodigal. Fine clothes. An endless supply of gold coins that he kept pulling out of his fancy purple pouch. Jovial laughter. *He's friendly to everyone, generous to all—*

and he's so confident! Alex thought. Even Prodigal's Jewish accent impressed him.

Alex's admiration was just what Prodigal needed. He thought to himself, *This really is me! I really am good!*

The two were inseparable from that evening on. In fact, Prodigal rented a large white stone mansion on main street for Alex and him to live in. He decorated and furnished it in high style. Then one day Prodigal held a party at his new home to show it off. He invited many prominent citizens from Antioch. Politicians, chariot racers, businessmen, and artists all came because they had heard about Prodigal and his money. There was an endless supply of food and wine with live music and dancing that lasted late into the night. Everyone had a good time. And all were impressed with Prodigal's fine taste, his party spirit, and his generosity.

Word around town about Prodigal of Nain spread fast. It wasn't long before Prodigal was known throughout the whole city as "the rich Jew with the morals of Daphne." (According to Greek mythology, Daphne was the mortal maid whom Apollo fell in love with. The temple of Daphne, which was full of prostitutes, was just five meters outside the city of Antioch.) But secretly people wondered about Prodigal. The whispers could be heard underneath the sound of shuffling feet in the city. "How did he get so much money? Why would a Jew live this way? Does he have a skill?"

In time Alex began to wonder, too. One morning at the breakfast table between sips of fresh squeezed orange juice Alex couldn't hold back his curiosity any longer. He asked the unspeakable. "Prodigal, I've never known anyone with as much gold as you. Where did you get all that gold?"

"What does it matter to you?" Prodigal responded. "I thought we agreed at the beginning of our friendship not to talk about our past. I never question you as to why you don't talk about or visit your family."

Tears began to form in Alex's eyes. "I'm afraid you wouldn't like me if you knew them. You see, we're very poor, and my father—." Alex swallowed, wiped his eyes, and looked up at Prodigal apologetically. "I'm sorry I asked. I'm just afraid we'll run out of money."

Run out of money! The words were like a jar of cold water from the Orontes River thrown into Prodigal's face. Prodigal looked straight at Alex with a startled stare. Then he dropped his head somberly.

"Prodigal, what's wrong?" Alex asked. "You look like you've woken from a wonderful dream, only to discover that it wasn't true and never would be!"

Quickly, Prodigal covered his wincing, reddened face with his hands. He jumped to his feet and rushed away from the table. He went into another room, flopped in the corner, and huddled in a fetal position on the floor.

He pulled out his pouch. He looked at it as he stroked the soft purple felt and picked at its gold embroidery, which his grandmother had stitched. He was afraid to look inside. He'd been trying not to think about it for days, but he knew it was almost empty. It's weight was so light that he hardly noticed it anymore, even though he wore it tied around his waist.

Prodigal shook the pouch and heard the clanking of just a few coins. He moaned silently, "What am I going to do? What am I going to do?"

Later in the day, after the time for the afternoon meal had passed, and his tears had long since been dried up, Prodigal opened his door and shouted, "C'mon, Alex! Let's go into town!" He had banished the negative thoughts; they would not bother him. Besides, he had a plan. The two young men saddled up their horses and rode into town.

When Prodigal saw the gold dome ahead he raised his arms and sang out, "Ah, the Purple Palace! The place of pleasure! The place where a man forgets about his troubles! This is the place for me!"

Alex too was excited. He too was trying not to think about the sense of impending doom that seemed to hang over their heads like a dark storm cloud.

Prodigal headed straight for the casino table. He didn't even turn to look when they walked past the stage where the band was playing and the women were dancing. He had a look of blind determination that said, "I've won big before, and I will again!" He threw down two gold coins to play his favorite dice game and exclaimed, "Alex, pick a number for us!" Alex picked a six, and Prodigal rolled a six. "Hey! We did it!" exclaimed Alex.

"Again," Prodigal motioned to the dealer.

"Six again!" Alex shouted. And Prodigal rolled another six. "Wow! We're rich! Prodigal, lets take our cash and have some fun!"

A man from the crowd that had begun to gather behind them urged, "This is your lucky day! Caesar has opened the door for you! Go on in!"

"Yes, Alex! Have you lost your mind? We're on a roll. The gods are looking down upon us. Pick a number again and we'll increase our winnings even more!"

"Si-i-ix." Alex could hardly get it out. It was a five. Alex knew it. The crowd sighed. With all eyes on him, Prodigal reached into his pouch, way into his pouch, feeling around all over, and he pulled out what he thought was his last coin and threw it on the table.

"Why, that's a rock!" laughed the dealer.

"He threw a rock, all right!" joked one of the bystanders.

Quickly Prodigal took back his rock and pushed his way through the crowd. Alex followed him out the door.

In the weeks ahead conditions deteriorated. If possible, things became even worse for Prodigal than having an empty coin purse. A famine overtook most of the Roman Empire. It hadn't rained much anywhere all winter. And now it was spring and still no rain. The crops were horrible. It was almost impossible to get food or goods from outside because almost no one dared to travel anywhere.

Conditions in Antioch, as elsewhere, were disastrous. Most people were out of work. Prices had soared so high that a loaf of bread cost two week's wages. Children were being sold as slaves to the rich to keep them and their parents from starving. Many people starved, and some of them lay dead in the streets with no one to bury them. People began to fear for their lives.

Prodigal and Alex survived longer than some people. They hocked furniture, their horses, jewelry, clothes—whatever they could. All just to get more food. Their goods had less value, however, in this poor country; no one could afford to pay much. In a few weeks they had nothing else to sell. Out of money, they could not pay rent; they could not buy food. All they had left were the clothes on their backs. Now their beds became the dusty, stone streets. The walls to their home were the storefronts. The roof over their heads was the night sky. The only light in their dark world came from the distant stars.

Their only hope was to beg from people who walked by them on the street. Occasionally a rare and bold merchant who was surviving the famine would walk by pushing a cart of food. This brought a surge of hope to the two vagrants. Prodigal did the begging for them both. He'd fall to the dirt on his knees, stretch out his left hand, lean his head back, and let out a drawn-out, pleading, moaning whine.

But no one gave him anything. The only way they kept from starving to death was by rummaging through garbage containers.

One day Prodigal did his begging routine in front of an out-of-town trader. This was only the second foreign traveler who had walked down the streets of Antioch since the famine started two months ago. Prodigal thought he might receive pity. When the traveler got close Prodigal saw that he was a Jew. In fact, it was Timothy!

"P-p-p-pro . . ." Timothy's face had a most ghastly look of horror.

"Yes, it's me Timothy. Pleeeeease help me. I'm so hungry!"

"Ah . . . ah . . . I . . . " Timothy was so shocked he didn't know what to say. He stood there for what seemed like minutes. He had a dumbfounded, blank stare above his gaping, speechless mouth. Finally Timothy blinked and spoke. "I had heard you were wasting your inheritance with foolish living, but I had no idea you had stooped to this! The shame you've brought to your family and to the village has come back to you. You know wise Solomon said, 'A dog returns to its vomit!'[1] You'll just have to go back home to the mess you made."

"Never! I won't go back!"

Timothy shook his head, turned, and walked away.

In shock, Alex looked at Prodigal. "You mean that was your father's inheritance money you wasted? No wonder you haven't gone home!"

Prodigal dropped his head in shame and walked away. He shuffled his feet as he walked down the street. He lifted his head, though, when he came across an overflowing garbage can outside a rich man's home. Prodigal ran toward this great treasure. He began rummaging through it, looking for leftover food. _Even if it's spoiled, it won't matter,_ Prodigal told himself. _I have to have something in my stomach._

Suddenly a starving beggar gone mad came from behind and attacked him. "Ah, food, food!" he ranted. "This is _my_ food! I saw it here first." The madman was swinging his fists wildly, screaming, foaming at the mouth, and trying to bite Prodigal. Terrified, Prodigal ran away. He and Alex hid.

That was another hungry night. Worse than that, though, the next morning Prodigal awoke to discover that he was alone. "Al-ex! Al-ex!" He waited. There was no answer. "Al-ex!" He walked up and down the street. "Alex!" He looked down alleys and inside the openings of the deserted shops. "Alex!" There was no answer. Alex was gone.

Horror gripped Prodigal's heart as he talked out loud to himself. "Was he killed and eaten by that madman? No! Maybe he went looking for food and fainted in exhaustion. But I can't find him anywhere! Oh, he's abandoned me! He must have gone back to his family and left me here! If there was hope of food at his home, why didn't he take me with him? Oh, if only I had a home!"

Prodigal was alone. His last friend had deserted him like the others. Now that he was out of money and in a desperate and pitiful condition no one cared about him. He had given to others, but now that he was in need no one gave him anything.

Just then Prodigal saw a man walking up the street toward him. The man was finely dressed and wore gold jewelry that sparkled. Obviously this was one of the wealthy citizens of Antioch. *Surely he has food to spare,* Prodigal thought.

Prodigal ran to the man and began wiping the dust off his shirt and pants. The man tried to shoo Prodigal away, but Prodigal wouldn't stop. He spit on the man's shoes and rubbed them clean with his shirt. He grabbed the man's sack to carry for him, and he pleaded, "Let me serve you! I promise I'll do whatever you wish. All I ask is that you give me the leftover crumbs from your table and the last drops of water from your cup. Please let me serve you, or I'll die of starvation!"

The man looked into Prodigal's face. With surprise he exclaimed, "You're Prodigal of Nain! The Jewish lad who threw that big party I went to a couple of months ago! What has happened to you?" The man felt sorry for him, but he still wanted to be free of such a nuisance. So he offered him a job he knew that any Jew with an ounce of dignity—even one who was desperate—would surely refuse. "All that I can offer you, son, is a job tending my pigs!"

"Oh, thank you, sir! Thank you! Thank you!" Prodigal threw himself to the man's feet and began kissing them. "I'll do whatever you wish! I am eternally grateful to you! God will bless you for your mercy to me."

"Oh, stop! Stop! Please stop! Rise to your feet! And no more of this silly God talk. I wouldn't want to count on the blessing of your God who has abandoned you in your deplorable condition!"

Prodigal followed his new master home, carrying the sack and hoping that his gnawing hunger pains would soon be relieved. He could hardly believe his eyes once he caught a glimpse of his master's home. Fig trees, date palms, and olive groves surrounded a marble mansion. The sight made Prodigal's mouth water.

Then the master turned to Prodigal and pointed. "There are the pigs, son. And here is the whip. Be careful with this. Pigs aren't like sheep. You have to drive them along. But never —and I mean never—never upset them! If you hurt or scare a pig, it'll turn on you, attack you, tear you to pieces, and eat your flesh!

"Lead them to that carob tree over there in that field. Below it are pods for the pigs to eat." Then he impatiently waved his hands back and forth at Prodigal and said, "What are you waiting for? Hurry along now!"

Prodigal did as he was told. Once at the carob tree, the pigs went wild. Chasing each other, smooshing snouts, bumping bodies, they were quite a sight to behold. Some rolled around on the ground, others jumped on top of one another in competition for the carob pods. Prodigal stood and listened to the pigs grunt and snort as they chomped on the tough pods. His stomach growled. "Oh, if only I were a pig!" he moaned. "Then I too could push my way into the herd and eat!"

When the pigs had eaten every last pod on the ground, he sighed and complained to the pigs. "Did you have to eat it all? Why didn't you save any for me? He led them back to the pigsty so they could drink from their trough. With a dry mouth Prodigal watched them slurp up the filthy water. Exhausted, he fell to the muddy ground and began to feel sorry for himself.

Just then his master approached him in the pigsty. Prodigal got on his knees and reported, "Master, I have done as you asked."

But his master had no food. "I'm sorry, lad, but I have little food for myself. I can give you only water. But I do have two questions that have been bothering me. Tell me, dear lad, why did you leave your home and your countrymen to waste all your gold? And now that you are broke, why don't you go back home?"

"Oh, I can't! Sir, you don't understand." Prodigal looked up at his master, but the man had already turned his back and was walking away. His master's questions wouldn't leave his mind. But Prodigal couldn't leave the muddy pigsty. Water, an occasional fruit from the trees, even pods with pigs were better than rummaging through garbage cans on the streets of Antioch. *Oh, to be back home again,* he thought. *But I can't go back. The villagers would mock me, Elder would torment me, and Father would not accept me.*

In despair Prodigal began to cry. He looked up into the sky and implored, "Oh, Father in heaven! I'm miserable! I can't help myself. And no one will rescue me. I'm stuck in this dirty pigsty. How I need Your forgiveness! How I need Your help to get back home."

WEEK 1

Pride Comes Before the Pigsty

Prodigal demanded, "Father, give me my share of the property that falls to me!" His words were an awkward and wordy way of beating around the bush. The most direct way to have expressed what he wanted would have been, "I want my inheritance." But Prodigal carefully avoided asking for his "inheritance" and instead asked for the "property" that would eventually fall to him.[2] Why is this? Because to have received his "inheritance" would have meant that he, as a Jewish villager, was accepting the responsibilities of managing his family's estate, caring for the family clan, and protecting the honor of the family and the entire village. Clearly, Prodigal wanted the privilege of wealth without the responsibility of considering the needs of others.

Furthermore, Prodigal shunned the responsibility of being accountable to his father. He wanted to prove that he could make it on his own in life. He wanted to be his own boss, with the freedom to do as he pleased. So he cut himself off from his roots, broke fellowship with his father, and left home to go to the far northern city of Antioch. In doing so he brought disgrace upon his father, his family, and the entire village.

After just a few months of prominence and pleasure Prodigal found himself lying in a muddy pigsty, longing to eat the pigs' food! From the muddy, smelly pigsty Prodigal finally admitted that he was truly miserable and that he was powerless to change his deplorable condition. For the first time in his life he looked to God instead of to himself, and he humbly asked for mercy. Prodigal had learned the hard way that "when pride comes, then comes disgrace, but with humility comes wisdom."[3]

Like Prodigal, we don't usually see the destructiveness to our self-su fficient pride until it has brought us to a pigsty

41

of disgrace. At first, our only thought is, *I want to do things my way! I don't want to be responsible or accountable to God or anyone else. I want my rights. I want the freedom to do as I please.* And so we walk out of the home that our loving heavenly Father provided for us—we leave God—and we travel to a far country where we live life our way instead of God's way.

This was true for Charles.[4] A self-made, successful investment banker, Charles had put himself through law school by waiting tables at night. He worked his way into a Fortune 500 company and eventually became a vice president. His oceanfront home and his Rolls Royce were two of the obvious displays of his material success. It wasn't until the economy bellied up and some large investments turned sour that Charles opened his eyes. What did he see? His neglected wife was having an affair. He hardly even knew his son or his daughter. Other than clients and colleagues with whom he had superficial business relationships, he had no friends who knew the real Charles. He had forgotten how to pray and didn't know God anymore. He, too, was living in a pigsty.

It took Charles a long time to get out of his pigsty. He wasn't able to work his way out. No one carried him out. He couldn't fix the mess he was in. Though he wished he could close his eyes and pretend it didn't hurt, the situation wouldn't go away.

Finally he sat there in that pigsty and opened wide his eyes and his heart. And with my help he looked at his business, his marriage, his children, his friendships, his spiritual life, and, most of all, himself. He felt the pain of it all. Then in humility he cried out to God for mercy.

Unfortunately some people are too proud to feel their pain and to ask God and others for help. They don't want to humble themselves. So they avoid this first step in their journey of healing, and they miss out on God's love and forgiveness.

Initially both Prodigal and Charles hid their emotional, relational, and spiritual pigsties with money and images of success. They avoided looking at the reality of their lives until they were up to their knees in pig feces! To many people, humility—to admit their need for help—is too painful, so they continue in their muddy mess.

"A man reaps what he sows," the Bible warns[5]. People who sow seeds of pride will reap destruction and disgrace in the end. Pride takes many forms—being self-sufficient, having no one to be truly honest with and accountable to, neglecting our needs and the needs of family and friends, avoiding right and responsible living by giving in to selfish gratifications and indulgences, distancing ourselves from God. The result is always the same: self-destruction.

We've all sown seeds of pride in our lives. We've all ended up in a pigsty before. Some of us, though, are quicker to humbly cry out to God for mercy.

Footsteps of Faith

1. Sometime this week read Jesus' parable of the proud pharisee and the humble tax collector in Luke 18:9–14. Both go to the temple. The pharisee goes to show off his image of success and righteousness. The tax collector goes to confess his sins and ask for mercy. Who is received by God? Who is exalted in the end? Which character are you like?

Received by God: _____

Exalted in the end: _____

Character I am like: _____

2. This week consider the areas in which you struggle with pride. Which of the following pigsties of pride are you living in? Check all boxes that apply.

    ☐ I rarely ask others to hold me accountable.
    ☐ I rarely share my feelings and my needs with others.
    ☐ I try to project an impressive image to others.
    ☐ I try to control people or circumstances.
    ☐ I'm so focused on my problems that I can't help others.
    ☐ I often disregard right, responsible living and give in to my impulses.
    ☐ I'm hurting in a relationship but I haven't talked about it.
    ☐ Spiritually I feel dead and empty.
    ☐ I'm alone with a problem.

3. Consider whatever pigsty you might be in and take some time alone with God. Follow Prodigal's example and pray his humble pigsty prayer: "Oh, Father in heaven! I'm miserable! I can't help myself. And no one will rescue me. I'm stuck in this dirty pigsty. How I need Your forgiveness! How I need Your help to get me back home!"

4. Perhaps you're the parent of a prodigal son or daughter. Or maybe you have a friend or other family member who is a prodigal. If so, pray again on your loved one's behalf and consider how you might help this person return to the Father.

WEEK 2
Quick Fixes Don't Work

Prodigal was tired of being known as the son of Father and the brother of Elder. He wanted to be in the spotlight. He was tired of arguing with Elder; he wanted to be free of conflict. He was tired of being responsible to Father; he wanted to be free to do whatever suited his fancy. He was tired of hearing from others in the village that his position and his blessings in life were gifts from Father; he wanted to make it on his own and prove himself. In short, Prodigal was tired of depending on Father for what he needed. He wanted to take what he thought was rightfully his and do with it as he pleased.

So Prodigal gave in to his insatiable impulses. He demanded that his father immediately give him his portion of the estate. As soon as he had the legal papers that designated him as the owner of one-third of the estate, he converted his property into fast cash. He was in such a hurry to sell his property, get his gold, and run away to do as he pleased that he practically gave his property away! He wanted spending money right now. He wanted the power to do as he pleased and to have whatever he wished. And he didn't want to work for it or wait for it.

Prodigal rode away from the sunrise and into the dark clouds on a black horse named Shadow. For a while, however, it seemed that he had ridden right into the sunrise. After all, his new friends in Antioch thought that the sun really shone on this young man. He had gold to spend, gold to share, and an endless supply of gold left over, or so he made it seem. He dressed in style, and he lived in a mansion. He indulged his sensual appetites in the Purple Palace, enjoying food, wine, women, entertainment, laughter, and gambling.

Prodigal justified all the pleasures and comforts of his new lifestyle with his generous contributions to Alex and to others. He was proud of his generosity, and he thought he was making friends. Indeed, people were impressed with him and befriended him, for a time.

Then in only a few months it all fell apart. The much needed spring rains never came, and famine struck the whole region. Prices soared. Prodigal's gold ran through his fingers like water. His power disappeared like a cloud of smoke, and his friends quickly deserted him. People were struggling to stay alive.

Prodigal's story is not new. We know that indulging yourself in pleasures doesn't bring true joy, impressing people with an ideal image of yourself doesn't bring you real friends, and trying to feel good fast only leads to feeling worse in the end. Nonetheless, many of us succumb to these temptations again and again. Why? Because, like Prodigal, we're looking for ways to escape from our problems and distract ourselves from our pain.

For instance, consider how four people I counseled tried to avoid their pain. An overeater who ate sugar foods whenever she felt depressed or lonely was trying to avoid the sadness and grief in her heart over years of empty relationships in which she didn't feel affirmed and valued. A perfectionist who tried to control, clean, or perfect something or someone whenever he felt anxious was trying to avoid looking at the reality of how out of control, messy, and imperfect he was inside. An empty mother who busied herself with her children, the home, and various errands and projects was trying to feel as though her life was significant, all the time thinking she was insignificant and inadequate. A troubled young man who studied his Bible to get God's answers for his problems was actually using the Bible to detach from his feelings.

These and other compulsive behaviors are quick fixes to emotional problems. They don't work, though. The way to deal with your problems is to begin by acknowledging and affirming the reality of how you feel and sharing those feelings with people you trust. As you get to know yourself and your needs, ask for what you need. Here are some ways you can ask a friend to help:

- "Can you just listen to me? I've been reflecting on how rejected I felt as a child, and I need your understanding more than I need your advice right now."
- "I've been sharing my depression with you for a long time now. You know me. What do you think is missing in my life?"
- "I know I made a mistake with this project last time, but I want another chance. I need for you to keep in touch with me on this and to encourage me along the way."
- "You really hurt me when you criticized how I handled that situation. You didn't hear the whole story, and I need for you to step into my shoes and see my side of things."

Recognizing our feelings and humbly asking for what we need is the first step in making life changes. This is very different from impulsively indulging in our wants in order to avoid painful feelings. It requires of you the patience to wait, courage to ask, trust to find someone who cares, and a tolerance for pain and stress. We must remember that no activity we use to feel better fast—whether food, sex, projects, pleasure, busyness, other people's problems, television, or religion —can satisfy in the long run the desires in our hearts. Still, such behaviors do represent patterns that are easier, more familiar, and probably more pleasurable in the short term than walking the road to recovery. That's what makes change so challenging.

Indeed, the hardest step in our journey of healing is the first one: humility. And most people, like Prodigal, need to be desperate and in a lot of pain before they're ready to begin. It's a rare person who seeks real change before hitting bottom in a pigsty. People like this are humble without being humbled. They're motivated to change not so much by pain as by their vision and hope of a better life.

Footsteps of Faith

1. Do you struggle with any of Prodigal's compulsions? Check any of the following behaviors that you struggle with.

☐ Alcohol or drug abuse   ☐ Overeating
☐ Sexual indulgence   ☐ Spending money
☐ Gambling/risk-taking   ☐ Pleasure-seeking
☐ Impressing people   ☐ Perfectionism
☐ Using entertainment   ☐ A constant need to
    to escape   help others
☐ Constant busyness

2. Unwanted feelings, unresolved issues, unseemly character traits, unmet needs—these are the parts of you that you've repressed into the darkness of your unconscious. This unwanted, dark part of you is like your shadow—it follows you around wherever you go and, as Prodigal learned, it even leads you into a pi,gsty if you don't deal with it. This week reflect on the uncomfortable feelings that your compulsive habit(s) have helped you avoid. Check any of the following feelings you have experienced.

☐ Depressed   ☐ Trapped
☐ Low self-esteem   ☐ Discouraged
☐ Bored   ☐ Afraid of rejection
☐ Resentful   ☐ Anxious to prove myself
☐ Lonely   ☐ Dissatisfied with life
☐ Lost   ☐ Confused
☐ Embarrassed of my needs

3. Express your feelings to God and to someone you trust. Then do as Jesus taught in Luke 11:5–13 and ask for

what you need and keep asking, seek for what you long for and keep seeking, knock on the door of opportunity and keep knocking. God promises to answer the prayers of those who have a humble and persistent faith.

4. Sometime this week consider the fruit of the Holy Spirit.[6] Part of receiving the Holy Spirit is to feed on these fruits. Do you have relationship with people in the Body of Christ who share these fruits with you? What fruits are you hungry for this week?

☐ Love	☐ Joy	☐ Peace
☐ Patience	☐ Kindness	☐ Goodness
☐ Faithfulness	☐ Gentleness	☐ Self-control

5. Which fruits of the Spirit do you have to share with others who are hungry?

The Beggar's Bondage

Prodigal ran out of gold. Food, friends, wine, pawnable possessions—they too were all gone. And he was alone. He had squandered his inheritance and gotten stuck in a famine.

He became a beggar living on the street. He whined and pleaded for pity from all who walked by, but no one gave him anything. Finally he competed with stray dogs, wild pigs, and beggars gone mad for food remains from garbage cans. He secretly hoped that perhaps his father or Timothy or someone—anyone—would rescue him. Week after week went by. No one came to his aid.

Prodigal's pleading, moaning, whining, and waiting to be rescued got him nowhere. He had tried to move people's hearts to feel sorry for him. He had tried to manipulate to get what he wanted. He had tried to make people feel guilty so that they would help him. It didn't work. His outstretched hands remained empty. His pleas were ignored at best and ridiculed at worst. His gnawing hunger pains grew worse by the day. Prodigal was desperate, so desperate that he surrendered his dignity as a Jew and hired himself out as a servant to tend the pigs of a wealthy Greek man. He plopped himself down in a dirty, smelly pigsty. He longed to eat the pigs' carob pods and to drink from their trough. But he didn't dare try to eat their food or drink their water lest they turn on him, attack him, and devour his flesh! He had been a slave to his lustful passions, and now he was a slave to a man who gave him only crumbs. He had hit bottom, and he was stuck there.

Hurting, love-starved people who are ashamed, confused, alone, and discouraged tend to become enslaved to someone or something. The emptiness inside needs to be filled; they can tolerate the pain no longer. During such times, addictions are born out of a compulsion to drink a shot, sniff cocaine, act out sexually (or fantasize about it), go on an eating binge, work constantly, or rescue another (or get rescued), to name but a few.

We are relational beings who need to be bonded and attached to loving people. But in the absence of healthy relationships with others, ourselves, and God we will become bonded to something else—anything else, whether drugs, obsessive thoughts, work, or some other god of our own making.

This is what happened to Prodigal. He bonded to his gold and to the pleasure, activities, and image it bought him. He attached himself to Alex by focusing on helping that poor peasant. This was a sick and unhealthy relationship because Prodigal used Alex to forget about his troubles at home, to justify his indulgent lifestyle, and to bolster his own insecure self-identity. When he was broke, he begged at the side of merchant's passing food carts. In the end he sold himself as a slave to a foreigner and worshiped at the feet of his new master.

It was out of Prodigal's unmet needs for love, significance, and peace that his compulsive, idolatrous behaviors emerged. The love of the Father was not in him. Instead, he loved the world and indulged in the things of the world through his craving for sinful pleasures, his lustful eyes, and his boasting about what he had and did.[7] He needed to go back home, face the consequences of the mess he made when he left, and discover the love of his Father, whom he never really knew.

He took his first step out of bondage in the pigsty and toward home when in humility he cried out to God for mercy. We need to do the same.

Footsteps of Faith

1. Do you, like Prodigal, need to change the way you ask for help? Take time this week to consider how you ask. Check the responses below that are true for you.

- ☐ I get others to take responsibility for my problems.
- ☐ I pray to be rescued from my pain.
- ☐ I roll the dice and hope I get lucky.
- ☐ Somehow I seem to make people feel guilty for not being more considerate of or helpful to me.
- ☐ I hint at what I want or am indirect in what I ask for.
- ☐ I don't ask for things much, but wait for others to offer.
- ☐ I ask for what I want, but I don't know what I really need.
- ☐ I am embarrassed of my needs and feelings.
- ☐ I ask for support while I take the steps to get my needs met.

2. Have you ever tried to get free from a compulsive behavior by exerting your willpower and discipline to "just say no"? Sometime this week read Colossians 2:20–23, where the apostle Paul says that disciplining yourself to try harder and do what you should is prideful and lacks value in restraining sensual indulgence. Usually, the harder you try to say no to a temptation the more you indulge in it.

3. Perhaps you have "white-knuckled" your way to abstinence. If so, consider if it has left you empty, flat, and superficial, or if you traded one compulsion for another one.

Usually a white-knuckled sober alcoholic becomes either a "dry alcoholic" or a workaholic (or co-dependent, a drug addict, a sex-addict, etc.). Read Matthew 12:43–45, where Jesus explains the danger of being delivered from evil without also being filled with good.

4. The way to overcome evil is to be filled with good.[8] Reconsider the fruits of the Holy Spirit that you hunger for (as you identified them on page 49). What steps can you take to begin satisfying your hunger? This week ask a friend to support you in this.

Asking the Right Questions

When his master approached him in the pigsty Prodigal got on his knees and said, "Master, I have done as you asked." Prodigal was waiting for food from his master to fill his hungry stomach. Instead, his master offered food for thought in the dish of two questions. "Dear lad, tell me, why did you leave your home and your countrymen to waste all your gold? And now that you're broke why don't you go back home?"

Prodigal didn't answer. Later he will, and then his master will know the reason for the senseless squandering of gold. He'll understand Prodigal's fear: the terror of returning home. But Prodigal isn't ready to answer the questions yet. First, he needs to ask them. And this is what he does while he is starving in the pigsty. "Oh, Father in heaven! Why did I leave home? How can I get back? I'm miserable! I can't help myself. And no one will rescue me. . . . How I need Your forgiveness! How I need Your help to get back home."

At first glance Prodigal's pigsty prayer may not seem to be worth much. But when we look closely we see that in it he is taking the first and hardest step of his recovery. Physically he hasn't moved an inch closer to home. He is still smack in the middle of the pigsty! But he has become honest; he has abandoned his denial. He has stopped indulging himself with pleasure to forget his troubles back at home. He's confessed his miserable condition and acknowledged that his desperate attempts to help himself by buying friends, gambling, begging—even rummaging through garbage and enslaving himself—were all a failure. He's taken responsibility for dealing with his problems rather than begging to be rescued. He knows that he needs God's mercy and has taken the humble step that those who are in a twelve step recovery program take: "We admitted that we were powerless over [our dependencies]—that our lives had become unmanageable."[9]

It's humbling to be honest about your troubles and your failed attempts to get free of them. It's humbling to take the time to ask such questions as, "Why did I get into this mess?" and, "How can I get out?" Even when you're in a pigsty it's easier to find a way to avoid your pain than it is to feel it. And it's easier to rush to find a quick fix or a way to be rescued than it is to keep asking the right questions.

Candice was one woman who took this step of humble honesty. She was an overeater who asked the right questions. "Why have I gained twenty-five pounds in the last four months?" and, "What can I do to change my out-of-control eating?" she asked me. The first thing we had to do was identify and discard all the false answers she had been telling herself up to that point. Her problem wasn't laziness, lack of discipline, having a sweet tooth, cheating on her diet, using the wrong diet, an unusually slow metabolism, or not praying hard enough. Diagnosing her real problem took some time, but what we uncovered was that she ate when she was alone and was feeling sad. And we also discovered that she hadn't grieved her father's recent death, she never felt understood by her mother, and she had no one in her life with whom she shared her inner feelings.

Uncovering the true nature of Candice's problem put us a giant step toward answering her all-important second question, "How do I change?" In the months that followed Candice began to let the tears of grief and sadness flow. And she allowed herself to feel the buried anger she felt toward her mother. She even opened up her heart to receive comfort and caring from me and from the women in her support group. She learned to check in with herself and ask, "How am I feeling?" before she ate. She learned to call a friend or write honestly in her prayer journal when she felt tempted to go on an eating binge. Then slowly some of the extra pounds began to go away.

You too can find freedom from destructive and painful patterns of behavior by following Prodigal's example and taking this first step of faith in which you humble yourself, face your pain, and ask the right questions. You'll need a friend to support you in this. And you'll need [a friend] to pray to your Father in heaven.

Where is God when you're hurting? Where is Father while Prodigal is wallowing in a muddy pigsty and offering his desperate prayer for help? He's right where Prodigal left him: home grieving for his lost Prodigal, waiting while his son learns from the painful consequences of his sins, reaching out to his son in the pigsty with invisible hands of support and guidance, praying for his son's change of heart. That's where our heavenly Father is, watching for His son's (and daughter's) return home, but not rescuing him.

Footsteps of Faith

1. Sometime this week ask the right questions, as Prodigal did. First, in view of your own struggles and issues ask yourself, "Why did I leave God's care and wisdom and go my own way?" Write down three reasons. (They probably relate to unmet emotional needs or unresolved issues.)

(1) _____

(2) _____

(3) _____

2. Later this week, with your desired changes in view, ask yourself, "What do I need to do in order to go home to my Heavenly Father's love for me?" Write down three specific things you can do this week to get started in the right direction.

(1) _____

(2) _____

(3) _____

3. Maybe like David in Psalm 10 you have asked, "Why, O Lord, do you stand far off? Why do you hide yourself in times of trouble?" (10:1). If so, follow David's example. When he was victimized he expressed his pain, his fears, his vulnerability, his grief, his aloneness, and his anger to God (10:2–11, 13). Then he cried out to God for mercy (10:12); and in faith he trusted that God felt his pain, and he waited for God to help him find his way out of his troubles (10:14).

4. Believing that God is truly with you in the valley of the shadow of death is the key to persevering through your journey of healing.[10] Take some time this week to read Hebrews 4:14–16 and 12:1–3. Consider that Jesus is able to sympathize with you in your weakness because He also suffered, even enduring the pain, victimization, shame, and rejection of the cross. He is your role model, the author and perfecter of your faith, and your high priest who represents you to God and God to you.

NOTES

1. Proverbs 26:11.
2. Fourteen times in the New Testament and four times by Luke the word *kleronomia* ("inheritance") is used. Here a rare word, *ousia* ("property,"), is used. It is used nowhere else in all the New Testament.
3. Proverbs 11:2.
4. In this and all other case examples, real names and identifying information have been changed in order to protect confidentiality.
5. Galatians 6:7.
6. Galatians 5:22.
7. 1 John 2:15–17.
8. Romans 12:21.
9. Step 1 of Alcholics Anonymous's Twelve Steps.
10. See my book *A Walk with Your Shepherd: The Twenty-third Psalm and the Twelve Steps to Recovery*, (Chicago: Moody, 1992).

"When he came to his senses, he said, 'How many of my father's hired men have food to spare, and here I am starving to death! I will set out and go back to my father and say to him: Father, I have sinned against heaven and against you. I am no longer worthy to be called your son; make me like one of your hired men.'"

Luke 15:17–19

STEP 2

Accurate Perceptions of God and Self

Pigsties Open Eyes

That first night at his master's house was not much different than the previous ones for Prodigal. For almost two months he'd been living on the streets. Now he was sleeping in the dirt again, only this time a pigsty floor replaced the stone street. Once again he was hemmed in, only not by storefronts but by pigsty fences. The roof over his head was just a different piece of the same night sky. The dim light in his dark world was just a different angle of the same distant stars.

But on this night, unlike those previous, his hope was completely new. Before he had put his hope in money, winning people's favor, gambling, and begging, which led him to a pigsty of despair. Now he put his hope in God and sought to find his way back home to his father.

That night Prodigal dreamed about going back home. Actually, he had a series of horrible nightmares. They began with him walking and walking and walking. Indeed, it was a 300-mile journey from the Syrian city of Antioch back home to the Galilean village of Nain. As he walked in the desert sun his body smelled of sweat, his bare feet were scalded by the hot sand, his stomach screeched with hunger pains, and his dry tongue stuck to the roof of his mouth.

Prodigal was dragging his feet across the sand when suddenly dozens of gigantic black snakes appeared. They slithered along at his side and their long red tongues kept hissing out at him the same taunting words of condemnation again and again: "Sss-sss, you're a failure! You've wasted your father's hard-earned money! Sss-sss, you're a failure! You've wasted your father's hard-earned money! Sss-sss, you're a failure . . ."

Then little black birds replaced the snakes. Hundreds of them swirled above Prodigal's head, diving at him, their sharp beaks snapping at his ears, neck, and thighs. Together the flock sounded like an off-key, out of harmony, out of sync chorus of cackling hecklers. Though all the birds were cackling at different times, they all had the same dreadful pronouncement, which they kept repeating: "Cawh, cawh. Your father hates you now! He and the others will never let you back into the village! Cawh, cawh. Your father hates you now . . ."

The nightmares were so real that even as he slept Prodigal was sweating and shaking, and he was trying to cover his ears with his hands. In the dreams, he was hot, exhausted, hungry, thirsty, and terrified, yet he kept walking the desert road toward Nain until finally he was at the outskirts of the village.

Ah, he was home at last! But his relieved smile was replaced with a startled panic when the street leading toward home suddenly was filled with a huge gang of boys from the village. They were marching toward him like attacking soldiers, and they carried big sticks held high over their heads.

They glared at him with hateful eyes! As the they marched they taunted,

Prod-i-goool! Prod-i-goool! You fool!
You took the gold and went away!
To us all you brought disgrace, we say!
So now we shall make you paaaaaaay!

Then the gang started beating him with their clubs. Prodigal fell to the ground with a loud scream. All at once each of the gang members kicked him. They kicked him so hard that he flew in the air, landing on the other side of the village.

There he lay, a heap at the gate to his father's house. And there stood Elder. Elder stomped his left foot on top of Prodigal's bruised chest. His teeth were clenched and gnashing. His arms were folded. Dropping down from his right hand was a long black whip. With his foot he pressed down on Prodigal's sore ribs, and then he snapped his whip again and again against the dirt, just inches from Prodigal's left ear. As he tormented and tortured his younger brother, Elder yelled out in sarcastic scorn:

I told you so!
I told you so!
Now you'll pay for your foolishness!
And when I say, "Do this!" you'll do this.
So the stalls you'll be cleaning.
The cattle feed you'll be eating.
From the trough you'll be drinking.
And in the chicken coup you'll be sleeping.
You've been sinning!
So now Father is going to give you a beating!

Elder roared with mocking laughter. Then he grabbed hold of Prodigal's arms and started dragging his brother across the stone walkway to the front door of the house. He was repeating again and again the final words of his horrid pronouncement of condemnation and doom: "You've been sinning! So now Father is going to give you a beating!"

Prodigal began to struggle and fight with Elder. Somehow he broke free and stood up. Then the front door to the house opened. Prodigal screamed "No! Please . . ."

He shook his head and slapped his face. He looked at himself and saw that he was indeed standing. He had heard himself scream. He could feel himself trembling and gasping for air. Then he blinked his eyes and squinted to see in the dim starlight. He didn't see his father anywhere. Nor Elder with a long, black whip. Nor the gang of mean village boys with their big sticks. Nor the hundreds of snapping, cackling little black birds. Nor the dozens of hissing, taunting gigantic black snakes. Just snoring pigs.

It was the middle of the night. Prodigal was tired, but he feared returning to sleep and having another nightmare. So he lay on his back on the dirt floor of his pigsty and gazed up at the distant stars.

He argued with himself. "I can't do it. I can't go home and face the scorn and condemnation of everyone in the village. I can't live off of Elder and work for him. I can't endure Father's disapproval. This shame is too much to bear! But I have to! I can't stay here. This hunger in my stomach is too much to bear. I've hired myself out to a strange man who won't even feed me. What can I do?

"How would Father treat me if I went home?" Prodigal wondered. "Would he beat me? Surely he'd criticize me for being so foolish. He'd point out my sinfulness and give me a long lecture. Maybe he'd send me outside to work, sleep, and eat with the hired slaves. He wouldn't even need to do any of this to punish me, though. All he needs to do is wait! While he waits inside the house, Elder, the men and women of the village, and the gang of boys will torment and abuse me! That's what Father has been doing. He's ignored me these months I've been destitute. If Timothy knew about my situation, then surely my father did. Why hasn't he sent me help?"

Prodigal folded his hands across his chest and his elbow landed on the rock in his pocket. He had forgotten about the rock. He pulled it out, and it sparkled even in the starlight. It was flat and smooth like the ones he and Father had once skipped across the lake. A smile came to his face and dissipated his fears. He pretended to skip the stone . . . One, two, three . . . He and Father would always count the skips out loud together. *Maybe Father would take me back home,* he thought.

Prodigal thought about what life used to be like as a son in his father's house. He remembered breaking bread with Father and talking together at the table for hours. And he remembered how Father always greeted him with a hug when he returned to the house from working out in the fields. He even remembered a little song about his father that he made up when he was a boy:

> *Why even if I were a mouse*
> *I'd live in my father's house!*
> *Why run in circles round and round*
> *And live alone on the bare ground?*
> *Inside my father has bread to spare,*
> *And smiles and hugs to share!*

As a boy, Prodigal would dance around as he sang that silly song over and over until Elder would scream, "Shut up! You're not a mouse, so don't act like one!" But Father liked the song. Prodigal realized that it was true—he was living like a scared little mouse running around in circles on the ground. His life had gone nowhere since he left home. He knew he belonged at home, but he was scared to go back.

Prodigal was stuck. He saw no good choices: go home and die of public humiliation or stay in the pigsty and die of hunger. His anxious thoughts swirled around in his head like a gathering tornado. Suddenly the thoughts stopped, as Prodigal saw a spot of morning sunlight peek over the horizon.

The sunlight reached across the miles of desert and farm-land, ricocheted through the leaves of the carob tree, and landed with a dance on Prodigal's cheek. It cast a sparkle in his eye.

"I know what I'll do!" Prodigal shouted, his exclamation startling the sleeping pigs into a hilarious commotion of grunting and bumping into each other. "I know I've sinned. I won't wait for everyone to scorn and condemn me. I'll con-fess my sin, but then I'll work off my debt. I'll go to my father and say, 'Father, I have sinned against heaven and against you. I am no longer worthy to be called your son; make me like one of your hired men.'"

Just then his master walked out of his house and toward the pigsty. Prodigal stood to his feet. He bowed his head and petitioned, "Master, I beg upon your mercy this morning. I thought upon your questions all night. I was foolish to leave my father's home and waste my inheritance. And I have suf-fered greatly for my sin. But now I have a plan to work off my debt and satisfy my righteous father. Even my brother, who despises me, won't be able to refute me! After many years of hard work I may even regain the respect of the village. Now please allow me to leave your service and go back home to my father."

"Dear lad, you have finally regained your good sense!" smiled the Greek merchant in reply. "Look son, you bound yourself to me, and you can set yourself free. But as payment for your service to me I'll give you some dried beans, nuts, and water for your journey. Furthermore, I'll have one of my servants give you a ride on the cart to the edge of town. From there take the coastal route back to Galilee. The first person you see who is on horseback, regardless of whether or not he has a cart, say to him, 'I am on a mission for my master Demetrius of Antioch, and I need a ride, please.' He will give you a ride as far as he is going. Do this until you reach your homeland."

Prodigal fell to his knees and joyously exclaimed, "Thank you, Master Demetrius, for your great kindness! God has used you to save my life!"

"No," Demetrius replied, "I am just paying you for your labor. You have saved yourself—like we all must do in this world. You Jews are the only people in this great empire who think you need a god to save you from sin."

Prodigal's nightmares of what it would be like when he returned home portrayed some real dangers. Everyone in the village knew how he had insulted his father and devastated the family farm by taking his inheritance money early, turning it into fast cash, and leaving town. And they had heard the news from Timothy of how Prodigal had squandered his money and become a destitute beggar. In fact, news of how Prodigal left home and how he wasted his inheritance would have traveled beyond the village of Nain. Among traveling merchants, for instance, one would tell another, "Did you hear about Prodigal of Nain? In Antioch they call him the rich Jew with the morals of Daphne."

So when Prodigal returned home he would have no secrets. His life would be like an open book of his sins and failures, many of which were exaggerated or even untrue. People in the village would have slandered his character; everyone in the community and in the family would be ashamed to associate with him. All would be angry at the disrespect he had brought to the village.

These attitudes would filter down from the respected men of the village to the women at the market, to the servants in the fields, and to the children playing in the street. Like most villages, Nain had a gang of boys who hung around in the streets. If given the chance, the gang would love to pick on an outcast like Prodigal and condemn him in order to avenge the village name.

As "the brother of Prodigal," Elder would have been the butt of many cruel jokes and tricks by the gang of boys. And how much more would the father of Prodigal be harassed and mocked. An adult was powerless against such a gang because it would bring dishonor to him to argue or fight with a boy. So whenever Elder or Father went into the village they

66

would hear about Prodigal from the gang of boys, as well as from the merchants and women about town. The old wounds of Prodigal's betrayal would be scratched opened again.

Because of these developments at home, Elder's disgust for his spoiled and lazy younger brother grew into a raging fire of bitter hatred. Elder's only peace was in his hope that he'd never see his brother again. But what about Father? What would be his attitude toward Prodigal?

Prodigal feared that his father would also be bitterly angry at him. _Surely Father will criticize and punish me and then send me away. At the very least Father will wait passively as Elder, the gang of boys, and others in the village attack me._ The best Prodigal thought that he could hope for was that maybe in time Father's anger would subside and he'd be pleased by Prodigal's hard work.

Put yourself in Prodigal's position. Put your father in Father's position. Would you dare to go back home? How would your father respond to you? How did your father respond to you as a child when you did something wrong, made a mistake, or disappointed him?

Some of the stories I hear in answer to this last question break my heart. And they come from adults who as children committed crimes much lesser than Prodigal's, or did nothing wrong except be within arm's reach or earshot of their father.

- One father beat his boy with an extension cord for quarreling with his brother.
- Another father called his daughter "lewd" because she wore a short skirt to church.
- Another father scolded his children for getting any grades less than an "A."
- Still another father screamed at his daughter when she spilled her fingerpaints on the carpet.
- One father called his son a "baby" because he was crying about being teased by the boys down the street.

You probably have heard similar stories. Perhaps you could add one or two of your own. Physical and emotional injuries from a father such as those above cut deep into a child's heart. The cut becomes an infected wound of shame, mistrust, or bitterness if it isn't followed up by Dad's saying something like, "I'm so sorry. I see that I hurt you. I lost control of my temper, I pressured you with unfair expectations, I judged you wrongly. Tell me how that felt for you. I'm going to try not to do that again."

Infected father-wounds long for the healing ointment of the heavenly Father's love. Yet, it is those who have been wounded by their earthly fathers who have the most difficulty emotionally trusting their heavenly Father. They may be slow to let any authority figure, any man, even any person, get close to their heartfelt hurts and longings. Even though they desperately need God's love, they keep him at arm's length emotionally because He is "Father."

Perhaps you have an unclear picture of your heavenly Father. Maybe you struggle to experience His love for you. Don't worry, Prodigal did also. He feared the worst and only hoped for a little better. But when he returns home he will be amazed by Father's outpouring of love to him. So will you if you continue the journey and follow Prodigal's steps of faith toward home.

Footsteps of Faith

1. This week think back to when you were a teenager and imagine that you are in Prodigal's position. You've insulted your father. You've disappointed him and made a mess of your life. How would your father respond?

☐ Give me a beating
☐ Offer silent disapproval
☐ Close the door in my face
☐ Ignore the problem
☐ Rescue me from the pigsty
☐ Say, "Don't cry!"
☐ Tell me, "It's no big deal."
☐ Have an honest discussion
☐ Show forgiveness

☐ Criticize me
☐ Use sarcasm
☐ Let Mom handle everything
☐ Say, "I told you so!"
☐ Say, "You have a lot of work to do to pay me back!"
☐ Use appropriate discipline
☐ Give me a second chance

2. Maybe you can identify with Prodigal because as a child you were picked on, rejected, or teased by a sibling or a peer. Did you feel safe talking to your father when you had hurt feelings? Why or why not?

_____

_____

3. Jesus said, "Anyone who has seen me has seen the Father."[1] He is the only perfect and complete representation of the heavenly Father's character. Consider Jesus' attitude toward children. Mothers brought their little children to Jesus, and He touched them, held them, and blessed them.[2] Sometime this week read Matthew 18:1–14, where Jesus demonstrated and taught that children are to be: (1) respected, (2) welcomed, (3) protected from sin, (4) not looked down upon, and (5) sought out when they are lost.

This week bring your inner child home to Jesus. Tell Him your inner thoughts and let Him love you.

WEEK 6
Hiding from Father in a Pigsty

Why would anybody hide in a pigsty? Because it's better to sleep in the slop with snoring pigs then to be attacked in the middle of the hot desert by huge hissing snakes and crazy cackling birds. Yes, these nightmares were only figments of Prodigal's imagination, but they represented the real terror of returning home to a hostile village crowd—and to an angry father.

"Oh, but Father wouldn't condemn his son—not this father," you reply to the scared son. Easy for you to say, for you know the end of the story. But put yourself in Prodigal's position; step into his footprints in the mud of his pigsty. Feel the mud between your toes. Smell the pig stench and hold your empty stomach with your hand. Imagine being alone in a foreign country far, far from home.

Then consider that your father knows where you are and that you're in a desperate situation. Furthermore, he has the means to help you, but he does nothing! You've been waiting for what seems like an eternity for someone to help you, but no one lifts a finger. In the midst of this dark isolation you too would fear the worst and hide in a pigsty.

The sadness of Prodigal's situation is that his fears about Father were misplaced. Father's heart was bursting with love for his son. His heart ached whenever he saw his sons' empty place at the table. He felt the slap in the face whenever he heard people in the village slandering his son. Father greatly missed Prodigal, and many times each day he looked toward the north to see if his son was coming home yet. Not a day went by that Father didn't pray for Prodigal's safe return.

Why didn't Father do something? Why did he just wait and wait? It seems he would have kept waiting even if it meant letting Prodigal die in that pigsty he was hiding in!

Father had to wait. Holiness demanded that he respect his son's freedom of choice to stay away from home and that there be consequences to sin. Wisdom insisted that he not rescue his son from those painful consequences, but that he allow him to be disciplined by them. Love required that he wait for his son's return home. So Father didn't cling to or control his son, he didn't rescue him as if he were helpless, and he didn't give up on him either. Instead, he waited for Prodigal to see the truth and return home.

It took some time in a miserable pigsty, but Prodigal finally saw the truth: he was wrong to leave Father the way he did; doing things his own way didn't work well; and now it was up to him to stop hiding and to face his fears of returning home. When he returned home and his eyes were opened to his father's love, he realized that in hiding from Father he was hiding from love.

Susan also was hiding from love. As a little girl she was told things like "You're too sensitive!" "Stop crying or I'll send you to your room!" In general she didn't receive attention when she expressed troubled feelings. She learned that crying and having emotional needs meant being rejected.

Even as an adult she had raised her hopes many times that maybe this friend would be loyal, maybe it was safe to share this hurt, maybe if she took the risk of investing in this group she'd be accepted, but each time it seemed that the results were the same: she was disappointed and rejected again. So she came to the conclusion that she just needed too much—her needs were bad and she should hide them.

At first, repressing her feelings and needs seemed to work for Susan. When she appeared strong, helpful, and cheerful, people liked her. But from time to time clouds of depression loomed above her head. She felt so alone and empty of love inside; no one knew how she really felt. Worst of all, she lived with a sense of shame about all the "bad" parts of her inside that she had swept away into a dark corner of her soul.

In therapy Susan realized how the very same defense mechanisms that she had used to protect herself from criticism and rejection as a child were now causing her problems. The hurting and needy parts of her inside that cried for love were hidden and remained unloved—even when love was available to her from other people and from God.

It took time, but gradually Susan began to reveal her inner feelings to people she trusted. Believing that her feelings mattered and that her needs were valid was a long uphill climb for her. She had to climb over the rocks of her past experiences and her own self-devaluations. But she continued in her efforts to come out of hiding and into relationship. As she accessed formerly lost parts of herself and experienced support, she felt more connected with God, too.

Footsteps of Faith

1. This week consider whether you hide from love. Maybe the very defense mechanisms that you developed to protect yourself from further injuries and disappointments as a child are now blocking the love you long for. Check the following defenses that you use.

☐ Isolating myself from others

☐ Blaming circumstances

☐ Repressing feelings

☐ Focusing on others' problems

☐ Getting others to rescue me

☐ Compulsive activity

☐ Presenting an ideal self

☐ Having all the answers

☐ Blaming people

☐ Minimizing my needs

☐ Analyzing without experiencing my feelings

☐ Substance abuse

2. Depending upon the feelings you associate with "father" it may be difficult for you to go home to your heavenly Father and trust that He will receive you with love. Write down the first six words that come to your heart when you say "Dad."

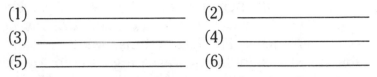

(1) _____ (2) _____

(3) _____ (4) _____

(5) _____ (6) _____

3. Perhaps you can identify with Prodigal's struggle: you believe in God's power to help you but you feel so distant from Him that you feel you're on your own. If you read David's personal thoughts in the Psalms, you'll learn that he often felt that way, too. This week read Psalm 32, which records an occasion when David's distance from God and his depression were a result of his hiding his sinfulness from God.[3] He began to experience God's unfailing love when he confessed his sins and expressed to God his feelings. After reflecting on David's example, consider what sins you might confess to God.

4. After reading the parable of the prodigal son, some people conclude that the father is too easy on his son. What they miss is Father waiting as Prodigal is destitute and famished in the pigsty. By not rescuing his son, Father used the natural consequences of Prodigal's sin as the means to discipline him. It took some time, but Prodigal soon was trained by this harsh, necessary discipline.

Read Hebrews 12:4–11 and notice the importance, method, and purpose in the heavenly Father's discipline. Perhaps, like Prodigal, you're being lovingly disciplined by God with hardships. If so, how do you feel about this time? Are you being trained?

The smooth skipping stone that Prodigal found in his pocket was put there purposely by Father. He knew that Prodigal would discover it in the bottom of his pouch at some point. When Prodigal first discovered it at the casino table he was angry that it wasn't a gold coin. He had been depending on his money, and now he was broke. He shoved the rock into his pocket. He continued to try to manage his life on his own. He hocked possessions, begged for bread, rummaged out of garbage cans, and hired himself out as a servant.

When none of these things worked and he was stuck in a pigsty, he finally pulled the rock out of his pocket and looked at it. Its sparkle shed light on his lost memories of his father and him laughing as they skipped stones on the lake, talking together as they broke bread at the table, hugging at the doorway after a hard day's work, dancing as they sang the funny mouse song.

When Prodigal held onto the rock Father gave him he changed: he came to his senses; he got in his right mind; he thought about Father's love and how much he needed him; he admitted that he couldn't manage his life without Father. Finally Prodigal understood that fulfillment was not in possessing wealth, impressing people, indulging in pleasure, or being free of accountability. He was finally ready to go home.

In my counseling office I have a pile of rocks on a table. Black, white, speckled, gray, or pink; big or little; round, jagged, or flat; smooth or rough—each rock is different. A few of the "rocks" aren't even rocks at all, but are petrified wood, acorns, or shells, which just look like rocks. Each rock would fit in the palm of your hand. Most would fit nicely in a pocket. Some would look nice on a shelf. Occasionally peo-

ple notice them and ask, "Why are those rocks there?" I usually answer their question with a question of my own, "What
does a rock mean to you?" I get all kinds of responses, but
for most people a rock symbolizes something solid and secure to hold onto. That is why David exclaims, "The Lord is
my rock, my fortress and my deliverer; my God is my rock in
whom I take refuge."[4] In fact, *rock* is used thirty-seven times
in the Bible as a symbol for God. It's an image for understanding God, one that I've found most people to be very
comfortable with.[5]

Occasionally, when it seems appropriate, I invite one of
my clients to pick out a rock from the pile in my office. I say
something like, "Find one that feels right to you. Look closely at each one. They are all different, and some aren't rocks
at all." For some of my clients who have developed a significant relationship with me, the select rocks are symbols of
their experience with me. Somehow in our relationship—I
think it's nothing short of miraculous—God's grace and truth
have come alive inside my clients' hurting hearts. For them,
taking a rock from my office symbolizes how they're interna-
lizing God's love as they've experienced it through me. They
want to hold onto that experience and take it with them
when they are alone in facing the challenges and difficulties
of their lives.

We all need a rock to hold onto. We need to take God's
grace and truth into our souls. This happens in godly relationships over time. And when it happens it changes us.
When you feel someone's gentle and consistent caring, then
you feel safe to open up and share your needs and your
hurts, you learn from their character and wisdom, and you
receive their feedback and guidance. Through this kind of
ongoing support in various life circumstances you begin to
see yourself differently and your life takes a new direction.

This was the case for a young woman named Sondra.
She had a Christian background, and God had been a very
important part of her life since she was a small girl. She

deeply wanted a close relationship with God and to honor him, but she didn't trust God deep inside her heart. She associated her heavenly Father with her earthly father, whom she didn't even know. When she was two years old he died. Her mother raised her in a Christian home, and Sondra had continued in her faith, but she never had a father figure whom she was close to. Her mother hadn't remarried until Sondra was in college, and Sondra avoided older men in her life —such as her uncle, pastor, and teachers—because she felt insecure around them.

Sondra became aware of how much she missed having a father in her life after listening to a talk I gave on the attributes of our heavenly Father as demonstrated in the parable of the prodigal son.[6] Her voice was trembling and tears were forming in her eyes as she told me how she longed for the kind of caring she saw in the father in this story. That day Sondra began to grieve her father's absence. About six months later, after continuing her grief process, Sondra told me that she felt closer to her heavenly Father. She sensed his love in a new way. She prayed as though she were talking with the daddy who loved to listen to her. Furthermore, she was feeling better about herself. She was more comfortable with herself and with her value as a woman and a Christian.

Like Prodigal and Sondra, you need to find a rock to hold onto and come to your senses. As you meditate on this narrative of Jesus' parable of the prodigal son, I hope that you too will discover your Father's amazing love for you.

Footsteps of Faith

1. Jesus paid humanity a tremendous compliment when in this parable He said that Prodigal "came to his senses"

when he came to faith and was ready to go home to Father. This week maybe you need to come to your senses by coming to believe your heavenly Father fully loves you. If so, then Psalm 103:1–8 is a rock you'll want to hold on to. In this passage God promises to benefit your soul in the following twelve ways. God will:

☐ Forgive your sins ☐ Heal your afflictions
☐ Help you out of the pit ☐ Be gracious with you
☐ Satisfy your desires ☐ Renew your strength
☐ Make you righteous ☐ Bring you justice
☐ Be compassionate ☐ Crown you with love
with you and compassion
☐ Be slow to anger with ☐ Abound in love to you
you

Take some time to meditate on this psalm.

2. Even though you probably believe the above descriptions to be true of your heavenly Father, you may still struggle to experience some of them. Check any of the areas above that represent currently unmet needs for you.

3. Usually the Father God's love comes to you over time through your personal relationships. Emotional injuries and disappointments from past relationships that need healing make the process of experiencing love all the more important and yet all the more difficult. Sometime this week talk with a friend about your unmet love needs.

The Face-Saving Plan

In the pigsty Prodigal took a big step toward home when he found his right mind and came to believe that Father could help him. Nonetheless, at this point he had very little grasp of the depth of Father's love for him. He felt ashamed and could not imagine that his father would forgive him. He thought it was all up to him to make things right.

So Prodigal had a plan to save himself from his shame. He would run the gauntlet through the angry and abusive mob in the village street, past Elder's condemnations at the gate, and to his father's feet. There he would receive his father's punishment. But then he would give his father the speech he had prepared and rehearsed in the pigsty.

With his head hung in shame, he would confess his sin and acknowledge his unworthiness to be accepted back as a son. Then he'd offer himself as a hired servant to his father; he'd hire himself out as a slave to his father just like he had done with his Greek master. In time he would regain his father's favor by working off his debt. He'd pay back his father for all the money he had wasted. This way he would "save face" and prove himself to be worthy of Father's acceptance and respect. Perhaps in time even Elder and the people in the village would respect him. This way, Prodigal thought, he'd be relieved of his shame.

Prodigal's failures in the far country had taught him that fulfillment was not in possessing wealth, impressing people, indulging in pleasure, or being free to do as he pleased. But he still had an important lesson to learn: he couldn't work his way to fulfillment. He thought that when he went home he could prove himself to be worthwhile and acceptable through working hard. This is the philosophy that his Greek master had been trying to teach him in the pigsty. It's also the philosophy that Elder lived by. It's probably a philosophy that you have been taught. Parents, teachers, employers, culture, and even church may have directly or indirectly taught you "work ethic" messages such as:

"The value of how you've spent your time is measured by what you've produced."

"You're acceptable if you do what others want you to do."

"You're valuable and worthwhile if you do well."

"Your accomplishments are the legacy you leave behind when you die."

"You can't count on anyone but yourself."

"Stay busy and you'll stay out of trouble."

"Successful people are happy people."

These are American values. They are not Christian values, although they sometimes appear to be. For instance, in Proverbs Solomon says things such as "The plans of the diligent lead to profit" and "He who works his land will have abundant food."[7] And in 2 Thessalonians 3:10 Paul says, "If a man will not work, he shall not eat." Indeed, work is necessary to living. But work is valuable and enjoyable only when it's something we want to do and it's balanced by rest and pleasure. This is what Solomon learned:

> What does a man get for all the toil and anxious striving with which he labors under the sun? All his days his work is pain and grief; even at night his mind does not rest. This too is meaningless. A man can do nothing better than to eat and drink and find satisfaction in his work. This too, I see, is from the hand of God, for without him, who can eat or find enjoyment?[8]

For many people, though, work is not something they enjoy, and it certainly isn't balanced by rest and pleasure. Instead, it is a matter of emotional survival. They *must* work to feel valuable, to keep themselves distracted from their internal anxieties, to forget about how empty they feel inside, to prove to other people that they are capable, to feel a sense of power and control, to get away from pressures or pain at home, or to . . . The list seems endless.

Elder was a workaholic by lifestyle, a legalist by religion. For him work was emotional survival: his sense of self-worth was conditioned upon his performance, as he thought he had to earn Father's approval. In the past, Prodigal had made the opposite mistake. He had been a hedonist by lifestyle, an abuser of grace by religion. He was lazy and spoiled. To him indulgence in pleasure made life worthwhile, so he did whatever he pleased—until he landed in a pigsty and his despair and his hunger led him home. But in returning home he was ashamed to face his father, his brother, and his neighbors. So he planned to pay off his debt and work his way back into favor by serving as a hired servant.

Prodigal's face-saving plan reveals a distortion in his view of himself and his father. He needed to understand that he couldn't atone for his sins by doing better; he couldn't earn Father's love by working harder. He needed to put his trust in Father and open his heart to mercy, forgiveness, free grace, and unconditional love. And he's about to do that. Then his eyes—and perhaps yours too—will see the Father's love in a new way.

Footsteps of Faith

1. This week consider if, like Prodigal, you're following Elder's bad example by using work to feel better about yourself. Which of the following messages have you accepted (even though you may try not to)?

- ☐ "The value of how you've spent your time is measured by what you've produced."
- ☐ "You're acceptable if you do what others want you to do."
- ☐ "You're valuable and worthwhile if you do well."

☐ "Your accomplishments are the legacy you leave behind when you die."
☐ "You can't count on anyone but yourself."
☐ "Stay busy and you'll stay out of trouble."
☐ "Successful people are happy people."

2. Both Elder and Prodigal struggled with feeling as if their worth and value were conditioned upon their performance and productivity. But until Prodigal's burst of false confidence in the pigsty, there was a big difference between Father's two sons.[9] Elder was proud that he had proved himself to be worthy, whereas Prodigal was ashamed that he couldn't prove himself to be worthy. Who do you identify with most closely, Elder or Prodigal? _____

3. This week meditate on God's grace to you, which the apostle Paul declared in Ephesians 2:8–10:

For it is by grace you have been saved, through faith—and this not from yourselves, it is the gift of God—not by works, so that no one can boast. For we are God's workmanship, created in Christ Jesus to do good works.

Notes

1. John 14:9.
2. Matthew 18:1–18; 19:13–15; Mark 10:13–16; Luke 18:16.
3. Other examples include Psalms 10, 13, 22, 60, 69, and 71. Note that unconfessed sin isn't always the reason David felt distant from God.
4. Psalm 18:2.
5. In my doctoral research study on the perceptions of God, I found *rock* to be the most popular among twenty-six symbols for God. The study surveyed 595 people in numerous evangelical Christian churches.
6. See Appendix 1, "Blessings and Curses from a Father," which contrasts the Father in Jesus' parable with sinful fathers.
7. Proverbs 21:5; 28:19.
8. Ecclesiastes 2:22–25.
9. See Appendix 2, "Prodigal and Elder Contrasted."

"So he got up and went to his father. But while he was still a long way off, his father saw him . . . ; he ran to his son."

Luke 15:20

STEP 3

Trust

Returning to the Father

The stirring of the chickens in the barn awoke Father early in the morning. He sat up on the edge of his bed and squinted to see in the dark. The dim light of the moon shone through the window, but the sun hadn't risen yet. He stretched his arms toward the ceiling, straightened his toes up and then down, and flexed his thighs and calves. Rubbing his eyes and then yawning, he considered lying back down.

Finally, after hesitating some time, he rose to his feet. He lost his balance and almost fell backwards onto the bed. "My, I feel like a stiff, wobbly old man in the morning!" he moaned.

Father walked to the dining area. He paused in front of the table. His eyes began to moisten as he saw the familiar scene: three complete place settings, a loaf of bread on a plate, and a full pitcher of wine.

It had been this way for almost seven months. No one was allowed to sit and eat at this table until the family could eat together. Each day Phillip baked a fresh loaf of bread and brought out a new pitcher of wine. Phillip thought it was a waste of precious food during the famine. Elder resented it. But Father was waiting for Prodigal to come home, and he wanted his son to be welcomed.

Father sat down at the table. Out the window he could see the sun rising. "Oh, what a beautiful morning it is!" Father exclaimed. "I wish Elder and Prodigal were at my side to enjoy it with me. But I see Elder's dishes in the washing area. He must already be working in the fields. And Prodigal is still away. But maybe he'll come home today. What do you think, Phillip? Is today the day?"

Phillip was just entering the dining area carrying a fresh baked pastry, cheese, and orange juice for Father's breakfast. He sighed, "Prodigal come home today? You know you've been saying that every day for months. Sir, I'm sorry, but I don't think he'll ever come home!"

"Come now, Phillip, where is your faith?" Father replied. "If you don't believe in Prodigal, then at least believe in Yahweh."

Later that morning Father went out to check on his vineyard. The vineyard, along with most of Father's land, had remained a lush green during the famine. That was because Father used the water from the lake on his property to water his plants and trees. He pulled one of the ripe grapes off the vine. A lump formed in his throat and his eyes began to tear as he thought about how much Prodigal loved to eat the grapes right after they were harvested.

Father tasted the juicy grape and looked north, in the direction where Prodigal had left. Just in front of him the cattle were drinking at their trough. Phillip was working in the vegetable garden. A neighbor's servants were working in one of the fields that Prodigal had sold. Beyond, Father could see that the village was just beginning to stir with people in the street. And past the village, way in the distance, Father could barely see some servants working in a field. But Prodigal was not to be seen.

As Father looked off in the distance he sang out the prayer that he had prayed every day since Prodigal left:

> You know I miss you, my beloved Prodigal, son.
> Soon the grapes will be harvested,
> And I pray you will be home with me by then.
>
> Your place at the table is still empty,
> Our bread is still unbroken,
> Our wine is still unpoured.
>
> Thus my heart is still empty,
> My thoughts of you unbroken,
> My love for you unpoured.
>
> I know I will see you soon, my beloved Prodigal, son.
> Your redeemed soul I will harvest
> When I find you coming home to me.

Prodigal *was* on his way home. He had taken the coastal route along the Mediterranean Sea. His trip across the desert had been nothing like his series of nightmares. It wasn't as hot as was typical for early summer, thanks to the clouds that had been blocking the sun. And he hadn't run into any hissing snakes or cackling birds! Further, he hadn't done nearly as much walking as he'd feared because he had received rides on carts for most of the three hundred mile trip home. The last ride dropped him off just ten miles outside Nain.

So far Prodigal's trip home had gone quite well. But he dreaded the final part—returning home. Just the thought of approaching the village sent chills through his body. His heart would begin to thump. His stomach would churn, his breathing would become shallow and rapid.

His mind would race. *How will I make it down the street past the gang of boys and the people in the village?*

Elder is going to beat me to a pulp if he gets his hands on me! And Father—what will he do? Will he listen to me? What if he doesn't even accept me back as a hired servant? I don't know where I'd go!

The more Prodigal thought about all that could go wrong, the more apprehensive he felt. His legs were becoming heavier as he neared the village. He wanted to turn around but he had nowhere to go; he could hide no longer. He had to face his father, Elder, and the others in the village; he couldn't escape the consequences of his actions.

So Prodigal shuffled forward, but now his head dropped in shame. He repeated to himself again and again, "Father, I have sinned against heaven and against you. I am no longer worthy to be called your son; make me like one of your hired men. Father, I . . ."

Father had gone out to the garden to see how the onions, cucumbers, beans, and other vegetables were looking. Phillip was still there plowing the dirt between the rows of vegetable plants. Suddenly, Father yelled out, "He's home! He's home! It's Prodigal!"

Phillip looked up and started to laugh at the old master. But then he stopped too; he saw a figure in the distance. And then he saw Father, running across the fields. Phillip was so startled that he dropped the hoe on his foot and fell backwards onto an eggplant!

Phillip couldn't believe his eyes. He had never seen his master run. He had never seen any man of such distinction, nor any man of his age run anywhere for any reason. But there went Father, tearing up the vegetable garden, then pushing through the cows, and then kicking up dust on the street! He was sprinting down the street as if he were in a foot race!

Phillip squinted to see the approaching figure in the distance. *How does he know that's Prodigal? But he must know or he wouldn't run like that!*

Phillip jumped to his feet, dropped his hoe, and ran after Father. *What would Father do? Would he beat Prodigal right there in the street? Why doesn't he just wait for Prodigal to get to the house?*

Just then, up ahead in the village, Sarah, one of the gossipy women of Nain, shouted out, "Look, it's Prodigal! The fool is returning home! He must be out of money! Ha! Ha! Ha!"

A small crowd of gapers began to gather and point at Prodigal. They could see him shuffling his way toward them down the street. His head was dropped in shame. His clothes were tattered and disheveled. He was covered in dirt from head to toe. And his hands were empty. Together their voices made quite a chatter as the crowd voiced slanderous thoughts about the town fool.

Others who heard Sarah scream were also gathering in the street to look at Prodigal. Among them were Joshua, the town mayor, and Rabbi Benjamin, the town priest.

Everyone's attention was on Prodigal until Sarah, who had turned around when she heard racing footsteps coming toward her from the other direction, howled in disbelief, "Oh, my goodness! Look over there! It's the Father of Prodigal *running*! He runs like a mad man! He's huffing and puffing and sweating! And look! His robe came untied! He's exposing his undergarments!"

Everyone turned to look at Father.

Tears were forming in Rabbi Benjamin's eyes, and there was a crack in his voice as he exclaimed, "See how he loves his son!"

This thought perturbed Joshua, who vehemently shook his head at Rabbi Benjamin and in his deep, gravel-sounding voice corrected the rabbi. "No, no, no! You don't understand!" Then pointing his finger at Prodigal and waving his Torah in the air above his head with his other hand, he angrily insisted, "This boy deserves to be punished severely! Justice must be enforced!"

Rabbi Benjamin was calmly stroking his long, gray beard as he responded, "No, Joshua, my friend. You are wrong. See the way this father runs? See how he shames himself? He has mercy on his face."

The boys in the street were also watching these events. Quickly they had put sticks in their hands, ready to poke, push, and punch Prodigal. But as Father came near they turned their attention upon him instead and a chant went up:

Silly old man.
Why do you run like a mad fool?
Silly old man.
Why do you expose your under-
garments to all?
Silly old man.
How can you love your stupid son?

But Father kept running toward Prodigal. The crowd and the gang of boys were all following behind him to see what would happen. But none of them ran. Even Phillip, as anxious as he was to see Prodigal and as much as he was curious, had gotten too tired to keep running. Only Father continued to run to Prodigal. He was gasping for air. Tears were streaming down his cheeks.

Prodigal stopped shuffling and stood still. He raised his hanging head and looked with wide-eyed amazement at his father running toward him with arms outstretched and open wide.

He's running! The villagers are mocking him, and his undergarments are exposed! But his arms are open to me. How can he love me this much?

It was as if he was seeing Father for the first time.

It had been seven months since Prodigal had left for Antioch. Everyone in Nain had given up on Prodigal. He might as well have been dead as far as they were concerned. And some people in the village would have been happy if he were dead! Upon hearing the news they would have shouted with scorn, "Good riddance to him! That sinful fool brought shame upon his family and his community! He got what he deserved!"

But that's not how Father felt. Every day since his son left home he went to the vineyard that Prodigal loved and looked north in the direction Prodigal had left. There were tears in his eyes, an ache in his heart, and the same prayer on his lips:

> You know I miss you, my beloved Prodigal, son.
> Soon the grapes will be harvested,
> And I pray you will be home with me by then.

> Your place at the table is still empty,
> Our bread is still unbroken,
> Our wine is still unpoured.

> Thus my heart is still empty,
> My thoughts of you unbroken,
> My love for you unpoured.

> I know I will see you soon, my beloved Prodigal, son.
> Your redeemed soul I will harvest
> When I find you coming home to me.

The father's love for his lost son is a picture of God's love for you. It's the theme of Jesus' parable: *God's love is looking for you.* No matter how lost you are in the far country, God's searching love can find you. No matter how deeply you've been hurt, God's healing love can comfort you. No matter how many times you've fallen into sin, God's hands of mercy can pull you back up onto your feet.

Jesus desired that we understand this. That's why he told the parable of the prodigal son as the final of three successive stories, all focusing on God's seeking love.[1] The shepherd with one hundred sheep leaves the ninety-nine sheep to find the one lost sheep and celebrates when he finds it. The old woman with ten silver coins lights a lamp, sweeps her house, and searches and searches until she finds her lost coin and rejoices when she finds it. And the father of two sons—the one indulging himself in the far country and the other slaving in the fields nearby, but each lost in his own way—looks for each of his sons and invites them into his house to celebrate his love. The father rejoices when he finds the first son. But the second son, the elder, he cannot find, even though he is nearby in the fields.

Unlike the elder son, Danny longed to be found by God's seeking love. He'd been a Christian since he was young boy. His parents taught him from the Bible and brought him to church. They provided well for him and his two older sisters. Danny never questioned that they "loved" him. In fact, he felt fortunate when he compared his childhood to that of many of his friends, who as children had experienced such family traumas as divorce, abuse, or an alcholic parent.

And it seemed that as an adult his life had gone pretty well too. He graduated from college as an accounting major with honors and now was working toward his CPA. He was active in his church, where he knew many people and everyone seemed to respect him. So why was he depressed?

Danny's life was flat, boring, and impersonal. He was detached from his feelings, so even when he was doing something "fun" he didn't really enjoy himself and even when he was talking with someone he didn't really feel understood or "connected." When a friend would surprise him and with sincerity ask, "How are you?" he always turned it around by asking, "How are you?" He wasn't used to answering that question. Most of the time he didn't know how he really felt inside or what he wanted for himself. He knew his thoughts. He knew what he was doing. He knew what other people felt or needed. But he didn't pay much attention to what _he_ felt and needed.

It had always been that way for Danny. His feelings and his needs were rarely the focus of attention. Now as he looked back on his life he wondered if his parents or anyone else really _knew_ him well enough to love him truly.

As a child Danny learned that his feelings weren't important. When he expressed sadness, fear, anger, or other emotions at home, his parents were uncomfortable. They didn't know how to deal with their own feelings, so how could they offer empathy and compassion for their son? And when he expressed his needs it just complicated family decisions, as four other family members expressed their needs. Furthermore, when he talked about something fun he wanted to do, a dream he had about his future, or an idea he was really excited about, somebody in the family seemed to find fault with it and burst his bubble.

Now, much of Danny's personal self was "lost." He had hidden many of his feelings, needs, values, dreams, and desires. These parts of him were lost in a dark, dusty corner of his unconscious. This began to change when he entered treatment for his depression. During the weeks he was in our program not a day went by that someone didn't ask him, "How are you, Danny?" Pretty soon he was wondering the same thing! When he finally began to open his soul, it was like watching a rose bud blossom and take in the warm sunshine. He learned what he had been missing out on: personal relationships. He was beginning to be found.

So it is with God's love. Sometimes we recognize His love in a story or a truth from Scripture and run to it. Other times, a sunrise, or a singing bird, or a quiet moment of reflection or prayer helps us know He cares. Usually, though, we recognize God's love most readily when He penetrates the lost, forgotten, neglected parts of our soul through the personal caring of people who, like God, are seeking to know us.

Footsteps of Faith

1. This week consider the two lost sons. Prodigal was lost in the far country, indulging his sinful impulses. Elder was lost in the fields, working to prove his worthiness. Neither knew the depths of father's love. (You may want to consult the descriptions of the two found in Appendix 1.) Which son are you most like? _____

2. You may feel distant from parts of your self. During the course of a typical day how much are you aware of your own feelings, needs, values, dreams, or desires? In your relationships how much of your personal self do you reveal? Depending upon your history of relationships, there could be several reasons that you hide or ignore parts of yourself. Check any of the following negative reactions you fear receiving when you express your feelings.

☐ Avoidance
☐ Judgment
☐ Harsh punishment
☐ Negativity and pessimism
☐ Abandonment
☐ The person takes it personally
☐ Condescending advice
☐ My feelings considered trivial
☐ Criticism
☐ Anger at me
☐ Sexual violation
☐ Disappointment with me
☐ Conflict
☐ Overwhelmed frustration
☐ An overreaction to what I say

3. Sometime this week meditate on Revelation 3:20. Jesus stands knocking at the door of your heart waiting for you to let Him in. He wants to know and love all of you, but He won't force His way in. But neither will He give up and go away. He waits, and when you open the door He brings both sides of His love: healing grace and revealing truth. Prayerfully invite Jesus into the dark corners of your soul, then open these same parts of your soul to a friend you trust.

WEEK 10
Father Wounds: Cause for Mistrust

As Prodigal returned home to his father he was terrified. He knew he had to walk past the gang of boys, the people in the village, and Elder just to get to Father. He expected to be bullied, beaten, and ridiculed. Maybe he wouldn't even be able to get through the crowd to get to his father. And what if he did? How could he face his father? *Will I even get a chance to talk to Father?* Prodigal wondered. *Perhaps he won't even acknowledge me. Maybe I'll be punished severely and thrown back into the angry mob.*

Prodigal was willing to face his fears because his needs were tremendous. He came to his father as a starving hired servant without a home. He was famished, destitute, ashamed, helpless, despairing. He had nowhere else to go and no one else to turn to. He had no friends. He felt all alone in a crowd of people looking at him with critical eyes. He needed food for his stomach, comfort for his wounds, encouragement for his heart, and forgiveness for his sin. Father was the only one who had the ability and the authority to provide these things. So Prodigal faced his fears, and he walked toward the unfriendly crowd looking for his father. He took a step of trust, and he was shocked by what happened. Father found him first! Father was looking for him. In fact, he was eagerly running out to greet him.

A father is very important to a child. Children look to their fathers for provision, protection, guidance, encouragement, security, warmth, and affection, among other things. Fathers are the first men in their lives, and by their example fathers teach their children what men are like. Sons need to feel bonded to and identified with their fathers and to have their masculinity affirmed—to feel that they belong with and will be respected by other men. Daughters need to feel embraced by their fathers and to have their femininity affirmed

—to feel that in men's eyes they are attractive, lovable, and worthy of respect.

The pain of an absent father is often a major factor behind such societal atrocities as gang violence, adolescent alcoholism, child pornography, teenage pregnancy and abortion, and teen suicide.

Some children with father-wounds are able to find more "acceptable" ways to deal with their pain. They may seek approval by trying to be the model student, star athlete, class president, homecoming queen or king. Other kids just drop out of the race for approval from their dads. They become high school dropouts, adolescent runaways, couch potatoes, depressed underachievers, lonely outcasts.

What was your childhood relationship with your father like? Were you found by your father? Did he push his way through the crowds of people, projects, and competing interests to find you and to express his love to you in personal ways? To whatever extent that he didn't find you, you will need to find him by taking three steps.

First, take a realistic look at your father's influence upon you. Sort out the good and the bad in your relationship with him. Thank him and God for the good that you received from your father. Acknowledge the bad too by confessing the sins of your father against you, sins of commission and sins of ommission.[2] Turning a light on your repressed, forgotten, or painful memories may be difficult. At first, probably something inside you will want to minimize the damage, protect your idealized image of him, or avoid the pain. Or you may find yourself taking the opposite approach, wanting to blame him for the problems you feel he created for you and expecting him to make it up to you now. If you take a realistic, balanced look at your father's sins, then feelings like emptiness, sadness, grief, shame, and anger will follow. Working through these feelings is a key part of the forgiveness process. The goal is to release yourself from resentment and your father from his debt to you. Ideally you and your father can talk about some of these things in a way that helps both of you.

Second, find a friend and tell him about your feelings toward your father. It helps if this person also has father-wounds, so that you can learn from each other. Whether you share with a friend, sibling, prayer partner, Twelve Steps sponsor, or support group is your choice. But do find someone. You can't do this alone.

Third, find a mentor. This is what Solomon meant when he advised, "Do not forsake . . . the friend of your father."[3] Even if you had a pretty good relationship with your father, you still need a guide and encourager as an adult. The greater your father-wounds, the more important this person is. Ideally this person will be older than you, the same sex, in a similar occupation or life position as you, and have a character that you respect and admire. But the only essential ingredient for this person to have is the last one in the list: he or she must be someone you respect and admire. Many people go through life without establishing even one significant relationship like this.

Finding a mentor can be scary. You may fear that this person will respond to you as your father and other authority figures have. You may feel judged, embarrassed, anxious, insecure, a need to please or to prove yourself, anger, rebellion, distrust, jealousy, and so forth. If this is you then you need to bring your father wounds to an understanding friend and to a mentor. As you do so, pray that the Father of Prodigal would find you!

Footsteps of Faith

1. This week consider your relationship with your father. The extent to which you experienced love from him has

a large impact on how comfortable it feels for you to take a step of trust and turn your will and your life over to the care of God.[4] On a scale of 1 to 10 with 10 being "very godly, near perfect" rate your father's expressions of love to in the following areas:

___ He provided for my basic needs.

___ He protected me from harm.

___ He guided me in ways that were good for me.

___ He gave me the support I needed to get through difficult times.

___ He encouraged me, but didn't pressure me, to become all that I needed to be.

___ I felt secure in his love for me.

___ He was open, warm, personable, and caring with me.

___ He showed me his love through affection without smothering me

___ He affirmed my gender identity.

2. Have you had a "friend of your father" to mentor and encourage you in life? The degree to which you have felt affirmed by a mentor will also affect your feelings toward trusting God. Check the feelings below that describe how you feel or act when you're with an authority figure:

☐ Fear of judgment   ☐ Embarrassment
☐ Anxious avoidance   ☐ Insecure
☐ Need to please   ☐ Need to prove myself
☐ Vulnerable   ☐ Needy
☐ Passive-aggressive   ☐ Anger or criticalness
☐ Jealous of his power   ☐ Distrust
☐ Rebellion or resistance   ☐ "I'd do it better than he/she."
☐ Cautious trust   ☐ Wanting to learn

3. Spend some time in prayer this week with your heavenly Father. Ask him to help you enact the three steps to healing your father-wounds: (1) forgive your father; (2) deepen your friendships with others who have father-wounds so that you can receive and give support; and (3) develop or deepen a mentor relationship.

4. When was the last time you and your father talked about your relationship? Maybe the two of you have never had an honest, loving discussion about how you each feel when you're together and what you each want for your relationship today.

As you progress in the healing of any father-wounds, consider whether it would be good for you to initiate such a discussion with your father. (Fathers, pray about talking with your children.)

WEEK 11

Shame and Fear: The Obstacles to Trust

Prodigal was returning to his father out of desperation. As he walked toward home he despaired over the mess he had made of his life, and he worried about how he would be treated. The weight of his guilt and shame dropped his head lower and lower; he wanted to start all over again, but it was too late. The weight of his fears and worries made his legs heavier and heavier; he wanted to turn back, but he had nowhere else to go.

The people in the village could see that Prodigal was ashamed and scared. They saw his drooping head, his tattered clothes, his disheveled and dirty appearance, his shuffling feet. The crowd gathered as Sarah shouted, "Look, it's Prodigal! The fool is returning home!" They mocked and slandered him as he approached the town. The gang of boys picked up their sticks and started shouting at him. Mayor Joshua pointed an accusing finger at Prodigal. Then with his other hand he waved the Torah over his head and in self-righteous anger he demanded, "This boy deserves to be punished severely! Justice must be enforced!"

Prodigal heard their insults and shouts of condemnation. He glanced nervously at the unruly crowd. He saw the gang of boys with their sticks. He swallowed hard and looked down at the ground. He continued shuffling forward. He was as helpless to save himself as a cow walking into the slaughterhouse to be butchered. He couldn't turn around; the crowd would chase after him and overtake him. So he prepared himself for their knives.

But he still had faint hopes that after he was bruised, beaten, and bloodied he could crawl on his hands and knees to his father. Then if he was received and after he was punished he would, with trembling hands and chattering teeth, offer his confession of sin and his promise to work off his debt.

Andy knew how it felt to be in Prodigal's shoes. As a boy he was skinny and freckled, and he stuttered. The other boys called him cruel names, such as "Skinny Andy," "Freckle Face," and the "Stuttering Stooge." One day after school Andy ran home when the other boys picked on him. His mother was scared for him. She planned to tell Andy's father about the tormenting boys, but Andy pleaded with her not to, insisting it would only make things worse. And he was right.

When Andy's father found out what had happened he was enraged. "My son won't be bullied!" he screamed at Andy. "Tomorrow you go back to school and show them what you're made of! Don't let them intimidate you!"

This just made Andy more scared of the bullies, and things didn't get any better. But Andy's father was a self-made tough guy who said he became a man while fighting in the Vietnam War. He was determined to toughen up his son and teach him to fight for himself like a man, so he signed up Andy for the school wrestling team.

"Somehow I made the team," Andy explained to me. "My father was so proud of me—until he came to my first match. I remember standing on the edge of the mat waiting for the referee to start the match. I looked at my opponent's mean, determined stare and looked away. I looked over at my father. He was standing to the side only fifteen feet from me. He gave me that 'C'mon, you can do it!' look that I knew all too well. To me that look meant, 'If you don't do it, then I'll be disappointed in you.'

"From that point on everything happened so fast. Before I knew it I was pinned to the mat, and I heard my dad groan. By the time I was back on my feet and I looked over at him he was gone. And that's pretty much the way things were between us. I wasn't tough enough. I never got his approval."

Now as a grown man who was married, had his own children, and was successful in business, Andy was still plagued with shame and fear. He was uncomfortable in groups of men because he feared being left out or judged. He avoided authority figures altogether because he resented people telling him what to do. He didn't trust older men, so he didn't let himself need their approval or encouragement.

Andy became successful on his own. He was like his father: tough on the outside, but inside still an insecure and self-conscious boy who avoided conflict and struggled for approval.

Andy needed the love Father displayed to Prodigal, but his fear of judgment, rejection, and failure kept him out of relationships with men, especially those whom he respected and admired. Andy had to work his way through his feelings of shame and fear. He began by challenging himself to take steps of initiative with other men. For instance, he joined a men's support group in his church. As he began to know the other men and they began to know him, he became more comfortable interacting with other men, and he felt better about himself as a man.

 _Footsteps of Faith_

1. This week consider how you feel when you're with a group of same-sex peers. Check the responses below that are true for you:

- ☐ Excluded ☐ Inadequate ☐ Jealous
- ☐ Anxious ☐ Depressed ☐ Superior to others
- ☐ Awkward ☐ Embarrassed ☐ Shy
- ☐ Afraid ☐ Vulnerable ☐ Ridiculed
- ☐ I'm more comfortable with members of the opposite sex
- ☐ I'm comfortable expressing myself and forming relationships

2. How does it feel for you to trust your heavenly Father? When you talk to God about your struggles, fears, and faults, how do you feel? Take some time this week to reflect on this. Most people idealize their relationship with God because they "know" that God is perfectly loving and they feel they "should" be able to trust Him completely. The degree to which you actually trust God is probably related to how you feel about trusting your father, authority figures, and other people.

3. Set aside some time to meditate on Psalm 25. Note how when David is experiencing difficulty in his relationships he talks to God about his feelings of fear, shame, loneliness, and distress (2, 16–20). He seeks God's mercy and love (6), knowing that if he trusts God with the anguish in his soul he will be comforted and guided in the right path (3–5).

4. Later this week, follow David's example and write a psalm of your own. Write down how you feel in your relationships. Perhaps you identify with David, Andy, or Prodigal. Read your psalm to a friend.

WEEK 12
"He Ran to Me!"

Father looked toward the north many times every day to see if his son was coming home, not only because he missed his son but also because he knew the trouble his son would face in the village. In past weeks he had heard Sarah's gossiping, Joshua's condemnation, Elder's criticisms, and the boys in the street singing their songs of ridicule. Everyone, it seemed, had something slanderous to say about Prodigal's foolishness. Like piranhas circling a lone fish, they were ready to attack Prodigal. Father wanted to save his son from this abuse.

When Father was standing in the garden and saw Prodigal way off in the distance he took off *running.* Yes, running. Father, a man of distinction, prominence, and wealth was doing what no other man in the village of Nain who was half his age or anywhere near his level of status had ever done! He tore up the vegetable garden, pushed his way through the herd of mooing cows, and kicked up dust on the street; he was in a foot race to get to his son before the abusive crowd did. Phillip was so startled at the sight of Father running that he dropped the hoe on his foot and then fell backwards onto an eggplant.

The scene was no less shocking in the village. The crowd of gapers and gossipers had gathered on the street to mistreat, mock, and malign the returning town fool. All eyes were fixed upon the fool until they heard Father's racing footsteps; then they turned to see what to them was a bigger fool. As he ran, Father was panting and sweating. He ran so fast that his robe came untied and exposed his undergarments, a tasteless action in Jewish culture. Now everyone's attention was fixed upon Father's public display of humiliation. Rabbi Benjamin was the first to understand at least part of the meaning of this. With tears in his eyes he exclaimed, "See how he loves his son!"

Some people have argued that the parable of the prodigal son is soft on sin, thinking that the father offers love and grace without taking his son's sin seriously. They think that the message of the parable is inconsistent with the message of the cross. What they don't see is this scene here: *Father is running to meet Prodigal.*

He identifies with his sinful son and takes upon himself his son's shame. He suffers the abuse and punishment due his foolish son.[5] The crowd turns from pointing at Prodigal to mock and slander Father. The gang of boys changes their song of ridicule from "Prodigool. Prodigool. You fool!" to "Silly old man. Why do you run like a mad fool?"

Other people wonder, "Shouldn't the father punish his son? Why is he wasting so much love on a fool?" Because Father is the real "prodigal!" He showers his son with his love and mercy![6] This is not the same as being soft on sin. He doesn't protect his son from the consequences of his sin. Prodigal experienced grief over losing his wealth, status, and friends. He felt the hunger of being a destitute and famished beggar. He experienced the terror of sleeping on the streets at night. He knew the hopeless despair of living in a pigsty. He felt the bondage of being a hired servant.

Actually, Father's incredible display of grace exposed the severity of Prodigal's sin. Until this point in the parable, Prodigal was still planning to work off his debt and make up for his sins. But now he sees how much his sin costs Father. He sees the humiliation, ridicule, and abuse that his father is experiencing on his behalf. And sees the joy and compassion on his father's tear-stained face and in his outstretched arms. With his jaw dropped open and his eyes staring at his approaching father, he realizes that he is seeing his loving Father for the first time.

In this parable Jesus is giving us a picture of what He—God in the flesh—did for us at the cross. He left His throne and the Father God in heaven and though "being in very nature God. . . [he] made himself nothing, taking the very nature of a servant, being made in human likeness. . . . he humbled himself and became obedient to death—even death on a cross!"[7] He became a sin offering for us. As God in human flesh He lived a perfect and sinless life. He fulfilled the requirements of the law, then chose to take upon Himself our sins and the punishment of death they deserved, so that we could be reconciled to God and know His righteousness.[8]

It's amazing but it's true. When we put our trust in God's gracious love for us expressed in Christ, we are saved from the shame of our sins and the fear of condemnation, and we are reconciled to the Father. And this is the Father we all long for! He empathizes with our pain, cares about our needs, identifies himself with us, takes away our shame, and fills us with His love.

Footsteps of Faith

1. Imagine yourself in Prodigal's shoes this week. But picture your _heavenly_ Father running through the hostile crowd to get to you. Through His Son Jesus, He's taking your shame upon Himself. Tears of joy are streaming down His cheeks because He has you back safe and sound. The Father's arms are outstretched to welcome you home.

2. David says of God, "You stoop down to make me great."[9] This is what Jesus did for us, and it's what Father did for Prodigal. It's the essence of encouragement. Somebody with authority whom you respect steps down to your level, empathizes with you, identifies himself with you, and gives you the courage to make it through tough times and to become all that you can be. In prayer, ask God to encourage

you this week and thank Him for His willingness to be involved in your life.

    3. Take a moment right now to consider what Jesus Christ has done for you at the cross. If you have never turned your will and your life over to the care of God by putting faith in Jesus as your Savior and Lord, then why don't you do so now? Simply confess your sinfulness to God, ask for His mercy and forgiveness, and then prepare yourself to begin to be changed by His love!

WEEK 13

Trust: Initiating and Being Responsive

When Prodigal saw Father's incredible display of love, he stopped his shuffling, raised his head, stood motionless, and stared. He was captivated by the sight of Father. There was his father running toward him through the crowd, exposing his undergarments, enduring the scorn and mocking, crying in joyous relief, reaching out to him with arms of love —all this for a despicable fool who had betrayed his father!

At first he couldn't believe it, but he soon did. He believed that Father loved him that much. He trusted in Father's mercy and it changed him.

Prodigal's trust in Father was a response to Father's expression of love for him. But it wasn't only a response. Remember the initiative he took. It was of his own accord that he left the far country to return to Father. He walked across the three hundred miles of barren desert. By heading toward the village he was facing up to the guilt of his sins and the fear of what he thought would be certain humiliation, condemnation, and abuse.

Returning to his father was a big risk. True, he was desperate and his only other apparent choice was to starve to death in the pigsty. Yet many people who don't take steps of trust die in pigsties of their own making.

Developing a trust that is balanced by initiative and responsiveness is essential to progressing forward in the journey of recovery. The alcoholic has to decide for himself to join Alcoholics Anonymous, to keep attending meetings, to work the steps, to pray to God, to call his sponsor when he's tempted to tip the bottle again. He also needs to be responsive in order to listen to his feelings, to discern how safe it is for him to share his needs with specific people, to base his trust in others on his experience of their character, to be open to God's love coming to him through the people in his

107

meetings, to apply from what he learns. This is the way the alcoholic turns his will and his life over to the care of God.[10]

Even if you're not struggling with an addiction to alcohol you also need to put our trust in the Father God's love and guidance. If you put your trust anywhere else you'll be trapped in an idolatrous bondage. "No one can serve two masters," Jesus explains. "Either he will hate the one and love the other or he will be devoted to the one and despise the other. You cannot serve both God and money."[11]

The things that can crowd God out of our lives are innumerable. For instance, the overeater needs to give up her compulsion to eat in secret in order to comfort herself and instead choose to express her feelings of depression, insecurity, and loneliness to God and to a friend. The pefectionistic housecleaner needs to resist her compulsion to clean and instead write a psalm to God about how anxious, inadequate, and out of control she feels. The adult child of a dysfunctional family needs to work at releasing his resentment by talking to his counselor and to God about his anger and his sadness over all the pain he experienced in his family.

It's difficult to give up the compulsions and destructive patterns that we use to avoid pain. That is why people in recovery often relapse. Thank God that mistakes, failures, and sins—though we commit them again and again—don't exclude us from the kingdom of God as long as we receive God's forgiveness and mercy. The difference between those who follow God and those who don't is not that followers of God don't fall down. It's that when God's people fall down they get up again with God's help, and they learn from their mistakes.[12]

Even the apostle Paul knew how it felt to relapse into old patterns. And he also knew how to get back on track by reconnecting with God's grace to him in Christ.

> I do not understand what I do. For what I want to do I do not
> do, but what I hate to do. . . . For I have the desire to do what

is good, but I cannot carry it out. . . . When I want to do good, evil is right there with me.

Who will rescue me from this body of death? Thanks be to God—through Jesus Christ our Lord![13]

A materialistic and dishonest man named Zacchaeus also learned to trust in Jesus.[14] He was hated by his fellow Jews because he served the Roman government as a tax collector, but his position had brought him great wealth. One day he heard that Jesus was passing through. He'd heard about Jesus' compassionate miracles and His wise teaching. He wanted to see Jesus, but the crowd was huge and unruly, and he was a short man whom no one wanted to help. So he took the initiative to run ahead of the crowds that surrounded Jesus and climbed into a sycamore tree so that he could see Jesus when He walked by.

Jesus saw Zacchaeus and said to him, "Come down! Let's eat dinner together tonight!" Everyone, including Zacchaeus, was shocked. Jesus was going to eat with such a despised sinner as this! But Zacchaeus responded to Jesus' invitation. He trusted Jesus because he wanted love and forgiveness. Then he demonstrated his new faith by renouncing his materialism and deceit, giving half his possessions to the poor, and paying back four times' worth to all whom he had cheated.

He took initiative to meet Jesus, and he responded to His love. He trusted God and was given a fresh start!

Footsteps of Faith

1. There are sacrifices we must be willing to make if we want to turn our lives over to God. Recovery from a destruc-

tive or painful way of life isn't easy. Old habits die hard. Perhaps you're trying to serve God and money (or something else). What in your life do you need to turn over to God?

_____

2. Sometime this week read Luke 9:57–62 and meet the three men who said they wanted to trust Christ but in the end did not. The first man said he'd follow Jesus anywhere but was not prepared for the difficulties of the journey. The second man wanted to follow Christ but first wanted to attend to his business and collect some money. The third wanted to go on with Jesus, but issues with his family held him back.

Perhaps you identify with the struggles of these men. Answer from your own perspective the following challenging questions Jesus asked of them.

> (1) Are you prepared to resist (with God's help) temptations to go back to destructive behaviors? Are you willing to uncover emotional pain you've repressed, injuries you've minimized, and past sins you've overlooked or haven't learned from?   _____
>
> (2) Are you willing to make sacrifices by investing your time, energy, and money in your healing and growth? You may lose popularity, pleasure, power—even success—to do so.   _____
>
> (3) Are you committed to work through past or present issues of family dysfunction that are hindering you?   _____

NOTES

1. Luke 15.
2. Nehemiah 9:2.
3. Proverbs 27:10.
4. This principle is embodied in Step 3 of Alcoholics Anonymous's Twelve Steps: "Made a decision to turn over our will and our lives to the care of God *as we understood Him.*"
5. This point is well established and illustrated by Kenneth Bailey in *The Cross and the Prodigal* (St. Louis: Concordia, 1973).
6. Lloyd Ogilvie makes this point in *An Autobiography of God* (Glendale, Calif.: Regal, 1981).
7. Phillipians 2:6–8.
8. 2 Corinthians 5:18, 21.
9. Psalm 18:35*b*.
10. As described in Step 3 of Alcoholic's Anonymous' Twelve Steps.
11. Matthew 6:24. In the context of this passage Jesus is referring to the bondage of materialism, but elsewhere in the Bible He and others apply the same principle to many other issues.
12. Proverbs 24:16.
13. Romans 7:15, 18*b*, 21*b*, 24, 25.
14. Luke 19:1–10.

"His father saw him and was filled with compassion for him."

Luke 15:20

STEP 4

Self-Examination

Looking into Father's Eyes of Compassion

Father continued racing toward Prodigal, pushing his way through the mocking crowds, panting for air like a tired dog, leaving a trail of sweat and clouds of dust behind him. Even as he ran his arms were stretched open wide, exposing the mercy in his heart.

Prodigal was standing, looking, waiting—now he blinked his eyes and shook his head in amazement. *Am I dreaming?* he wondered. *How can he love me this much? That should be* me *running the gauntlet through town!*

Father was racing closer and closer, his feet pounding the dirt road. The ground itself seemed to rumble with excitement. Prodigal braced himself, closed his eyes, and winced, thinking his father would tackle him in love—or in anger! *Is he mad at me?* Prodigal wondered. *Is that why he's chasing toward me?*

Then Father suddenly pulled up his stride and came to a halt. *What will he do? What will he say?* Prodigal worried, his eyes still closed. He heard his father panting. He heard his arms drop to his side. He felt Father standing there right in front of him, toe to toe, nose to nose, breath to breath, heart to heart. There was a long silence . . .

Finally, Prodigal opened his eyes. He looked at his father. He watched as the tears continued to swell in his father's eyes and roll down his cheeks. Prodigal wanted to say something, but the words wouldn't come. So much time had passed. So much had happened. What could he say?

Finally Father broke the silence, "My son, I've missed you more than you know."

"You did?" Prodigal exclaimed in amazement. I don't know what to say Father. I—"

"Yes, son. I've so much longed for this moment. Remember the meal we never finished the night before you left? It's still waiting. We couldn't eat at the table as a family without you there. So each day I had Phillip put out a fresh baked loaf of bread and a pitcher of wine in hopes that you'd be back home to eat with us.

"As time passed and the famine got worse and worse my heart grew heavier and heavier. I had heard that you were in trouble. Then Timothy told me how bad things had gotten for you, and my grief couldn't be contained. How eagerly I longed for you to come home! How I wished I could feed you! How anxious I was to restore your soul! But I had to wait for your return; I couldn't rescue you from yourself. I knew that it was only a matter of time before you'd come to your senses and find the courage to come back home.

"Every morning I went out to the vineyard you love, and I thought of you and prayed for you. And every day, all day long, in all that I did I looked north, watching for your return. I wanted to be the first to greet you when you returned home. I knew that people in the village were angry at you. I heard them slander you to one another. Their words were like

114

knives piercing my heart! I knew the ridicule and abuse you'd face in the village, and I wanted to save you from this."

Just then the people who had been trailing Father as he raced through the village caught up with him. All were confused by the unexpected events they had just witnessed. All were buzzing with curiosity, wondering what would happen next. Of course, Sarah was the first and the noisiest arrival. She could be heard muttering over and over, "This father is a bigger fool than his son!" Then Timothy, Joshua, Rabbi Benjamin, the gang of boys, and the others from the village arrived. Phillip was the last to reach the scene. He was exhausted—and a bit embarrassed that he couldn't keep pace with an old man!

Father and Prodigal were so engrossed in conversation that neither of them paid notice to the bystanders. With his eyes still fixed on his son, Father exclaimed, "And now, son, I'm so glad I have you back home safe and sound! But I look at you and my heart still aches for you. You look exhausted. You've traveled so far in the hot sun. And this without shoes! Your feet must be raw and blistered. How did you survive the famine? You must be starving! Oh, look at these scratches on your arms and legs. Did you get these living in the streets? And . . . and . . . Oh, son! I smell the pigs! How did you ever endure such shame and such despair?"

At this Sarah pointed at Prodigal and shrieked, "Swine! Swine!" And everyone backed away a few strides holding their noses and grimacing. Prodigal dropped his head in shame. Father reached out and put his hand on Prodigal's bare shoulder, exposed by a tear in his tattered shirt, and whispered in his ear, "You're still my beloved son, and you always will be."

"Oh, Abba!" Prodigal replied as he buried his head into Father's chest. "Abba, I've missed you so much! Even when I had all of Antioch wrapped around my little finger, I was empty inside. The gold, the impressive image, the fancy living, the wild partying, none of it made me as happy as I am

115

now to see you, Abba! But, fool that I was, I had to lose it all to see that it was your love I longed for!

"It was horrible, Abba," Prodigal cried, his tears falling onto Father's chest. "I lost everything! All the gold you gave me is gone! I gambled away my last coin! Then came the famine. I had to hock the shoes on my feet to get bread! I lived in the streets with Alex, a friend I made. We begged from all who passed by us. We fought with wild pigs and beggars gone mad for the remains from garbage cans. Then one night Alex, my only friend who hadn't abandoned me in my despair, he left me too! I was all alone, Abba! No one would help me!"

Prodigal took in a deep breath, closed his eyes, and exhaled. "Then, I hired myself out to serve a wealthy Greek man named Demetrius. He wanted to get rid of me, and so he offered me a job feeding his pigs! I was so desperate I took it! But he gave me no food. I would have eaten the pigs' carob pods but I couldn't! I slept in a dirty pigsty but even there I was an outcast!"

"Son," Father's voice was cracking with emotion, "you must have been so lonely, so sad, and so embarrassed. How did you ever see hope in the midst of such despair?"

Prodigal pulled his head out of Father's chest, looked into Father's eyes, and continued, "Yes, Abba. I felt all of that and more."

"Tell me, son."

"Well, I finally came to my senses! I did find hope, Abba. I called out to God for mercy. And I decided to find a way back home. But I was so scared! I was terrified to face the village and Elder—where is Elder, anyway?"

Father looked around him, but his other son was not to be found. To have both his sons reconciled to himself and to each other was a wonderful, but fading, thought. "Son," Father replied, as he refixed his gaze upon Prodigal, "let's not concern ourselves with Elder just yet. He's probably working so hard in the fields that he doesn't even know you're home!"

"But *you* knew I was coming home, Abba! You believed the best in me even after I had done the worst! Abba, I feel silly admitting it now, but I was even scared to come home to you. I guess I didn't really know you then like I'm starting to know you now."

Still looking right into Prodigal's eyes, Father chuckled, "Yes, son! And I have so much more of myself to give you! You just wait and see. You can't imagine the blessings I have in store for you!"

Prodigal was startled. Such knowledge! Such love! It was too much for him to grasp. It felt bad and good at the same time. He looked away from Father and shook his head. Tears of grief—and joy—streamed down his cheeks. He covered his face with his hands, but try as he did he couldn't get the image of Father's eyes out of his mind. He kept thinking about his Abba's eyes . . .

> *Eyes that know me deep inside.*
> *Eyes that see my sinful pride.*
> *Eyes that see past my dirt.*
> *Eyes that love me and heal my hurt!*

Meanwhile, Joshua was quite upset about Father's apparent disregard for justice. He leaned over and muttered in Rabbi Benjamin's ears, "I can't keep quiet any longer! This is ridiculous! All this weeping over nonsense and this display of affection is making me sick! The issue here is the law! Prodigal should have known better than to commit such vile sins, and now the law must be enforced. Certainly, Benjamin, you agree that he should be punished?"

"Oh, no, I don't, Joshua," the misty-eyed rabbi replied. "Where is your compassion for a lad in distress? Can't you see that the issue here is love? Father loves his son dearly. Besides, it isn't long until the Day of Atonement, and we'll then offer up the necessary animal sacrifices."

This argument between Joshua and Rabbi Benjamin was nothing new. For years they had been debating between themselves and even in front of the villagers about justice versus love. Joshua was so upset because this turn of events threatened his prominent position. Father's display of loving kindness and mercy had tipped the scales in Rabbi Benjamin's favor. Until now the mayor had been the leader in the village whom everyone turned to for answers. Of course, Rabbi Benjamin was elated. He thought that perhaps now everyone would see his point that love is more important than justice. *Maybe now the village of Nain will finally see the day when the priesthood is esteemed in its rightful position of superiority over the government!*

Prodigal was oblivious to Joshua and Rabbi Benjamin's debate. (For that matter so was everyone else except Father, who knew their thoughts.) Prodigal was still feeling the impact of Father's eyes, and he was lost in silent thought. Father's incredible display of love as he ran through the town and his deep compassion shown up close had shone a light into his soul and exposed the darkness there. It wasn't a pretty sight to look at, but he did anyway.

Prodigal began to take inventory. First, he considered how he had been sinned against: Timothy, who took advantage of his impulsiveness; Alex, and others in Antioch, who used him for his money; the passersby who mocked him when he was living in the street; Alex, who left him. These things angered Prodigal. He needed Father's help to forgive and be released from his resentment. His heart also was heavy with hurt, and he needed greatly his father's love.

Then he looked at his own sins: insulting and rejecting his father, being greedy for money, pridefully thinking he could run his own life, foolishly doing as he pleased, projecting a false image in Antioch, manipulating people to get his way, harboring resentment toward Elder.

The weight of these sins made Prodigal's face-saving plan to work off his debt to Father seem impossible. Father's incredible display of love by running through the village and enduring the scorn and mistreatment of the crowd in Prodigal's village made Prodigal's plan seem ridiculous. How could he make up for all the pain he caused Father? How could he do enough to repay Father for this enormous sacrifice of love?

He couldn't. He couldn't.

WEEK 14
You Need Compassion Too!

Father had compassion for his prodigal son. He sensed the ridicule and abuse his son would face in the village. He saw his son's dejected face and shuffling gait. He smelled the dirty stench of the pigsty on his son. He listened to his son's cries about all the troubles he experienced. He tasted the tears as he cried with his son. He touched his son's shoulder, exposed by the tear in his tattered shirt. He felt his son's sadness, loneliness, shame, fear. He knew his son needed food for his stomach, forgiveness of his sins, and restoration of his soul.

Like Prodigal, we long for someone to step into our shoes and to feel our feelings. We yearn to be fully known and fully loved. Our heavenly Father did this for us by sending His only Son, Jesus, to be born into this world and live as a man. Jesus experienced pleasure and pain, leisure and hard work, success and struggle, hope and disappointment, friendship and loneliness, acceptance and rejection, joy and sadness, satisfaction and hunger, security and temptation, confidence and embarrassment. In His earthly life He received peace and anger, praise and criticism, blessing and mistreatment. He lived a life similar to ours; He understands what we feel, and He wants to help us. And because He lived without sinning He has the right to forgive our sins.[1]

Unfortunately, many people who believe in Jesus Christ and who try hard to follow Him still struggle to experience in their hearts this compassion from God. They read about Jesus' life in the Bible, they pray to God, they attend church— and yet, though they may receive guidance and encouragement, they still lack a tangible sense of God's compassionate love in their hearts. Why would a committed Christian struggle to experience God's love?

That is exactly the question Rick asked when he first visited me. "I think I'm having a midlife crises, and I can't pray my way out." As I got to know Rick, I became impressed with his intelligence, his success as an entrepreneur, and his dedication to his family and to God. But I could also see that he was depressed and that something was missing in his life. And in my relationship with Rick I didn't feel I was getting closer to him with time. He wasn't personal with me. Mostly he talked with me about problems he was having that related to his work. Sometimes he would talk about his feelings, but even then he seemed far away. He didn't feel his feelings in the here and now. Even though he came to me asking for help, he wasn't vulnerable with me; he didn't seem to let himself need my caring.

When we explored Rick's current and past history of relationships, we discovered the same pattern. Though he was married and had friends, all his relationships lacked intimacy and warmth. And to whatever extent he developed closeness with other people it was largely due to their being vulnerable with him. Rick had what he thought was a fairly "normal" childhood. There wasn't any obvious trauma in his past. The only lack we discovered was he had received little compassion as a boy.

One day Rick said of his father, "I knew he loved me. He was just too busy to notice my feelings." Rick said his mother was known for keeping the house clean and calm for Rick's father. "I abided by the rules," Ron told me. "As long as I stayed out of trouble and kept my feelings to myself my parents were happy with me."

"But surely there were times when you had trouble keeping so quiet," I interjected. "What did you do when you were upset or disappointed?"

"Oh, I went outside and shot hoops," Rick answered almost immediately. "I played basketball by myself for hours. Sometimes I played with friends too. Of course, later I played competitively at school. Those were the happiest times of my childhood!" All of a sudden Rick got quiet for a long moment. "You know what I just realized?" he continued. "I do the same thing today! When I feel depressed or if things aren't going well at home with my wife or my daughters I just go and do something to clear my mind. I feel my best when I'm either out on the court or at work engrossed in a project."

Rick decided it was time to take a different approach. He chose to pay more attention to his feelings. When he was depressed he expressed his feelings to me, his wife, or his friend, who, because he had just been through a divorce recovery program and was working through his own depression, was sensitive to Rick's feelings.

Rick's approach seemed to work. About a year after I met Rick he didn't seem depressed, and he had a much more dynamic and real relationship with God and with others. He spoke of tearing up during worship at church, of his love for his daughters, an improved marriage, and a "best friend" with whom he not only played tennis but at times shared heart to heart.

Rick had experienced God's compassion in his relationships, and it made the world a place where he could be honest and real.

Footsteps of Faith

1. This week consider your relationships. Do you struggle to experience the compassion you need? If your answer to any of the questions below is "yes" then you may want to follow Ron's example by making some changes in your relationships or by developing some new relationships.

(1) Are you more comfortable listening to others' feelings than sharing your own? _____

(2) Do you allow other people's needs to crowd out or minimize your needs? _____

(3) Do you feel as if you need too much? _____

(4) Do you feel guilty or embarrassed when you share your feelings with a friend? _____

(5) Do you talk about your feelings without experiencing them? _____

(6) When you share your feelings with a friend, do you walk away feeling like you're no different inside? _____

(7) Do you measure yourself based on your productivity rather than your experience? _____

(8) Do you lack a current relationship in which you consistently find the compassion you need? _____

2. Prodigal had his father. Rick had a friend, his wife, and his therapist. Who do you have to show you compassion? Do you have a friend who wants to know what it feels like to walk in your shoes? If not, sometimes the best way to find a friend is to be a friend to someone. Look for someone who needs compassion, and then maybe you can start putting each other's shoes on!

3. In compassion the Spirit of God searches out our hearts, seeking to restore our souls and aid us in our journey of healing.[2] His compassion opens the door to our soul so that we can take inventory of our sins and our hurts. With this in mind, set aside time in the next few days to meditate on and pray David's prayer: "Search me, O God, and know my heart; test me and know my anxious thoughts. See if there is any offensive way in me, and lead me in the way everlasting."[3]

WEEK 15

Justice and Love

Father's display of compassion toward his son outraged Joshua, who regarded Prodigal as a despicable and sinful fool. The town mayor muttered to Rabbi, "Prodigal should have known better than to commit such vile sins, and now the law must be enforced!" He wanted justice preserved and thought that this could only be done through swift and strict punishment. He wanted Prodigal punished for his sins in front of the whole town: "Everyone must know that sin has consequences and that Nain is a just city!" he explained.

Rabbi Benjamin had a very different view. Yes, Prodigal had sinned, but it would be atoned for when the animal sacrifices were made. The rabbi thought that the issue here was love, a Father's love for the son, who was dear to his heart. He wanted Nain to be a village where love was preserved over justice, relationships over law. Then the people would be free from condemnation, and the priest, not the town mayor, would lead Nain.

Neither the mayor nor the rabbi had the answer to the problem of what to do about Prodigal's sins. Had Prodigal focused on the town mayor's condemnation of his sins he would have hidden in shame and found no forgiveness. Had he focused on the rabbi's blind love he would have overlooked the gravity and the immensity of his sins, and thus he still would have found no forgiveness. Clearly, Joshua and Rabbi Benjamin were not concerned about Prodigal's needs for forgiveness and restoration; each was interested in improving his position of authority in the village at the expense of the other.

Father had the answer, though. He took on himself the punishment for sin that the village would have meted out on Prodigal. As the one who Prodigal had sinned against, Father had the authority to forgive his son, and he chose to show compassion and to forgive Prodigal. Love _and_ justice were preserved. Both had to be there. If it wasn't for Father's expressed love, then Prodigal would have been too scared and ashamed to take inventory of the dirty wounds in his heart. But Father's humiliating demonstration, in which he bore the ridicule and mistreatment justly due his son, let Prodigal recognize the seriousness of his sin.

What a Godsend! (I use that word literally.) Love and justice, grace and truth, freedom and responsibility had become one in Father's compassion. In Father, mercy and righteousness kissed each other; sympathy and morality linked arms.

In response to this compassion Prodigal was freed from his shame. He buried his head in his father's chest and opened his soul to the one who knew him and still loved him. Tears of grief flowed like a river over all the pain he had experienced. As Prodigal sighed in regret over all the sins he had committed, his wounds were being healed and his sins were being forgiven—his recovery was progressing forward.

Can you imagine yourself standing in Prodigal's place? Perhaps as a child you did; you stood toe to toe with your father and shared a hurt with him or talked with him about a wrong you committed. What was that experience like? I hope those were times when, like Prodigal, you received your father's compassion. Unfortunately, for some people those times were very hurtful. They heard things like:

- "Haven't you cried enough about that? It's time to forget about it and move on."
- "Don't cry over spilt milk."
- "Don't be a crybaby!"
- "How could you do that? You should have known better!"
- "Just don't make the same mistake again!"
- "Don't cry or I'll give you something to cry about!"
- "Look at what a mess you've made of your life. When are you going to get your act together?"

It's not just fathers and town mayors who may say shame-inducing things like this to us. Such comments can come from anyone. When they come from someone you trust, especially if you're a child, they tend to get deep inside your heart. And once they get inside it's hard to get them out. I know because I hear many people who say these kinds of condemning things to *themselves*. Their tone of voice or even their exact words are a parent's, yet it's coming from their own minds and mouths! The tragedy of this is magnified when people pass on these same messages to their friends, their spouse, and even their children.

Other people as children had a very different kind of parent. Instead of encountering strictness and judgment they received permissiveness and reassurance. When they talked about an injury or a struggle they received such verbal or nonverbal messages as:

- "Don't worry. Everything will be OK."
- "There, there. Cheer up. Don't feel that way."
- "It doesn't matter if you do wrong."
- "I'll just pretend you didn't do that."

Parents, like the town rabbi, sometimes go to this other extreme and adopt a *laissez faire* approach. Often their own parents were too strict or harsh, and now they want to avoid hurting their children in the same fashion they were hurt. Although this approach is a lot "nicer" and doesn't inflict sharp wounds, it leaves you, the child, feeling as though you don't matter that much, which in a different and more subtle sense also leaves you feeling ashamed. Blind love and empty reassurance lack the substance of compassion. Permissiveness undermines our need for justice and boundaries.

Like Prodigal, we need both love and justice. We experience these when we meet our heavenly Father as Prodigal did, toe to toe, eye to eye, heart to heart, tear to tear.

Footsteps of Faith

1. Sometime this week review your relationships with your parents and others whom you've relied upon for caring and guidance. Maybe some of these people are like the town mayor. If so, then you must have felt judged, pressured, or wounded. Note any of the messages below that are similar to ones you've heard.

- ☐ "Haven't you cried enough about that? It's time to forget about it and move on."
- ☐ "Don't cry over spilt milk."
- ☐ "Don't be a crybaby!"
- ☐ "How could you do that? You should have known better!"
- ☐ "Just don't make the same mistake again!"
- ☐ "Don't cry or I'll give you something to cry about!"
- ☐ "Look at what a mess you've made of your life. When are you going to get your act together?"

2. Maybe some of the people you relied upon were like Rabbi Benjamin. If so, you probably felt as though you weren't important enough to be fully known and fully loved. Check off any of the messages below that you were given.

- ☐ "Don't worry. Everything will be OK."
- ☐ "There, there. Cheer up. Don't feel that way."
- ☐ "It doesn't matter if you do wrong."
- ☐ "I'll just pretend you didn't do that."

3. What kinds of messages do you give to other people? Are you more like the just mayor or the loving priest? Have a friend help you answer that question. If you live by and give

messages like the town mayor, then probably you're some-what compulsive, perfectionistic, and legalistic. If you're more like the priest, then you're likely somewhat impulsive, messy, and permissive.

4. Set aside some time to read Mark 1:40–45, the story of the man with leprosy who was healed by Jesus. In that day lepers (those with skin diseases) were ostracized by society; no one dared get near lepers for fear they would catch their disease. But Jesus touched this leper, healing his disease and its shame and restoring him to the community. As a part of the restoration process the healed man went to the Temple and offered sacrifices for cleansing and forgiveness, which would have included confessions of sin. This week pray that Jesus would touch your soul by healing your injuries and your shame, helping you develop relationships, and giving you the courage to confess your sins.

Oh, Abba!

When Prodigal meets his father upon returning home from the far country he meets his father like never before. The encounter is like the grand finale at a fireworks show. Multicolored surprises of love start bursting forth one after the other, filling the sky and the heart with beauty! Father's gift of compassion is just the beginning. Father hints to Prodigal and the others that he has more gifts to give. Indeed, still ahead in the story are bountiful blessings and symbolic serendipities such as a hug, a robe, a ring, sandals, a party, and much more. The anticipation of even more surprises to come makes the excitement all the greater!

This first fireworks of compassion is a show in itself. When Father grieved over his son's absence and longed for his son's return home in spite of his son's sin against him, the first pyrotechnic display shot skyward. It exploded with color when Father spotted his son and ran down the village street and endured the scorn and the abuse that his son deserved. And now, just when we think the color and sparks will die out and fall to the ground, this same fireworks of compassion issues a second display, as beautiful as the first: "You're still my beloved son, and you always will be!"

What Father had demonstrated in action was now spoken in words. Words of sensitivity, tenderness, mercy, gentleness, and patience. Words spoken to a sinner overtaken by pride, greed, and lust. Words spoken to a castaway rejected by all except beggars, garbage cans, pigs, and . . . the one who spoke!

Who is this old man who spoke? Who is he really? "Father" doesn't quite fit him, so Prodigal exclaims, "Oh, Abba!" *Abba*, the Aramaic term for *Daddy*, captures Prodigal's warm, intimate feelings for his father.

Prodigal finally saw his father's heart. He saw it because he had been humbled, like a baby boy crawling on his hands and knees with a loaded diaper and crying screams of desperation. Humbled, yet trusting, Prodigal now brought his soul's pain. He wanted his Daddy and no one else would do!

My son David's very first word was "Da-da." He used it all the time when he was a baby. When he wanted out of his crib in the morning. When he wanted to eat. When he wanted out of his high chair. When he wanted to be held. When he wanted anything! When he felt sad, happy, angry, or content—no matter what he felt, it was always the same: "Da-da! Da-da! Da-da! Da-da!" It was the only word he knew, so he used it hundreds of times every day.

I wouldn't have been sure that "Da-da" really meant me, his daddy, except for the fact that every night when I came home from work it was the same routine. He'd hear the garage door open and close. His Mommy would say, "Da-da is home, David!" David would crawl toward the door to our garage and with a look of anticipation he'd exclaim, "Da-da! Da-da! Da-da! Da-da!" When he saw me the "Da-da's" got louder and louder until I reached down and picked him up and gave him a big squeeze. Then he was all smiles—and so was I!

I've been told that it's the same with Jewish babies. Their first word is "Ab-ba," which is Hebrew for "Da-da." I know it isn't fair to mothers. They bear the pregnancy, go through labor, and endure more than their share of dirty diapers, runny noses, crying, screaming, and mindless hours of child's play. Yet "Da-da" may still be their child's first word!

Maybe it has something to do with what the apostle Paul said: "Because you are sons, God sent the Spirit of his Son into our hearts, the Spirit who calls out, 'Abba, Father.'"[4] There is something deep inside of us all that longs for the love of our heavenly Father. For young children who don't yet have that capacity for faith in God that longing can only be filled to the extent that they are affectionately and lovingly bonded with Daddy, Mommy, and their other caretakers.

Many of us don't appreciate the great privilege of being invited to call God "Da-da." This is a relatively new concept, one introduced by Christ and His apostles. In the Old Testament God was known as the "God of our fathers," "Lord Almighty," and "Creator." References to God as "Father" in the Old Testament are usually used in a prophetic sense, suggesting that He will ultimately be revealed and understood that way. And on the rare occasions when an Old Testament writer speaks of God as "Father" in the Old Testament what is meant is "Father of Life" or "Creator," never "Abba, Father." God was to be feared and revered. People were even careful not to speak His proper name "Yahweh."

It wasn't until Jesus came and gave us a more complete picture of God that people understood that in addition to being reverenced as "Lord Almighty" and "Creator," God was to be embraced as "Father," even "Daddy." Thus, in the New Testament the references to God as "Father" are abundant.

Theologically, you probably understand God to be "Father." But how about emotionally? Do you experience God as "Daddy"? In a survey I conducted of almost 600 church-attending Christians about the images of God they had, 64 percent admitted to having some difficulties experiencing God as their "Daddy." Depending upon your experiences with your own father and other authority figures, you too may struggle with knowing God as "Daddy" (or even "Father."[5]) Don't let yourself miss out on this part of the fireworks show. If you miss the impact of God's being your Daddy, then you'll miss out on so much of God's compassion. And you need this compassion to enable you to examine the hurts and sins in your soul and progress in your journey of healing and growth.

Footsteps of Faith

1. Sometime this week write a letter to your father about your relationship with him. Express your regrets (things that you wish had been different between you) and your thankfulness (things you're grateful for from your father). Write this letter even if you don't want to send it to your father or even if he has passed away.

2. Another time this week write a letter to your heavenly Father about your relationship with Him. Just as you did with your letter to your father express your regrets and your thankfulness. Be sure to send this letter to God, reading it to Him in prayer.

3. After you've finished both letters—do wait until after you're through with both or it'll ruin the effect—compare the two.

4. This week when you pray to God pray "Dear Abba . . . " At the end of the week note how you feel. What is it like for you to talk to God as your "Daddy"?

WEEK 17
Tears of Grief

There was Prodigal, looking into the eyes that looked into his eyes. It was a special moment. Father and son, eye-to-eye. In the silence, Prodigal looked deep into Abba's eyes and knew his dad as never before. And he realized that his dad knew him completely, yet loved him completely. The good and the bad—and it seemed mostly bad to Prodigal—did not alter Father's steady love.

For Prodigal the experience of being fully known and fully loved was so otherworldly, so overwhelming, so incomprehensible that he looked away, shook his head back and forth, and finally covered his face as tears of grief streamed down his cheeks. Looking into Abba's eyes had left an indelible image inside Prodigal. His thoughts formed into a spontaneous poem that captured his tears of grief and turned them into tears of joy:

> *Eyes that know me deep inside.*
> *Eyes that see my sinful pride.*
> *Eyes that see past my dirt.*
> *Eyes that love me and heal my hurt!*

I imagine that's what the apostle Peter saw in Jesus' eyes. Peter had some dramatic moments with Jesus, when no doubt they looked into each other's eyes. One time Jesus and His disciples were talking about how some people who had heard Jesus teach and had seen His miracles thought Jesus to be just another prophet. Jesus looked at Peter and asked, "But what about you? Who do you say I am?" Peter looked at Jesus and answered wisely, "You are the Christ, the Son of the living God." This was a high point in Peter's life, and Jesus pronounced blessing upon him for his great confession.[6]

But just minutes later Peter made a huge blunder. Jesus had explained to Peter and to the other disciples that as the Christ He would suffer and be crucified and then be raised to life on the third day. After hearing this Peter pulled Jesus aside, looked Him in the eyes and rebuked Him, declaring, "Never. . . . This shall never happen to you!" Jesus then corrected Peter sternly, telling him that he didn't understand the mission of the Christ and that his words of opposition were from Satan.[7]

Less than a week later Peter was one of only three disciples who climbed a mountain with Jesus and at the top saw Jesus transfigured. Jesus' face shone like the sun and His whole body gleamed with white light. Peter and the others then heard a voice from heaven proclaim that Jesus was God's beloved Son and they should listen to Him.[8] What a moment of ecstacy for Peter! What a roller coaster ride he'd been on. In a week's time he made the greatest confession in history, been given the most foolish rebuke in history, and witnessed the most spectacular event in history.

A few months later he was at the Last Supper, the most famous meal in history. Yet, from this high point he fell even farther and harder than before. Peter and the other eleven disciples were eating bread and drinking wine with Jesus. Shortly after they celebrated the first Communion, Peter and some others were arguing about which of them was the greatest disciple. Jesus corrected the proud Peter and warned him that he would fall upon hard times, but Peter responded by making yet another foolish boast, claiming that he was ready to die for Jesus if necessary. Jesus corrected him again and told him that in just a few hours he would three times deny that he even knew Jesus.[9]

Sure enough, that night Jesus was betrayed by Judas and arrested by Temple guards under Roman authority. Peter and the other disciples fled, abandoning Jesus. But Peter secretly followed Jesus as He was led away to see what would happen. Then, while Jesus was being unjustly accused of crimes He didn't commit, Peter was spotted by people who knew him to be a disciple. Three times Peter denied that he knew Jesus; the last time he was so angry and emphatic about the denial that he cursed. Immediately Jesus turned and looked straight at Peter. Their eyes met. Peter ran away and wept bitterly. He cried about his hurt, and he cried about his sin.[10]

The next day Jesus was crucified, and Peter was in despair. But then on the third day Peter's despair turned to joy when Jesus rose from the dead, as He said He would! Then Jesus reappeared in His resurrected body to Peter in order to reinstate Peter. There they were again— Lord and disciple— face to face, eye to eye. Three times Jesus asked Peter if he loved Him. Each time Peter answered, "Yes, Lord." Each time Jesus then said, "Feed my sheep." Each denial was forgiven. Each affirmation of love was encouraged.[11] The up-and-down and up-again and down-again Peter had been given yet another chance at restoration by Jesus. Peter made good on his second chance. He became an apostle in the new church and a hero in character and deed for people struggling in their faith.

Have you looked into Jesus' eyes lately? When was the last time you took a step of trust and opened your heart to a friend in the Body of Christ? When you do this, God's eyes of compassion will search into your soul and elicit tears of grief over what you see and what you don't see. Grieving over your sins and the sins of others against you is at the very heart of your journey of healing and personal growth. In the end, "Those who sow in tears will reap with songs of joy."[12]

*Footsteps
of Faith*

1. This week consider how you may be like Peter. Note any of the following negative characteristics of Peter's that are true for you.

☐ I often say things that I regret later.
☐ I compete against other people, trying to prove that I am better than them.
☐ In my life very high points seem to be followed by very low points.
☐ When I get overconfident I make big mistakes.
☐ Sometimes I abandon a friend in need because it's too stressful for me to remain loyal.

2. Perhaps Peter can be a role model for you in your own journey of healing and growth. Which of the following positive attributes of Peter's do you need to develop?

☐ The courage to get back up on my feet and try again after I've fallen flat on my face
☐ The willingness to examine myself
☐ The freedom to cry over my hurts and my sins
☐ The feeling that I am loved in spite of my faults
☐ The confidence that I am completely forgiven for all my sins
☐ The determination to succeed when given second chances

3. Consider Jesus' beatitude: "Blessed are those who mourn for they shall be comforted" (Matthew 5:4). That beatitude would suggest that Jesus is referring to the importance of mourning over our poverty of spirit. Grieving is

essential to emotional healing, to spiritual growth, and to happiness in general. This week pray that God would help you to process any unresolved grief. Perhaps you need to mourn over one or more of the areas below. Check any that apply.

- ☐ Sins I have committed that have hurt God, others, and myself
- ☐ Opportunities for doing good that I have neglected
- ☐ Hurts over ways I have been sinned against
- ☐ Emptiness from love I've needed but didn't receive when I needed it
- ☐ Grief over a loved one's death
- ☐ Grief over the ending of a relationship

WEEK 18
It's Time to Take Inventory

After looking into Father's eyes of compassion Prodigal began to take inventory of his feelings. He felt hatred toward Elder for all his criticism and condemnation. He felt bitter at Timothy for not giving him a fair price for his inheritance property. He felt ashamed over the way he had been used for his money by Alex and others in Antioch. He felt the sting of being mocked by passersby when he lived in the streets. He felt betrayed by Alex. In all these ways he had been wronged and injured. The injuries were like infected wounds in his soul. He needed to work at forgiving to find peace and to be released from the festering resentment that was poisoning his soul.

Not only had Prodigal been sinned against, but he had sinned too. Even though it hurt, he knew he had to be honest and admit his sins. Looking inside, he could feel his resentment toward those who had wronged him. He admitted that he tended to repress his anger and sometimes lost his temper at Elder, or even Phillip, who usually was just an innocent bystander. Furthermore, he had to admit that his brother was right in saying that he was lazy and didn't do his share of work around the farm.

Then Prodigal thought about how he had left home and insulted and betrayed his father by selfishly demanding his inheritance. He acknowledged that greed had taken control of his heart and that the prideful desire to run his own life without being accountable to Father had driven him to a country far away from Father's loving care. He knew that in the far country he heaped his sins one on top of the other, foolishly wasting his inheritance money, projecting a false image to impress others, and indulging in all sorts of sinful pleasures.

The damage sin created in his life was obvious. He stood before Father famished, broke, covered in dirt, barefoot, half-dressed in tattered and torn clothes, and carrying the stench of pigs. He had come home to Father lonely and ashamed. The pain and destruction in his life had made clear to him that he was powerless to manage his life on his own. In desperation, he turned his will and his life over to Father's care.

One part of Prodigal resisted surrendering. One stronghold of pride was still left. It was exposed by Father's amazing display of compassion when he ran down the village street through the hostile mob and satisfied both justice and love. Only then did Prodigal realize he couldn't save face. Up to his neck in debt, he couldn't shovel his way out; having betrayed Father, he couldn't effect a reconciliation. So he admitted his pride and surrendered himself completely to Father. Now his only hope was for Father to be merciful.

Thus Prodigal took a big step toward forgiveness and change by examining himself thoroughly in the light of Father's all-knowing love. This kind of self-examination is like open-heart surgery. If not done right it will kill you, and even if it is done right it will leave you in pain and exhausted. Perhaps in your journey of healing you've trembled and quaked inside upon taking this fearful step called _inventory._ Maybe you've felt the shame of opening up an infected wound or a cancerous growth of sin to someone you hoped was the compassionate surgeon you were trusting him or her to be.

As a psychologist, sometimes I feel like a surgeon of the soul. It seems that everyone responds differently when they enter the operating room. Unfortunately many people fail to apply God's simple wisdom revealed through the prophet Jeremiah: "You can't heal a wound by saying it's not there."[13] Here are six people I've counseled who have resisted the painful—but necessary—surgery:

- A young man addicted to speed thinks he's ready to begin a recovery program but doesn't make it through withdrawal: he failed to recognize his physical dependency.
- An overeater indulges in a whole bag of potato chips while watching television: she failed to recognize her loneliness.
- A mother loses her temper at her daughter: she failed to recognize the anger that had been building inside her for days.
- A husband is gently confronted by his wife for neglecting the family to work for hours in the garage and he's defensive: he failed to recognize his compulsion to be productive.
- A Christian is proud of his commitment to have a daily quiet time but struggles to feel close to God: he failed to recognize his pride and self-sufficiency.
- A young woman frequently cuts off stressful relationships by blaming the other person; in therapy she denies the pattern: she failed to recognize her habit of projecting badness onto others.

It's painfully hard to be honest about our flaws, faults, and foibles. Forces of denial, deceitfulness, and defensiveness fight against emotional honesty. Yet this fourth step in our journey with Prodigal is critical. To progress in our personal and spiritual growth we must take inventory with a ruthless honesty and a persistent regularity. This is such an important step and one that is so easy to gloss over that Alcoholics Anonymous' Twelve Steps program (and similar recovery programs) requires this step twice.[14] (Probably even more times than that, since most people work through all the steps more than once.) Step 4 is: "We made a searching and fearless moral inventory of ourselves" and Step 10 is: "We continued to take personal inventory and when we were wrong we promptly admitted it."

Footsteps of Faith

1. Set aside a few minutes this week to consider Matthew 20:29–34, the story of how Jesus healed two blind men who desperately wanted to see and pleaded for mercy from Jesus. In compassion Jesus touched their eyes, and they could see again. This week ask Jesus to touch your spiritual eyes with His compassion to help you to see what sins you need to recognize.

2. It's time to take inventory of our sins. Are you ready? Have you prayed that your eyes would be open, as the above Footstep of Faith requests? Now we will use the Ten Commandments as a yardstick to measure your motives and your actions. As you recognize your need, I hope you will sense the Father's compassion, as Prodigal did.

(1) Do you have any gods besides God? Perhaps someone or something controls your heart instead of God. Consider how you spent your time last week, the things you've thought about and done. Did you neglect to involve God in any of these things? _____

(2) Do you turn God into an idol of your own making? Is your perception of God limited to only certain aspects of His character? (To help you with this you may want to consider the attributes of love from 1 Corinthians 13:4–8, the fruit of the Spirit from Galatians 5:22–23, or

the examples of support that David sought from God in Psalm 20.) ____

(3) Do you misuse the name of the Lord? Do you ask him to do things that are inconsistent with His character? ____

(4) Do you respect the Sabbath? Do you acknowledge your needs for rest and worship by regularly setting aside one day from your busy schedule? ____

(5) Do you honor your father and mother? This means you respect the influence they've had in your life, being grateful for the good you've received from them and forgiving them for the bad. ____

(6) Do you carry hatred or resentment in your heart toward anyone? Do you condemn, criticize, or discourage others? ____

(7) Do you carry lust in your heart for anyone? Lust may express itself in fantasies about selfish sexual gratifications or a secret longing to be free from your commitment to love your spouse. ____

(8) Do you steal from others? Do you use manipulation, guilt, playing the victim, or expectations of payback to get what you want from others rather than taking the initiative to ask them for what you want? ____

(9) Do you lie to others? Do you minimize or distort the truth in what you say or don't say to others? Do you project a false image of yourself to others? ____

(10) Do you covet what others have? Do you feel jealous of other people's opportunities or achievements? ____

3. If you are like most people, you had at least a few "yes" responses in the above inventory. It hurts to see our sins, and once we see them we may be tempted to try to make up for our sins or to work ourselves out of debt. This is a common reaction to guilt. If this is true for you then follow Prodigal's step of faith by acknowledging your pride and putting your trust in Father's mercy.

4. Later this week follow the advice of Leviticus 26:39 and examine how the sins of your parents have affected you, whether by the lifestlyle they modeled or the way they interacted with you. Use the Ten Commandments as yardsticks for them just as you did for yourself. Note any similarities between your parents' sins and your own. Consider how they need mercy, just as you do. Then ask God to guide you in the process of forgiving your father and mother.

NOTES

1. Hebrews 4:15–5:1, Mark 2:10.
2. Zechariah 10:6.
3. Psalm 139:23–24.
4. Galatians 4:6.
5. See William Gaultiere, "The Development and Preliminary Validation of a Measure of God's Image," doctoral disseratation (U.S. International University, 1989). In that same study I found that 26 percent of those surveyed admitted to having some difficulties experiencing God as "Father."
6. Matthew 16:13–19.
7. Matthew 16:21–23.
8. Matthew 17:1–9.
9. Luke 22:7–34.
10. Luke 22:47–62.
11. John 21:15–19.
12. Psalm 126:5.
13. Jeremiah 6:14 TLB*.
14. Steps 4 and 10, Alcoholics Anonymous' Twelve Steps.

*_The Living Bible._

"The son said to him, 'Father, I have sinned against heaven and against you. I am no longer worthy to be called your son."

Luke 15:21

Seeking
Father's Forgiveness

Prodigal was still pensive; Father was still patient. To the eavesdropping bystanders the silence seemed unending. The onlookers stood there impatiently waiting to see what would happen next, as they each had their own agenda for this meeting between son and father. Finally, after many minutes of silent reflection and careful inventorying of his soul, Prodigal looked at his father again. He looked deep into the eyes where he had found knowledge and compassion, and he dropped to his knees.

There, on his knees at Father's feet, Prodigal said, "Father, I have sinned against heaven and against you. I am no longer worthy to be called your s—"

"Well, it's about time you admitted it!" Joshua screamed, cutting off Prodigal's confession and waving his Torah in the young man's face. "An unworthy sinner you are indeed! More than that, you're a wicked boy! You've committed vile sins! You know what we do with rebels, thieves, gamblers, drunks, and adulterers? We stone them! That's what I'll have done to you if you step foot within the city limits of my town! You ought to turn right back around and walk back to the pigsty. That's where you belong."

"Joshua!" Rabbi Benjamin elbowed everyone who was in his way and stepped between prosecutor and defendant. Sarah and the others gasped in astonishment. They had never seen Rabbi express anger like this! The rabbi's anger was fierce, and he began a stern rebuke. "What are you doing, Joshua? Are you going to beat up this poor lad with the law? Can't you see he's brokenhearted? Look at his face. He's been crying over his sins. We've heard his confession. He's suffered enough. Let's forget about his sins and welcome him back home. Nain is my town and it's a town of love, not—"

"What?" Joshua shoved the rabbi. "I'm the town mayor! I make the rules! You say the prayers. Got it?"

"You won't tell me what to do anymore!" Rabbi Benjamin defended himself.

Prodigal was the rope in a tug-of-war for power. He was being pulled, stretched, and yanked by two people who despised each other. Phillip was feeling for Prodigal, and he pleaded, "Please stop this arguing! Just stop! I can't take this tension anymore! Can't we just get along? Let's all forget about our differences and go home. OK?"

"Bu-bu-b-but Phillip, I have sinned." The accused, still on his knees, trembled and stuttered as he bravely continued his confession of sin. "I told Father that I didn't want him anymore, just his money. I turned my back on the one who loved me. You know I did this! You warned me before I did it. Remember?"

"Oh, Prodigal!" Phillip wiped the sweat off his brow in exasperation. "Please don't incriminate yourself further. Can't you see? Enough damage has been done already. Just ask for forgiveness and forget about it. It's water over the dam. Let's not talk about it. It's upsetting me, and you're only making things worse."

"Phillip, I have to talk about it! I can't hide these sins any longer! They've been leading me to ruin! My bitterness at Elder led me into a life of laziness. My resentment of Father's authority led me far away from his love. My greed led me into the life of a famished beggar feeding out of garbage cans. My impulsiveness led me to be enslaved to my passions and to other people's approval. My pride led me into a pigsty. Do I need to go on, Phillip?"

"Please don't. I'm feeling sick to my stomach thinking about what you did. All the money you lost. For years and years we've all worked so hard to make this farm productive, and you threw a third of it away in just a few months! And even worse, from the time you were a boy I helped your Father raise you in righteousness and in Jewish integrity, and you forsook it all in a palace of sin and a pigsty of disgrace! I wish you would have listened to me. I wish you would have listened . . ." Phillip's voice trailed off to a mumble.

"I agree!" Sarah bellowed. Then she turned toward the prostrated, penitent Prodigal and pointed her finger at him. "You ought to be ashamed of yourself, young man. It's like doing it all over again to talk about such things!"

"Eh, eh, eh." Timothy cleared his throat to speak. "We all know Prodigal has sinned, and sin has its consequences. It's because of Prodigal's sin that God sent the famine in our land. We're all suffering because of him. So I agree with Joshua. Send him back to the pigsty!"

"Yeah! Let's get him!" the gang of boys hollered in evil delight as they approached the kneeling Prodigal with sticks in their hands and rage in their hearts.

Within seconds the gang had attacked. They swarmed upon their victim. They pounded their sticks, kicked their feet, screamed obscenities, and taunted the fool who had destroyed their city's reputation:

Let's have some fun
And beat this bum!
He brought shame upon Nain,
So let's put him in pain!
We'll watch him pout, pout.
And then we'll throw him out, out!

Joshua cheered them on. Rabbi wept. Sarah kept shrieking. And Phillip winced while covering his ears. Timothy nodded in self-righteous pity: "Well, it's too bad, but he has sinned." The beating continued. Sticks cracking against bone. Thumps of fists and feet against flesh. Screams of hate. Screams of agony. Spats of blood flying.

Finally Rabbi Benjamin could stand it no longer and yelled, "Stop this! This is wrong! Father, do something! Father—" Rabbi looked around but couldn't see Father. "Father, where are you? How could you leave your son at a time like this?" Turning to the others he persisted, "Where did he go?"

Mayor Joshua had a sinister smile on his face, "Benjamin, suddenly you seem concerned about justice! OK, boys, that's enough. Leave the sinner be."

Like trained attack dogs responding to the command of their master, the boys stopped immediately. One by one, panting in exhaustion but smiling and barking out words of congratulation to one another, they peeled themselves off of their victim until he was exposed.

"Oh, my! It's Father!" Sarah fainted.

"Dear God, help us!" Rabbi Benjamin rushed to Father's side. Father had placed himself between the gang of boys and his son to protect his son and to take the beating for him. No one had noticed his leap to cover his son, least of all the wild boys. Father looked beaten, but he was breathing. He had a bruise on his cheek, a black eye, and a bloody nose. He was covered in dirt. His clothes were ripped, tattered, and in disarray.

"Are you OK? Can you stand up? Oh, you must be in such pain!" Rabbi winced.

"Yes, I'm OK," Sarah interrupted, thinking Rabbi was concerned about her, since she had fainted. She blinked her eyes and looked around. Everyone was huddled around Father, whom Sarah had forgotten. Realizing that no one was going to come to her aid, she let out a loud moan and whined in exasperation as she helped herself up, "Well, I guess I just have to take care of myself!"

Meanwhile, Rabbi was attending to Father. "Here, let me help you to your feet."

"Ooh, ooh, ooh! Thank you, Rabbi. Yes, I'm OK. Just a little bruised and banged up." Father forced a smile as he straightened up. Then he turned to his son who was lying in the dirt face down, and he extended his hand to help him up. "Dear son, are you OK?"

Prodigal cocked his head back and looked up. "Abba, why did you do that for me? I deserved that beating, not you!"

As Prodigal stood up, Father looked at him. "Yes, son, justice has been served. I've taken upon myself the judgment and the punishment you deserved. You are forgiven all of your sins." Then turning to address the crowd of onlookers, Father explained. "None of you have the right to judge Prodigal's sins! You too are sinners. Prodigal has confessed his sins, and I have forgiven him. Now who among you will follow his example and receive forgiveness?"

It was quiet. No one had the courage to speak. Finally after several long seconds of silence Father spoke. One at a time he rebuked everyone for their sin against Prodigal. He began with the mayor. "Joshua, you have neglected two important matters of the Torah, that the greatest commandment is love and that Yahweh alone is Lord and Judge. And Rabbi, can't you see that justice had to been served—and it was? Don't be blind to the meaning of my running through town and now enduring this beating. Open your eyes now and see that I have offered the necessary sacrifice for sins!

"Phillip, Phillip, Phillip. When will my love be enough to make you secure? You must understand that closing your eyes to conflicts doesn't create peace. And Sarah, I know your heart. You're taking mental notes of everything you see and hear so that you can gossip to the whole town! Timothy, how could you condemn my son after you took advantage of him in his moment of foolish desperation. And boys, all of you, please look at me. Go back to your fathers and ask them to teach you from the Torah."

Father stepped aside to stand next to Prodigal, and the villagers watched motionless, stunned into silence. No one dared speak his thoughts, though each was quietly murmuring against Father. Joshua was angry that Father had insulted him by suggesting he didn't know his Torah. Rabbi was stroking his long, gray beard and trying to understand the purpose of Father's sacrifice when the animal sacrifices had always been sufficient for sin in the past. Sarah was repeating in her mind, *I don't gossip! I just pass on the news to people who are concerned. I don't gossip* . . . Timothy was trying not to feel guilty, and the boys were mumbling under their breaths about the suggestion that they "go back to their fathers." But no one heeded Father's invitation.

WEEK 19

When Your Conscience Condemns You

Here it is, the scene you may have expected. In a way, everything that has happened up until now in our story has been drama building up to this point: Prodigal's public confession of his sin. Perhaps when you first heard the beginning of the story of the prodigal son, you wondered, *Will he confess his sins? If he does, will he berate himself for them? Will he minimize them? Will he try to save face and make up for his sins? Or will he speak the truth of his sins and throw himself upon Father's mercy?*

Finally, our questions are answered. Yes, Prodigal confesses his sin, but no sooner does he do so than he is castigated and condemned by a Torah-waving, throat-screeching, fanatical religionist. "Unworthy sinner!" "Wicked boy!" "These are vile sins—stone him!" "Send him back to the pigsty!" The town mayor's reprimand of the penitent Prodigal is like the pounding of a gavel on an exposed heart that brings bruises and blood. But, as we will discuss later, the town mayor had no real authority in this trial. It was Father's response that mattered, and it was to him that Prodigal was making his appeal.

Everybody has at least one condemning town mayor in his or her life, and some people live with one every minute of every day: their conscience. Our conscience serves a purpose, but it cannot bring healing. It is like the rebuking fans at a basketball game. Recently I was watching a high school game, and a player on the visiting team committed a foul. When the referee blew his whistle, many of the home-team fans immediately stood. Pointing their fingers at the visiting player who committed the foul, they began to chant, "You! You! You! You! You!"

When you sin you need your conscience to blow the whistle, to convict you so that you repent and seek God's forgiveness in Christ. But you don't need your conscience to stand up, point a critical finger in your face, and scream, "You! You did it! You're a bad person!" A condemning conscience like that makes you want to crawl into a hole and hide in shame.

This was the case for Alexandria. One day with about five minutes left in her counseling session she abruptly paused and looked at me with tentative eyes. Her breathing became very shallow and rapid and her lips started to quiver as she forced out the words, "I have something I'm afraid to tell you."

"Maybe it's best for you to wait until next week to tell me since we're almost out of time today," I replied.

"No. I can't keep it from you any longer." Of course, my curiosity was really peaked now. Alexandria had sought my help for her depression five months ago. In that time she had shared many things with me, but clearly there was something important that she hadn't told me yet. Then she blurted out, "I've been stealing food at the grocery store and then eating it all in the car."

She picked up the pillow on the couch, buried her face into it, and dropped her head into her lap. I heard her mumble, "You must think I'm a bad person." I thought about the last few seconds. When she confessed her stealing to me I hadn't frowned at her, or grimaced, or gasped, or raised my eyebrows, or anything else. As I listened my face was blank. In the history of my interactions with her I had demonstrated an empathic concern for her welfare and shown God's forgiveness for her sins. Clearly she was projecting her own self-critical and self-condemning thoughts about herself onto me.

"It seems that you're feeling ashamed," I commented. Alexandria nodded, her face still buried in the pillow. I continued, "There's so much more we need to talk about on this subject, but I'm afraid we're out of time for today. Maybe before our next session you can write down what you're afraid I think about you now, and then we'll continue our discussion next week."

Alexandria returned with a list that made me sound like Joshua sounded to Prodigal:

"Thieves don't enter the Kingdom of God!"

"You broke one of the Ten Commandments and you better not do it again."

"You're a bad person."

"You should go to jail for what you did."

"You're hopeless. I don't want you as a client anymore."

A lump gathered in my throat as I said, "This is how you feel, Alexandria?" She nodded. "What would your dad say to you if you told him about your stealing?" She began to sob hysterically. She answered my question. Alexandria had told me about her father in previous sessions. Clearly she had internalized into her conscience her father's harsh, critical, and condemning attitude, and it spoke to her all the time— when she was late to an appointment, when she lost her temper at her daughter, when her husband didn't like the meal she cooked, when her friend didn't say hello to her at church, and when she stole food at the grocery store. No wonder she was depressed.

Alexandria needed to have her conscience transformed. As it was, when she sinned—or just made a mistake or disappointed someone—she felt a sense of condemnation that let her to hide in shame. Instead, when she sinned she needed to feel the "godly sorrow"[1] that leads to repentance and reliance upon God's forgiving grace. As she confessed her sin to me, I had the opportunity to offer her God's forgiveness.

Footsteps of Faith

1. Perhaps like Prodigal and Alexandria you also need to make a confession of sin. Set aside some time alone this

week to write down your bad parts, whether they be expressed in behavior, words, motives, or thoughts.

_____

_____

_____

2. Read what you wrote down in question one. How do
you feel about yourself in view of your sinfulness? Perhaps
you hear some of the following statements from your conscience. Check any that apply.

☐ "You ought to be ashamed of yourself!"
☐ "You're so bad no one could love you."
☐ "You'd better hide out until you straighten out."
☐ "You screwed up again!"
☐ "If you ever do that again you'll be in big trouble."
☐ "How could you do that? Why didn't you _____
    instead?"
☐ "Shape up or ship out!"

3. If you checked some of the statements above, then
you've been dialing the wrong number! You're conscience is
wired to the accuser, Satan,[2] rather than to the Comforter, the
Holy Spirit.[3] The spirit of Satan and the Spirit of God are competing for the phone line to your conscience.[4] Read and meditate on the following truths from Romans 8, promises for
every believer in Jesus Christ. Then thank God for His promise of forgiveness as we confess our sins and ask Him for His
comfort.

1) "There is no condemnation for those who are in
   Christ" (v. 1).
2) "The law of the Spirit set me free from the law of sin
   and death" (v. 2).
3) "The Spirit himself testifies with our spirit that we are
   God's children" (v. 16).

4) "The Spirit helps us in our weakness" (v. 26).
5) "All things work together for good to them that love God" (v. 28 KJV).
6) "If God is for us, who can be against us?" (v. 31).
7) "Who dares accuse us whom God has chosen for his own? Will God? No! He is the one who has forgiven us and given us right standing with himself" (v. 33 TLB).
8) "We are more than conquerors through him who loved us" (v. 37).
9) "Nothing can ever separate us from his love" (v. 38 TLB).

4. Which list, the one of accusing statements (in Footstep 2 above) or the one of comforting statements (in Footstep 3), better reflects what you heard as a child from your parents? _____
Which list better reflects what you say to your children or your friends? _____

WEEK 20
Are Your Problems Caused by Sin?

Ever since Timothy had bought Prodigal's inheritance property at a ridiculously low price, he felt guilty. He knew he had taken advantage of Prodigal in his moment of weakness. But every time somebody in town spoke negatively about Prodigal, Timothy's conscience eased a little. His attitude was "Yeah, Prodigal got what he deserved. It's not my fault he was so foolish. He shouldn't have wasted his inheritance. If he hadn't sinned, then maybe he wouldn't have gotten into such a mess." And Timothy went even further than that. He announced to everyone, "It's because of Prodigal's sin that God sent the famine in our land. We're all suffering because of him!"

Timothy believed in a just world, at least in the lives of other people. His line of reasoning was, *People get what they deserve, so those who have problems must have done something wrong.* Yet when Timothy had business problems because of the famine, it was Prodigal's fault, not his own. Thus he blamed other people for their problems and for his problems! This way he always looked good, and he had a delusion of control over his destiny: *As long as I do what's right then things will go well for me.*

At first glance Timothy's opinions might seem ridiculously superstitious and harshly judgmental, and they are. But they are also very common. Most people usually view other people's problems as being a result of something those people did wrong or didn't do right. Yet many of these same people believe that their own problems are caused by circumstances beyond their control or people who have wronged them in some way. Sometimes those who make excuses like this for themselves are actually feeling guilty and are fighting against the conclusion that their problems are their fault.

You may wonder, *Then whose fault is it when some-body has problems?* That is exactly the question the disciples asked Jesus. They had encountered a man who had been born blind, and they couldn't figure out whether this man was blind because of his own sins or his parents' sins. "'Neither this man nor his parents sinned,' said Jesus, 'but this happened so that the work of God might be displayed in his life.'" Then Jesus healed the man.[5] Jesus showed us that some of our problems aren't directly related to our sins or others' sins against us but are simply a part of living in an imperfect world. That's a scary thought. It means that bad things happen to good people, and it means that bad things happen to careful people!

Giving up your delusion of control over what happens to you in life is difficult. It requires taking a posture of trust. You need to trust that when bad things happen you haven't been abandoned by God, you won't be destroyed, and you can mature through this difficulty. This is a vulnerable position to be in and will inevitably bring up insecure and fearful feelings, especially if personal experience has taught you that it isn't safe to depend upon anyone but yourself.

Some people do realize that they can't control everything that happens to them, but they go to the opposite extreme and give up responsibility for their life altogether. They just "go with the flow." "I let happen what happens," the passive person says. These are irresponsible people and no better off than those who are hyper-responsible.

Jesus made this clear on another occasion to some self-righteous people who thought that both the Galileans who were murdered by Pilate and the Jews who died when the tower in Siloam fell on them must have been sinners; otherwise God would not have let them die that way. Jesus rejected that conclusion, indicating that those people weren't necessarily any worse sinners than their neighbors who didn't die. Then Jesus gave a stern warning to those who questioned him: "But unless you repent, you too will all perish."

What did Jesus mean? He explained the meaning by telling them a parable about a fig tree that wasn't bearing fruit in season. The diligent owner dug around it, fertilized it, and waited another year. At that point if there was still no fruit then he'd cut it down.[6] Thus, Jesus illustrated the point that we are all responsible to bear fruit. Even if our problems are not directly related to our own sins—and some of our problems aren't—we're still responsible to learn from our problems and work through them so that we can bear fruit in our lives.

Footsteps of Faith

1. Timothy tried to absolve himself from guilt by blaming Prodigal for his problems. Do you sometimes do this?

2. When Job was suffering, his "friends" had some very uncompassionate and untruthful words for him.[7] Among other things, they told him that he was suffering because God was punishing him for his sins and that he shouldn't be upset about his suffering.[8] Have you heard things like this when you were going through a hard time? Have you said these things? _____

3. Consider the difficulties that you are experiencing in your life. Which of the following attitudes do you have about these problems? (Check all that apply.)

☐ "If I hadn't done _____, then I wouldn't be in this position."
☐ "If so-and-so hadn't done _____, then I wouldn't be in this position."

☐ "Life isn't fair. Circumstances left me in this position."

☐ "I want to learn and grow through this situation."

☐ All of the above are partially true.

4. Do we live in a just and predictable world? This week consider the following principles from the Bible: "A man reaps what he sows."[9] "[God] punishes the children for the sin of the fathers to the third and fourth generation."[10] "[God] causes his sun to rise on the evil and the good."[11] "Endure hardship as discipline. . . . God disciplines us for our good that we may share in his holiness."[12] These verses speak of four truths that need to be held together:

(1) There are consequences to our actions.
(2) We are affected by other people's actions.
(3) "Good" people experience good and bad in life, and "bad" people experience good and bad in life.
(4) We are responsible for how we respond to the circumstances we encounter.

5. This week pray the "Serenity Prayer," which is used in Alcoholics Anonymous and other Twelve Step recovery programs: "God grant us the serenity to accept the things we cannot change, the courage to change the things we can, and the wisdom to know the difference." Do not simply pray in fatalistic acceptance, but trust God to lead and control your life, knowing He is all-wise and all-powerful.

WEEK 21
Sweep It Under the Rug!

Phillip was listening to Joshua condemn Prodigal, and it was making him very upset. As the family servant, Phillip had helped Father raise Prodigal and grew to love Prodigal as himself. In fact, he loved him too much; he overidentified with Prodigal. It wounded him to hear Prodigal criticized, it ripped his heart to see Prodigal tugged between Joshua and Rabbi, it drove him crazy to hear people arguing.

Phillip had problems with his boundaries (his sense of himself as a separate individual). He was scared of feeling separate from other people, so he avoided conflict at all costs. "Please stop this arguing! . . . Can't we just get along? Let's all forget about our differences." He tried to excuse Prodigal's sins: "Please don't incriminate yourself further! . . . Enough damage has been done already! Just ask for forgiveness and forget about it." He wanted the past to be past: "It's water over the dam. Let's not talk about it. It's upsetting me, and you're only making things worse." When Prodigal persisted in trying to work through the conflicts and in confessing the truth of his sins, Phillip made one final effort to silence him through guilt: "I'm feeling sick to my stomach thinking about what you did. . . . We've all worked so hard [for you]. . . . I wish you would have listened to me."

Recently I was discussing differences between Eastern and Western culture with some friends, Jason and Sue, who have done missions work in various Eastern countries. They told me that people in the East won't talk about their conflicts and sins as people in the West do, but will go to great lengths to avoid discussion of subjects that can be emotionally uncomfortable. It was interesting for me to hear this couple describe Westerners as honest and forthright. Sometimes in my work with people of Eastern background I have also noticed this general cultural difference, yet from all back-

160

grounds I've found people who have "The Phillip Syndrome," in that they avoid conflicts, excuse sins, try to forget the past, and repress anger.

Maybe people avoided conflict in the family you grew up in. When there was tension, family members just swept it under the rug. There was a need to keep the family room clean by hiding the dirt. And in some families it seems to work—for a while. People look happy, successful, and as though they get along until somebody trips over a dirt bulge in the rug. Dad loses his temper and inspires fear in everyone, Mom has a "bad day" that leaves a cloud of depression in the home, one child starts abusing drugs, another child becomes mouthy when told to do something, a third child acts happy on the outside but is sad and lonely on the inside. There is no real intimacy in a home like this, and personal growth is stunted as well. When instead of avoiding inevitable relational conflicts we speak the truth in love[13] by respecting our own feelings and others' feelings, then we not only resolve our differences over time, but we deepen our relationships and smooth out some of the rough edges of our character.

Often the same people who avoid relational conflicts excuse sins, their own and others'. *If conflict is dirty and to be swept under the rug, then certainly sin needs to be hidden too,* they reason. Indeed sin *is* bad, but when it's hidden it is evil. All sins can be forgiven except those that are hidden. Unfortunately, some people learn to feel so guilty and so ashamed of their badness that the only way they know to deal with it is to hide it in fear. Their attitude is, *If others see my badness, then I'll be destroyed by rejection, condemnation, or punishment. And if I see others' badness, then they'll be destroyed.* Acceptance, compassion, and forgiveness are missing when we don't feel safe enough to confess our sins one to another so that we can be healed.[14]

If you can't talk about conflicts and sins then you certainly can't talk about the past because it will be full of both! Neither can you talk about your anger, of which you will also be full. When past conflicts aren't healed and past sins aren't forgiven, injuries and resentments are carried forward into the present and repeated again and again in the future. Anger gets acted out in passive ways or in aggressive ways rather than assertively.[15]

Often people ask me, "Why bring up the past? I can't change what happened, and I don't want to stir things up." I reply, "You can't change the history that's been written, but you can change you, and part of you is still stuck back there. The hurt and anger you feel today is because you haven't resolved your issues from the past." The key to resolving your past issues regarding unresolved conflicts and offenses is in confessing your sins and the sins of others against you.[16] This is a process; over time and with support from someone you trust, you talk through your anger, fear, hurt, shame, and any other related response. As you do this, you find that you begin to experience the forgiveness you need and to release the forgiveness that others need.

Footsteps of Faith

1. Are you a conflict-avoider? Do you try to keep the peace at any price? Perhaps you know someone who is like that. Consider Phillip's conflict-avoiding statements and put a check mark in front of any statement you have said or thought during a conflict.

☐ "Please stop this arguing!"
☐ "Can't we just get along?"
☐ "Let's all forget about our differences."

2. Do you excuse your sins or other's sins? Do you minimize the bad to keep yourself or others from being rejected,

condemned, or punished? Do you know someone who fits these descriptions? Consider Phillip's sin-excusing statements; then put a check in front of any that you have said or someone has said to you.

☐ "Please don't incriminate yourself further!"
☐ "Enough damage has been done already!"
☐ "Just ask for forgiveness and forget about it."

3. Do you try to forget unresolved conflicts and unconfessed sins from the past? Have you failed to learn the lessons from your history so that you stop repeating it in the present? Do you know someone like this? Consider the following statements of Phillip's, which reflect his desire to forget the past:

"It's water over the dam."
"Let's not talk about it."
"It's upsetting me."
"You're only making things worse."

4. Consider these statements of Phillip's, which reflect his repressed anger and the guilt he was sending in Prodigal's direction:

"I'm feeling sick to my stomach thinking about what you did."
"We've all worked so hard (for you)."
"I wish you would have listened to me."

Do you repress your anger? Do you convert your anger into guilt, putting others or yourself on guilt trips? Do you know someone who does this?

5. Before this week is over meet with a friend and talk about what you learned this week. Perhaps the two of you together can encourage one another to do the following things as a response to the Phillip Syndrome:

(1) Speak the truth in love in your relationships.
(2) Confess your sins and the sins of others against you.
(3) Learn the lessons you need to from your past so that you don't repeat the painful experience.
(4) Express your anger in assertive, not aggressive or passive ways.

How to Confess Your Sins

Prayers spoken, eyes searching, arms outstretched, ears listening, tears visible, heart opened—these were the demonstrations of Father's compassion toward Prodigal, and they led Prodigal to take inventory of his sins and to confess them to Father. He dropped to his knees and confessed: "Father, I have sinned against heaven and against you. I am no longer worthy to be called your son." Wait a minute! That's different than the confession that Prodigal prepared in the pigsty and rehearsed in the desert: "Father, I have sinned against heaven and against you. I am no longer worthy to be called your son; *make me like one of your hired men*" (emphasis added).[17]

What a difference there is between those two confessions![18] Instead of trying to make up for all the money he lost and work off his debt as a hired hand, he dropped to his knees and waited for mercy at his father's feet. Unlike when he left home, Prodigal now knew how much Father loved him, and he couldn't insult that love a second time by exerting a proud self-reliance as he had before. So he confessed that he had sinned against "heaven" (he was too reverent to speak the name of Yahweh from his sinful lips) and against his father. He confessed that he was not worthy of acceptance; he did not deserve forgiveness. Note that Prodigal didn't say he was worthless; to the contrary, he demonstrated faith in Father's love, daring to believe that to Father he was of great worth and value, even though he had sinned and couldn't make up for his sinful acts.

It wasn't easy for Prodigal to offer this confession of sin. No sooner had he opened his mouth than the mayor screamed condemnation, the rabbi minimized his sins, Phillip excused his sins, Timothy blamed the famine on his sins, and Sarah shamed him for talking about his sins. Furthermore, the gang of boys tried to ridicule and abuse him for his sins.

In spite of this opposition Prodigal confessed his sins: he admitted that he had wronged his father, Elder, and others; he talked about how his sins of resentment, greed, impulsiveness, and pride had led him to ruin; he took responsibility for his actions and for his response to the way other people treated him. Everyone listened to Prodigal's confession, but no one was willing to forgive except Father, and that was enough.

By profession I'm a psychologist, but sometimes I feel more like a priest in a church confessional than a psychologist in a doctor's office. That's because day after day people similar to Prodigal come to my office and confess their sins to me. For all these people—whether depressed or anxious, facing a relational problem, or dealing with compulsive behaviors, or something else—their struggles have been impacted by sin. They've been sinned against, they've made wrong choices, or they've dealt with the circumstances of their life in unhealthy ways, but they haven't yet confessed these sins and found healing and forgiveness. They are consulting me in part because they need to do as the apostle James suggested nearly two thousand years ago: "Confess your sins to each other and pray for each other so that you may be healed."[19]

Often the nature of our sins requires more than confession to God alone. That's why Step 5 of Alcoholics Anonymous' Twelve Step recovery program is "We admitted to God, to ourselves, and to another human being the exact nature of our wrongs." When you confess your sins privately and quietly it's too easy to gloss them over, minimize their impact in your life, avoid the shame that you feel, and fail to take responsibility for changing. But when you confess your sins to another person, a clear element of accountability appears. Furthermore, confessing your sins to another person helps you to experience tangibly and more fully the healing and forgiveness that God offers.

Of course, the person whom you chose to be your priestly ambassador of God's reconciling love is very important. You need someone who will offer you both sides of love: grace and truth; forgiveness and accountability. With such a person you'll grow to feel safe, and then you can confess specific sins, experience the cleansing you need, and take responsible steps toward change.

This is what Jesus offered the woman caught in adultery. The Pharisees and the teachers of the law brought her to Jesus and questioned him. "Teacher, this woman was caught in the act of adultery. In the Law Moses commanded us to stone such women. Now what do you say?" Jesus paused, bent down, and started writing on the ground with His finger. The religious leaders harangued Him with questions and sneered at the woman. Jesus kept writing with His finger; perhaps He was writing on the ground the names of each of the religious leaders. Then He stood and replied, "If any one of you is without sin, let him be the first to throw a stone at her." Then He stooped down to write again. Maybe now He was writing down the sins of each accuser beside his name. However it happened, the religious leaders became convicted of their sins, and one at a time they each walked away until only Jesus was left with the woman. Then Jesus, the one who was without sin and who had the right to stone her, said to her, "Has no one condemned you? . . . Neither do I condemn you. . . . Go now and leave your life of sin."[20]

Footsteps of Faith

1. Set aside some time this week to reconsider what you discovered when you examined yourself against the standard of the Ten Commandments (see Week 18). Find a friend you can trust and confess those sins to this person. Then note how you feel. (You may want to check more than one box.)

☐ Embarrassed   ☐ Guilty
☐ Afraid of rejection ☐ Afraid of being judged
☐ Minimizing of my sins ☐ Evasive
☐ Pressured to make up for my wrongs
☐ Sad about how my sins have hurt me or others
☐ Frustrated because I know I'll repeat these mistakes
☐ Encouraged and helped to do what's right in the future
☐ Forgiven, cleansed, and purified
☐ Accepted in spite of my sins

2. How did your friend respond to your confession of sin? _____

Perhaps you received one of the responses that Prodigal received from those who listened to his confession:

- Judgment and condemnation (Joshua)
- Softness and acceptance without accountability (Rabbi)
- Overlooking and minimizing (Phillip)
- Shock, embarrassment, or discomfort (Sarah)
- Blame for how your sins have hurt them (Timothy)
- Ridicule or abuse (the gang of boys)
- Understanding, mercy, and forgiveness (Father)

3. After David committed adultery and murder he tried to hide his sins for a whole year. Only when he was confronted by Nathan did he confess his sins. In Psalm 32 David described what he experienced before and after he confessed his sins. Which describes better how you feel?

	Before		*After*
☐ Deceitful	☐ Wasting time	☐ Truthful	☐ Forgiven
☐ Depressed	☐ Anxious	☐ Secure	☐ Protected
☐ Burdened	☐ Tired	☐ Delivered	☐ Instructed
☐ Guilty	☐ Lost,	☐ Loved	☐ Trusting
☐ Stuck	confused	☐ Joyful	

Joshua, Timothy, and the gang of boys thought justice would be served if they punished Prodigal for his sins. Rabbi and Phillip thought love would be served if they excused Prodigal's sins. Sarah was shocked by the whole situation, but she was taking notes so that she could pass the gossip in town! It was Joshua's group, led by the gang of boys with sticks in their hands and rage in their hearts, that prevailed. They jumped on their victim, pounded with their sticks, kicked with their feet, screamed obscenities, and taunted the fool:

> *Let's have some fun*
> *And beat this bum!*
> *He brought shame upon Nain*
> *So let's put him in pain!*
> *We'll watch him pout, pout*
> *And then we'll throw him out, out!*

It was a gruesome, gut-wrenching display of violence coming from a gang of boys who used punishing Prodigal as an excuse for unleashing some of the hate inside themselves. Rabbi Benjamin was furious seeing all this and, seeking justice, started screaming of all things, "Father, where are you? How could you leave your son at a time like this?" Joshua was delighted! Prodigal had been punished and Rabbi had finally conceded defeat, so he called the attack dogs off their victim.

Then came the shocking revelation. It was Father who had been attacked, not Prodigal. Father hadn't disappeared, as Rabbi thought, but had thrown himself atop his kneeling son just a split second before the gang pounced on him. No one saw it until afterward.

Eventually Father explained to everyone why he had leapt into the fray. He took upon himself the punishment that

Prodigal's sins deserved; he sacrificed himself for his beloved son. Justice and mercy were served at the same time. But no one understood. Father offered forgiveness to the others as he had to Prodigal. But no one admitted his need. So Father confronted each person for his sins against Prodigal. But no one else sought forgiveness.

It was the same when Jesus told the parable of the prodigal son. A crowd of Prodigals—the tax gatherers and "sinners"—had gathered to hear Jesus speak. These dejected outcasts were reaching out for the mercy Jesus offered them. The Pharisees and the teachers of the law complained and muttered against Jesus. They didn't understand how Jesus could forgive these sinners, nor did they understand that they too were sinners who needed forgiveness.[21] Their god held aloft law and justice without grace and mercy, and they appeared to follow the commandments perfectly; but their hearts were full of greed, self-indulgence, hypocrisy, and wickedness.[22] They were blind to God's love, and they were blind to their sin.

Shortly after Jesus told the parable of the prodigal son He pointed out to these religious leaders just how blind they were by telling them another parable about a rich man and a beggar. The rich man lived in luxury every day of his life. At his gate lived a beggar named Lazarus, who was covered with sores and longed to eat the crumbs that fell from the rich man's table, but the rich man showed no pity. Eventually they both died. The rich man, who had depended upon his wealth, went to hell, and Lazarus, who had depended upon God (Lazarus means "God is my help"), went to heaven with Abraham, the father of faith. The rich man was being tormented in the fires of hell, and so he cried out to Abraham to have Lazarus dip a finger in water, reach down to hell, and cool his scorching tongue. But it was too late.

Therefore the rich man begged Abraham to send Lazarus to warn his five brothers before it was too late for them, too. Abraham told the rich man that his brothers only needed to listen to Moses and the prophets and they too would be saved. But the rich man insisted that, if Lazarus were raised from the dead and went to speak to them, then they would listen.

"If they do not listen to Moses and the Prophets," father Abraham replied, "they will not be convinced even if someone rises from the dead."[23]

And that is what happened. The same religious leaders who murmured against Jesus and sneered at Him for healing the sick, forgiving sinners, and teaching about God being a loving Father were the ones who would later condemn Him to death, jeer as He was lashed with whips and pierced with a crown of thorns, and watch with approval as He was nailed to a cross and let hang to die. Three days later Jesus was raised from the dead; still they weren't convinced that He was the Son of God, who sacrificed Himself for their sins, willing to offer forgiveness.

Footsteps of Faith

1. Have you, like Rabbi Benjamin, ever wondered where the Father was when you or someone you love was suffering? This week reflect on these times of suffering. How did God respond to your pain or hardship? He wants to be with you in difficulty and to help you through those hard times. Just as Father didn't abandon Prodigal but took the blows from the gang upon himself, so also God didn't abandon you in your suffering but took the blows upon Himself when Jesus died on the cross.

2. Have you relied upon Christ's finished work at the cross whereby He paid the price for your sins and forgave you?

Have you confessed your sins and called out for God's mercy? Have you extended this mercy to those who have sinned against you? Pray that God would help you in these matters.

3. Sometime this week read Mark's account of the last week of Jesus' life on earth (Mark 11–16).

NOTES

1. 2 Corinthians 7:9–10.
2. Revelation 12:10*b*.
3. John 14:16, 26, 15:26, 16:7 KJV.
4. 2 Corinthians 10:3–5.
5. John 9:1–3.
6. Luke 13:1–9.
7. God referred to Job as "blameless and upright, a man who fears God and shuns evil" (Job 2:3). God rebuked Job's friends: "You have not spoken of me what is right, as my servant Job has" (Job 42:7).
8. Job 4:8; 20:29; 15:3.
9. Galatians 6:7.
10. Numbers 14:18.
11. Matthew 5:45*b*.
12. Hebrews 12:7,10*b*.
13. Ephesians 4:15.
14. James 5:16.
15. In Proverbs 14:7 Solomon points out the two basic kinds of mistakes people make with their anger: losing their temper (aggressiveness) or being crafty and manipulating (passive-aggressiveness).
16. Leviticus 26:40–42.
17. Compare Luke 15:21 with 15:18*b*–19.
18. Many theologians interpret the two confessions as being different because the father interrupted Prodigal, as if his love was too great to let his son degrade himself. I have used the interpretation that Kenneth Bailey offers in _The Cross and the Prodigal._
19. James 5:16.
20. John 8:1–11.
21. Luke 15:1–2.
22. Matthew 23:25, 28.
23 Luke 16:19–31.

"He . . . threw his arms around him and kissed him."

Luke 15:20

STEP 6

Reconciliation with God

Embracing the Father

While everyone else was quietly murmuring under his breath against the truth of Father's rebuke, Phillip was lost in thought. He was replaying in his mind the tape of Father's words to him. "Phillip, Phillip, Phillip. When will my love be enough to make you secure? You must understand that closing your eyes to conflicts doesn't create peace. Phillip, Phillip, Phillip. When will my love be enough?"

Suddenly, Phillip was startled to see his master reach out to Prodigal, give him a big hug, and kiss him on the cheek again and again. Then Phillip heard his master exclaim to Prodigal, "Son, I love you! I'm so glad to have you back home! Know that no matter what people say about you, I'll always stand beside you."

"Oh no!" Sarah gasped. She turned to Joshua with a disgusted expression on her face. "Ewhh! How could anyone hug someone who smells like swine!"

Joshua was shaking his head back and forth and frowning as he said, "This just isn't right. It just isn't right. The forgiveness was bad enough, but this is even worse!" Joshua never had been comfortable with expressions of affection, especially in public and especially between men.

But Father and Prodigal weren't the least bit concerned about what Sarah or Joshua or anyone else thought. They continued embracing and squeezing one another and crying their happy tears. This was their moment, their time to celebrate! They had been separated by 300 miles of barren desert and by seven months of unforgiven sin. Though bystanders had mocked them and a violent gang had attacked, now they were reconciled. Now they were standing strong together!

As they stood together embracing, Prodigal rested his head on Father's chest. He buried his head deep into his father's strong yet soft chest. As he rested there he heard his father's heartbeat. *I love the sound of Abba's heartbeat!* Prodigal thought. The rythym reminded him of the waves from the Mediterranean he had heard along the coastal route home, near the desert's edge. Later he would compose a poem celebrating his father's steady love:

> *Abba's heart beats for me*
> *Like the waves of the sea.*
> *Thaugh-thump. Thaugh-thump. Thaugh-thump.*
> *Waugh-woosh. Waugh-woosh. Waugh-woosh.*
> *I am here. I am here. I am here.*
> *I love you. I love you. I love you.*
> *The strong, steady rythym never changes,*
> *The soothing, satisfying sound never ceases.*
> *When I stop to listen close*
> *The pace of my life slows.*
> *When I breathe in*
> *I feel Abba's love for me.*
> *When I breathe out*
> *I feel my love for Abba.*

Father seemed to know his son's thoughts behind the budding poem. He whispered, "It's good to have you back with me again." Then he patted Prodigal on the back, stepped to the side, motioned with his arm, and said to everyone, "Well, what do you say we head on home now!"

Rabbi Benjamin looked up with a start. His head had been bowed reverently during the embrace between Father and Prodigal. Teary-eyed, he asked Joshua for a handkerchief.

"Oh, take your snivels somewhere else! I've had enough emotion and affection today to last me a lifetime!" grumbled Joshua.

"I agree," echoed Timothy. "Besides, I need to get back to my business in the shop! It's almost time for the evening prayers, and I haven't done any work all day!"

Just as everyone started back toward the village Phillip shouted, "Wait! Wait! Master, I need you too! Please forgive me too! I don't want to avoid conflict anymore. I want to stop burying my feelings. I want to. be truthful. I want to experience real closeness, master."

Father rushed over to Phillip, embraced him, and kissed him again and again on the cheek, just as he had done to Prodigal. "You're my son too, Phillip! I've always loved you like my own. Of course I forgive you. And from now on I want you to call me _Father_."

"Me, call you father? Wow . . . _Father_!"

"Yes, Phillip! You're my brother!" Prodigal chimed in, as he also gave Phillip a hug, making it a group embrace.

"Here we go again!" muttered Joshua. "I can't believe this! You'd never see this in my courtroom."

"Joshua, don't you see?" Rabbi Benjamin exclaimed while emphatically raising his hands toward heaven. "That's your problem! You're missing out on love! Love is the answer."

"Another lecture, eh, Benjamin? Well, I just don't see the justice in closing our eyes to sin. It's just not right to be hugging and kissing a swine-smelling sinner!"

Then Father turned to Prodigal and Phillip, too, and sang out with a heart set free:

> *Come with me, my sons!*
> *Put your hands in mine.*
> *Now that we're together*
> *Let's skip our way home!*
> *'Cause I have still more blessings to give.*
> *Yes, I have still more blessings to give.*

And what a sight it was! Three men gleefully singing, holding hands, and skipping along. In the middle was a bruised and beaten-up old man, on the right a dirty and disheveled vagrant, and on the left a sweaty servant. Trailing behind these unlikely merrymakers was a gossiping gaper, a grumbling grinch, a mumbling merchant, a pious priest, and a band of boys.

Healing Hurts from an Abusive Father

The sight was moving: Father and son reunited with enthusiastic embraces, kind kisses, and wonderful whispers. It did not move Joshua, though. He was shaking his head back and forth and frowning as he complained, "This just isn't right. It just isn't right." To him Prodigal was a "swine-smelling sinner" who ought to be beaten and sent back to the pigsty. *Anyone who would hug someone like this is a fool!* he thought.

As we've seen again and again in our story, when it comes to showing love toward his son, Father gladly plays the role of the so-called fool. He believed in his son when others gave up. When others stood still, he ran to greet Prodigal. When others were judgmental, he showed compassion and embraced his son. When others tried to beat Prodigal, Father protected his son. Father wasn't ashamed of Prodigal; he loved him even though he was a sinner and even though he smelled like swine.

Imagine yourself being that close to your father. A warm embrace, a kiss on the cheek, a whisper of love—

"I don't want Father to touch me!" cried Sandra, a woman I was praying for. "My father molested me!" The woman began sobbing right there in my church office. I was her college pastor, and I thought I was helping her when I prayed for her that God would be like the Daddy she never had, that her Father God would hold her in his lap, look into her eyes, and say, "I love you."

As I looked into Sandra's tear-filled eyes and listened to her story of how her father had abused her sexually, I understood why it didn't feel good to her that God promised, "I will be a Father to you, and you will be my sons and daughters."[1]

Sandra isn't alone. Studies suggest that as many as one of every four girls and one of every seven boys have been sexually abused by an adult. And in almost half of those cases, the trusted adult is the child's father or step-father.[2] But these are not the only people who have trouble with God being called a *father*. Many other people, even though they have not been sexually abused by their fathers, also have trouble when God is presented as their "Father." They, too, are hesitant and fearful about letting a heavenly Father get too close to them because their earthly father injured them in other ways. They may believe the heavenly Father is loving and gentle, but in their hearts the word *father* has different associations for them. They remember painful wounds from their past. Listen to their cries with me. (Maybe one of these cries is yours, too.)

"I hid in my room and tried to cover my head with my pillow while my father beat my mother again and again, but I still heard her screams."

"It hurt when my father jokingly called me by nicknames like "Stooge," "Trouble," or "Dumbo.""

"When my father came home drunk I tried to stay away, because he'd say mean things to whoever got in his way."

"Every Saturday my dad had a huge list of chores for me to do before I could play. If I didn't do them all perfectly then I got a long lecture about my failings."

"My dad is a nice guy, but he has a lot of problems. When I was a kid it seemed like I was the one who would listen to him. Not anymore."

"When my father was upset with me and my two younger brothers he lined us up in the backyard and with our pants down to our ankles he'd give us the switch. What I hated most was the waiting. I was the last to get punished so I had to wait and listen to my brothers scream."

Our heavenly Father isn't like those human fathers. Jesus promised that if we go to him for bread we will not receive a stone instead, or if we ask for an egg we will certainly not receive a scorpion.[3] Yet that is what has happened to some people with their own fathers. They trusted their fathers and were violated. Indeed, fathers can easily deceive their vulnerable and trusting children with bad gifts that look good. A little, round limestone on the seashore looks like a loaf of bread, and a scorpion at rest with its claws and tail folded in looks like an egg.

For people who have been deceived and wounded by their fathers emotionally, distinguishing father from Father is a difficult process. One prayer isn't enough. In fact, as I learned several years ago, it can cause a lot of damage. Sermons, explanations, and even Bible verses about the character of God aren't enough either; for many people they do little to change the emotional associations of the word *father*. When we approach our heavenly Father we bring with us memories of our earthly father and of other authority figures who have been important in our development.

So how can you join Prodigal in receiving Father's warm embrace? How can you get close to your heavenly Father if you're carrying father-wounds in your heart? By following Sandra's example of forgiving her father. At first, forgiving her father's incest was the last thing she wanted to do. But as she spent month after month processing painful memories and working through her feelings of confusion, shame, anger, and hurt she began to realize that forgiveness—releasing her father from all he owed her—was good for her. It was freeing her from her prison of resentment. She found that she had more energy and hope for life. She started to trust that there were men who were different from her father, men who weren't abusive, controlling, and manipulating, men who had their anger and their sex drive under control. Courageously and carefully she began to trust other men, such as her counselor, a boyfriend, and her best friend's husband. Through this healing process Sandra began to see her heavenly Father more clearly and felt closer and closer to Him.

Footsteps of Faith

1. This week imagine yourself in Prodigal's place, receiving a hug and a kiss from your father. How would that feel for you? Was your father affectionate with you? How did/does his affection (or lack of affection) feel for you?

_____

_____

_____

2. What feelings come to your heart when you say, "Dad"?

☐ Fear	☐ Disappointment	☐ Sadness
☐ Anger	☐ Anxiety	☐ Shame
☐ Inadequacy	☐ Pressure	☐ Guilt
☐ Love and hate	☐ "Who is he?"	☐ Abandonment
☐ Empty void	☐ Loneliness	☐ Distance
☐ Worry	☐ Love	☐ Joy
☐ Peace	☐ Pride	☐ Affection
☐ Security		

3. Were you deceived by your father? Maybe he said or did some things that were supposed to be "good for you" but they wounded you. Check any statements below that apply.

☐ His spankings left marks, bruises, and shame.
☐ I was touched by him in sexual ways.
☐ He teased me in a way that hurt my feelings.
☐ He called me nicknames I didn't like.
☐ His lectures were condemning or insulting.
☐ He bragged about my achievements to others to bolster himself.

☐ I could never measure up to his expectations for me.

☐ The time I spent with him seemed to be for him and not me.

4. Make it your prayer this week that God would help you to follow Sandra's example by forgiving your father for his sins against you and also by working to develop safe relationships with other people, including men and authority figures.

Healing Hurts from a Neglectful Father

The display of affection between father and son brought a gasp from Sarah. *How could such a distinguished man shower warm embraces and tender kisses upon such a sinful, sweaty, and smelly adolescent?* Joshua also was disgusted. In his view it wasn't appropriate for men to be affectionate, tender, or tearful, particularly in public. Joshua was a man of the law, not mercy; facts, not feelings; strength, not sensitivity.

Father was a different kind of man. Jesus' story line and his choice of words in his parable make this clear. Although Father was an older man, a man of distinction, prominence, and wealth, he was nonetheless a man who panted, grunted, and sweat as he ran a footrace through the village to reach his son before the crowds did, a man who was overtaken by compassion in his innards, a man who kissed his son again and again. Indeed, Father was a man marked by characteristics such as humility, gentleness, empathy, mercy, tears, and affection. Yet he was still a "macho man," a man's man, who was confident, sound-thinking, strong, and just. He demonstrated this when he protected his son from the hostile gang of boys and when he rebuked the mocking group of bystanders. The best thing about Father, though, was that he brought all of himself—gentleness and strength—in a personal way to his son.

Do you know a father like this? What kind of a man was your father? Leah answered this question in a letter she wrote to my wife and me after reading my book *Mistaken Identity.*

> My heart yearns and aches for a real love relationship with God, but the images in my mind and heart confuse and frustrate me. It's easier to see Jesus as loving and forgiving, but when I think of God, the Father . . .

Growing up, my father didn't have much time for us kids, and I always felt like I was in his way. I felt that I didn't deserve his time. And when he gave me his time, his face revealed how I had disturbed or interrupted his schedule. I was always scared to go to him or ask him for anything. I just didn't want to bother him. . . .

I never liked my father, which has caused me tremendous guilt, because I thought we're supposed to have all these great feelings towards our parents.

I just hope that I can develop positive, nurturing relationships so that through them, I can _feel_ and receive the love of God. Please pray for me and all the other people who are struggling with negative God images.

I do pray for Leah and people like her who are crying out to know their heavenly Father's love. Unfortunately, people like her are often forgotten, and their needs are minimized. Leah wasn't abused, beaten, or abandoned by her father. She didn't live in fear of drinking binges, angry arguments, or a night without food on the table. But she did feel alone; her longing to feel close to her father and to know that she was special to him was unfulfilled. On most of the rare occasions when she did feel somewhat close to her dad she regretted it because she felt his impatience and his judgment, not the caring and acceptance she wanted.

People who have been victimized, criticized, or betrayed by a parent or someone else they love usually feel violated or ashamed. Their pain is acute, sharp, and they may find themselves in crisis. People who have been emotionally neglected feel as though they don't matter much, and often think such neglect is no big deal. Their pain is so chronic, so dull, so familiar that they may not even notice it. Their feelings and needs never mattered before so why should they now? Questions such as, "How do you feel?" and, "What do you need?" have never been relevant to them. (Victims of abuse may have also felt neglected _except_ when they were being abused.)

The opposite of love is not hate, abuse, or criticism. It's indifference. If your father failed to show you his love in personal ways, then you probably felt unimportant, forgotten, lost, neglected, alone, fatherless. Unfortunately, one of every four children in America—more than 15 million—is growing up in a home without a father present.[4] And in many of the homes where the father is present physically he is absent emotionally.

One survey found that when troubled daughters needed comfort they went first to music, second to girlfriends, and third to television. Dad was ranked thirty-fourth on the list.[5] Another survey found that when teenaged sons were struggling with problems, only 7 percent went to their fathers for support. Father was the last help on the list, after friends, female friends, mother, others, and nobody.[6]

Perhaps you didn't feel as close to your father as you wanted to be. If so, then just as I prayed for Leah I pray for you, too, that you would know that you are indeed special to God. For God is "a father to the fatherless, a defender of widows. . . . God sets the lonely in families, he leads forth the prisoners with singing."[7] "The Lord watches over the alien and sustains the fatherless and the widow."[8] And Jesus promised to us, "I will not leave you as orphans; I will come to you."[9] *But God hasn't come to me yet,* you may be thinking. *I feel fatherless and lonely. What about me? Why haven't God's promises come true for me?*

It's hard to trust in and experience God's love when it wasn't modeled to you. God, as "the Father from whom all fatherhood derives its name,"[10] is the role model for fathers and the source of all fatherly love. Thus, in the ways that your father neglected you or wounded you he failed to carry out God's commission, failed to represent effectively the one who gave him the name "father." So now as an adult you need to find your fatherless child inside and bring him or her to your heavenly Father and to trustworthy people. You need to seek help with this, and other people need your help too.

This is one purpose of the church—to "defend the cause of the weak and the fatherless"[11] and to share food with the alien and the fatherless.[12]

Footsteps of Faith

1. Consider life with your father when you were a child. Was his personality balanced like that of Prodigal's father? Which of the following attributes were true of your father's character at home:

- ☐ Strong
- ☐ Self-respecting
- ☐ Sound-thinking
- ☐ Just
- ☐ Industrious
- ☐ Respectful of boundaries
- ☐ Serious
- ☐ Steady

- ☐ Gentle
- ☐ Humble
- ☐ Sensitive
- ☐ Merciful
- ☐ Personable
- ☐ Affectionate
- ☐ Playful
- ☐ Enthusiastic

2. Women, rate your husband, boyfriend, or other man in your life according to the attributes above. (Men rate yourselves.) Rate the person from 1 to 10, with 1 indicating that the characteristic was fully absent and 10 indicating that the quality was fully developed.

- ____ Strong
- ____ Self-respecting
- ____ Sound-thinking
- ____ Just
- ____ Industrious
- ____ Respectful of boundaries
- ____ Serious
- ____ Steady

- ____ Gentle
- ____ Humble
- ____ Sensitive
- ____ Merciful
- ____ Personable
- ____ Affectionate
- ____ Playful
- ____ Enthusiastic

3. Do you feel sad when you imagine Father's expression of tender affection and compassionate love for Prodigal? Maybe you missed out on those personal expressions of love from your father. If so, take some time to grieve and express your loss. This week write a letter to your dad expressing your sadness about the things you wish he had shared with you. (Do this even if your father has passed away or even if you wouldn't want to mail the letter.)

4. Jesus taught us, "Blessed are those who mourn, for they shall be comforted."[13] A practical way you may want to apply this is to read to a close friend your sad letter addressed to your dad.

WEEK 26

Two Hearts Beating as One

Not surprisingly, Prodigal fell deeply in love with his father. He was enthralled at a father who wanted him back after he had insulted him, wasted his inheritance, and brought disgrace to the family. Prodigal was simply responding to Father's love—a love so deep that Father had run to greet him, wiped his tears, forgiven his sins, endured the beating he deserved, and hugged and kissed him again and again. Once lost in a far country of sin and despair in a pigsty of disgrace, now Prodigal was at home and reconciled to his father.

So there they were, father and son embracing. Father had his arms wrapped around his son. Prodigal had his head resting on his father's chest, listening to the heart that beat for him. Later he composed a poem about his father's love:

> *Abba's heart beats for me*
> *Like the waves of the sea.*
> *Thaugh-thump. Thaugh-thump. Thaugh-thump.*
> *Waugh-woosh. Waugh-woosh. Waugh-woosh.*
> *I am here. I am here. I am here.*
> *I love you. I love you. I love you.*
> *The strong, steady rythm never changes,*
> *The soothing, satsifying sound never ceases.*
> *When I stop to listen close*
> *The pace of my life slows.*
> *When I breathe in*
> *I feel Abba's love for me.*
> *When I breathe out*
> *I feel my love for Abba.*

When was the last time you heard God's heartbeat? Some people like Prodigal hear it in the waves of the sea or in the heartbeat of a trusted friend. Others hear it in the whispers of the wind, the drops of rain as they fall, the ticking of a clock, or the words of a wise person. God's heart is always beating; His voice is always speaking. It doesn't matter where you hear it as long as you hear it, and the more you hear it the better. You know you've heard God's heartbeat when your own heartbeat slows down and you find yourself reflecting upon things that really matter in life. That's because God's heart beats slower and stronger than ours.

We all long to have our hearts united with our heavenly Father's heart, don't we? His heart whispers to us, "Be still and know that I am God,"[14] and our hearts unite with His when we reply, "Abba, Father!"[15] Being reconciled to God like this is our greatest need in life. The Creator has set eternity into our hearts, and only that which comes from the Eternal God will satisfy our souls.[16] Yet, since the fall when Adam and Eve sinned, the entire creation has been subjected to the frustration of longing for glory and perfection but being in bondage to decay.[17]

The path to freedom and reconciliation begins by being adopted into the family of our heavenly Father. This requires a rebirth, which is followed by a gradual transformation into the likeness and glory of God's only Son.[18] And, as anyone who has watched the delivery of a newborn knows, birth is a painful experience, both for the mother and the child (and often for squeamish fathers). The apostle Paul explained that spiritual birth is the same way. We groan in pain, struggle with weaknesses, and must fight against opposition.[19] And the transformation process can be even harder than the spiritual birth. Yet just as the refiner's fire that brings the gold's impurities to the surface for removal, so also suffering purifies and betters the Christian.[20]

That is the way it was for Prodigal. Because of his sins, the sins of others against him, his disconnectedness from God, and circumstances out of his control, he suffered greatly. He ran out of money, couldn't find work, and was abandoned by his friends. He became a beggar in the streets, scrounging around for food in garbage cans, mocked by passersby, and attacked by madmen. Finally, he realized that he needed his father and so returned home.

And what did he find? The blessings that Prodigal encountered when he reconciled with Father are amazing. We're only halfway through our story and already Prodigal has experienced the blessings of Father's patience, respect, initiative, compassion, forgiveness, and affection. And look at the new fruit in Prodigal's character: humility, changed perceptions of God and himself, trust, self-examination, repentance, and intimacy with Father. Truly the hardships and suffering Prodigal had encountered were being worked for his good,[21] as he was in a process of being healed and transformed by Father's love. His heart was becoming one with Father's heart.

Footsteps of Faith

1. Most people struggle to experience intimacy with the heavenly Father. Often a number of distractions must be dealt with or put aside in order to hear God's heartbeat. Which of the following things distract you from your Father's love? Check all that apply.

☐ A hectic and overcrowded schedule
☐ Racing thoughts that won't stop
☐ Worrying about things that trouble me
☐ Pressure to finish all the things on my "to do" list
☐ Guilt over my sins, mistakes, or failures
☐ Feelings of unworthiness or shame
☐ Future plans or hopes that I'm excited about
☐ Anger at God over ways I've been disappointed by Him

2. Perhaps you are troubled about some things that haven't yet worked out for your good. If so, apply God's prescription for anxiety, echoed by the apostle Paul in Philippians 4: "Do not be anxious about anything. Instead, talk to God about all the things that trouble you and ask Him for what you need. Then thank Him that he hears you and be patient for His response. You'll find that the wonderful peace of God will guard your heart and your mind from anxiety."[22] Bring your worries to Him in prayer.

3. Sometime this week set aside time to listen to God's heartbeat. Go to the ocean, a lake, a park, or your backyard and listen to the sounds of creation. Or you might rest your head on a loved one's chest, and let God soothe your soul through the words of a friend. Or you may want to go to a quiet place to pray. Pray that the Father would speak to you and draw you close to Him as you quiet your soul and listen.

Embracing the Father

Phillip had served Father faithfully for years. He took care of Father when he was sick, he made meals, he ran the household, he worked in the fields, and he helped raise Elder and Prodigal. Always Phillip's first thought was, *What would Father want me to do?* Phillip was devoted to Father and thought he had grown to know his master well. But things changed when Phillip saw Father's incredible expressions of love toward Prodigal. Phillip saw Father race through the village to get to Prodigal before the taunting and abusive mob did. He heard the conversation between Father and son and saw the compassion in Father's eyes. He was shocked when Father stood between the gang of boys and Prodigal and received upon himself the beating due Prodigal.

When Father embraced Prodigal in spite of his sins, Phillip cried. He wanted that kind of father and son relationship too. And he knew he needed to be forgiven as Prodigal was.

So Phillip shouted, "Master, I need you too! Please forgive me! I don't want to avoid conflict anymore. I want to stop burying my feelings. I want to experience real closeness, Father. Help me learn to serve you with love, joy, and peace."

Father was overjoyed. Phillip opened his ears to the truth of Father's words. He opened his eyes to the beauty of Father's expressions of love to Prodigal. He opened his heart to the forgiveness that Father had for him. He opened his arms and embraced Father as his own father. Yes, Father adopted his servant as his son! And he embraced his new son, kissed him again and again on the cheek, forgave his sins, and loved him completely, just as he had done for Prodigal. Like Prodigal, Phillip was reconciled to Father. So with the noisy argument between Joshua and Rabbi fading into the background, Father, Prodigal, and Phillip joined hands, sang about God's forgiving grace, and danced their way home.

Like Phillip, we need a father to embrace. I remember my own dad wrestling with me when I was a small boy. We would roll around together all over the carpeted family room floor. I'd pound on his chest, and he'd pull me to himself and give me a big bear hug! Then I'd scream with delight as I felt his squeezes, rubs, and pats. We made a lot of noise (much to the dismay of my mom!), but no one got hurt. We both had fun, and I felt so special to my dad. I've enjoyed passing on this little father and son ritual to my own son, David. He has enjoyed it every bit as much as I did. I remember when he was not even two years old, and he'd look at me sitting in our family room and exclaim, "Da-da! Da-da!" and then he'd come toddling toward me with both arms stretched out wide in anticipation of a big bear hug! And before you know it we were rolling around on the carpet, just as my dad did with me when I was a boy.

Few things in life feel better than a hug from someone you love. Arms wrapped around you and squeezing you close have a way of saying, "I love you!" How much children need this from their fathers! They long for their father's loving touch, tender affection, and encouraging embrace. Touch from someone you trust is a powerful way to take love into your soul. It sensitizes even the most calloused skin. It loosens the most rigid body. It warms the coldest personality. It softens the hardest heart.

Johnny longed for this kind of touch from his dad. He recalled waiting up at night for his dad to come home from the bar. Many nights he fell asleep on the sofa waiting. When Johnny got older he stopped waiting for his dad and started hanging around with the wrong crowd of kids in the neighborhood. It wasn't long before a sensitive boy became a callous adolescent. His appearance even changed. He looked hardened, rigid, angry, resigned to a wasteful life. His previously warm personality seemed so cold. His once soft and impressionable heart was now hardened. Johnny missed out on a father's affectionate touch. He had waited and waited for a hug, a hand to hold, a pat on the back—something—until finally he could wait no more and gave up.

I met Johnny when he was a young adult and had just finished a recovery program for an addiction to cocaine. He had made a new start. He made friends in his recovery group who helped support his sobriety. He worked through his father-wounds in his treatment. He even found an older man in his church to befriend and disciple him. Over time Johnny's heart softened. He shared his tears and his longings, and he found hands to hold, pats on the back, and hugs. His heart even softened to the heavenly Father, and he told me that daily he prayed, "My Father in heaven, holy is your name. . . ." He is on his way to accepting fully his Father's love.

Footsteps of Faith

1. Did your father show you his love with hugs, pats on the back, kisses on the cheek, or a hand to hold? Did you get the affection you needed from your father? Was it appropriate? Consider how your father's touch (or lack of touch) has impacted your life.

2. Have you ever felt "touched" by God? Recall to mind past experiences in which you have felt the Father coming close to you.

3. This week follow Johnny's example and pray to your heavenly Father using "the Lord's prayer" as a guide (Matthew 6:9–13). Pause as you pray each word and each phrase,

considering the meaning of what you're praying and how it feels for you to pray these things to the Father.

> Our Father in heaven, we honor your holy name.
> We ask that your kingdom come now.
> May your will be done here on earth, just as it is in heaven.
> Give us our food again today, as usual, and forgive us our sins,
>   just as we have forgiven those who have sinned against us.
> Don't bring us into temptation,
>   but deliver us from the Evil One. Amen.
>
> Matthew 6:9–13, adapted, TLB

4. Maybe, like Phillip, you also would like to be adopted as a child of your heavenly Father. If so, then do as Phillip did. Call upon the Father's love, confess your sins to Him, and open your arms wide to let Him welcome you home with an embrace.

NOTES

1. 2 Corinthians 6:18.
2. Lynn W. England and Charles L. Thompson, "Counseling Child Sexual Abuse Victims," *Journal of Counseling and Development* 66 (April 1988): 370–73.
3. Matthew 7:9–10; Luke 11:11–12.
4. Research study conducted at the University of Pennsylvania, as cited in David Stoop, *Making Peace with Your Father* (Wheaton: Ill.: Tyndale, 1992), 13.
5. Study by the National Center of Fathering, as cited in Stoop, *Making Peace*, 15. For information, contact the center at 217 Southwind Place, Manhattan, Kansas, 66502.
6. "Whom Male Teens Confide In," *USA Today*, October 11, 1989, p. 6.
7. Psalm 68:5–6.
8. Psalm 146:9.
9. John 14:18.
10. Ephesians 3:15.
11. Psalm 82:3; Deuteronomy 10:18.
12. Deuteronomy 24:19; 26:12.
13. Matthew 5:4.
14. Psalm 46:10.

15. Galatians 4:6.
16. Ecclesiastes 3:11*b*.
17. Romans 8:19–21.
18. Romans 8:22.
19. Romans 8:22, 26, 31–39.
20. 1 Peter 1:6–9.
21. Romans 8:28.
22. This is my paraphrase of Philippians 4:6–7.

"But the father said to his servants, 'Quick! Bring the best robe and put it on him.'"

Luke 15:22a

Wearing Father's Robe of Righteousness

Father led the way as he, Prodigal, and Phillip sang and danced through town and toward home. Sarah, Timothy, Mayor Joshua, Rabbi Benjamin, and the gang of boys all followed behind. Each resisted the temptation to stop in town and return to the activities he had been doing before Prodigal showed up. They were curious to see what would happen next. They wondered what Father meant when he sang out to Prodigal, "Yes! I have still more blessings to give!"

When the home of Father became in view, Prodigal exclaimed, "I'm home! I'm home at last!" He ran toward his home and swung open the front gate to the courtyard. Suddenly his mind flashed back to his nightmare of returning home and being kicked and tormented by Elder.

"Where's Elder?" Prodigal turned around and yelled at the others who had been running after Prodigal.

Phillip had been leading the march this time. (Apparently encountering Father's love had put some pep in his step too.) He reached the gate right behind Prodigal and replied, "Oh, I'm sure he's working in fields. Why, you should have known that, Prodigal!"

"I guess things really haven't changed around here since I left!" Prodigal laughed as he headed down the stone path toward the house. The wooden door had been left standing wide open, but Prodigal knew better than to go charging in as if he owned the place. He pulled up his stride and stood in front of the short, narrow opening. He turned around and watched as Phillip arrived, then Father and the others.

Everyone was standing in front of the door waiting when Father abruptly turned to Phillip and urged him, "Quick! Bring the best robe and put it on Prodigal!"

Prodigal's eyes bulged, and he looked over at Father with his jaw dropped open in amazement.

Phillip thought he was hearing things. He looked at Father and stammered, "Wha-what do you mean? Bring the-the-the *what*? F-f-for whom?"

"You heard me, Phillip! Bring my best robe and put it on my son!"

"You don't mean your ceremonial robe?"

Father nodded.

"But Father"—Phillip tried to reason with him in vain— "surely you don't want him to wear your robe. He's been rolling around in the dirt feeding pigs! He's sweaty from walking in the hot sun!"

At the sound of this Joshua's face reddened with anger, and the mayor shouted, "You can't do this! Keep him in his rags!"

"This time I agree with the mayor!" echoed Rabbi Benjamin, who was also quite offended. "If he wears your robe,

Father, it will be defiled! Why it'd be like bringing a pig into the synagogue!"

Father looked at them both sternly and insisted, "It's my robe, and I can give it to whom I wish! Phillip, are you doubting my love again? Now run along. You heard me say, 'Quick!'"

At once Phillip rushed into the house. He hurried over to the chest in Father's private room. Opening the cover, he carefully pulled out the ceremonial robe. It was beautiful! The robe was purple and covered with green emeralds, stones that represented the tribe of Judah. On the edges was an ornate, blue fringe. The robe carried the fragrance of the incense used in the synagogue. This robe was originally made for Father's great, great grandfather, who was still known as a great father in the tribe of Judah, and he had passed down this robe to his son, who passed it down to his son, and so on until it was now in the possession of Father. Each of these great men of Judah had worn this robe in countless religious ceremonies and festivals.

Phillip carried the robe back out, and without further questioning he stood in the doorway and, as he had been ordered, began to put the robe on Prodigal.

Prodigal stopped Phillip and looked at Father. He dropped his head and said, "I am not worthy."

Father replied, "I have loved you and forgiven you. You are my son, and I have made you worthy. Now please stand under the threshold and receive my righteous gift."

Prodigal looked up at the sacred stone threshold just above the door. Every Passover Father sprinkled the blood of a choice lamb upon it as a reminder of their deliverance from slavery to Pharoah. Prodigal bowed reverently under the threshold and then reached out his arms one at a time and slipped them into the large sleeves that Phillip held open for him.

Once he had the robe on Prodigal felt the soft linen against his arms, shoulders, and neck. He smelled the fragrant incense. He looked at his new royal appearance. Then he stood a little taller and stuck his chest out and held his head high, thinking, *I don't feel like a filthy sinner anymore. I feel righteous now. And I certainly don't look like a pig-herding slave anymore. I look like a nobleman.* He glanced past the open door into Father's house and thought to himself, *I don't belong in a pigsty. I belong in Father's house!*

Beaming with pride, Prodigal looked over at his father. "Thank you, Abba! You have delivered me! You have made me worthy. I am honored by your gift."

"You swine-smelling sinner! You don't deserve to be honored!" Mayor Joshua fumed with anger. "Take that off right now, or I'll have you punished!"

"Yes, please take the robe off, Prodigal!" urged Rabbi Benjamin. "You can't represent our village when you haven't washed and you haven't offered a sacrifice for sin! I won't let you into the synagogue in such a state!"

"No! I won't take the robe off! Did our forefathers deserve to be delivered from the hand of Pharaoh? No, it was because of His mercy that Yahweh delivered them from slavery. Neither do I deserve my deliverance and the mercy I have received. But Father has chosen me! He gave me this robe for me to wear, and I will wear it with pride. This robe I am wearing shows that Father has cleansed me and that he stands with me."

Joshua and Rabbi were both shocked. They had just been lectured and rebuked by a young man, a sinner at that! But they remained speechless because it was clear that Father was indeed standing with Prodigal.

The gang of boys, though, cared nothing about what God did for their forefathers nor what Father did for Prodigal. They wanted to have some fun so they began to mock Prodigal, bowing down before him and waving their hands up and down as though he were a king. Prodigal was not humored. "Get up, boys! Get up! You don't know what you are doing. I am like you. Apart from this robe of my father's, I am nothing. Father is the king! He is the holy one! He is the one we ought to worship."

The gang of boys stopped.

Father was standing behind Prodigal, on the other side from the gang of boys. He was smiling his approval.

Prodigal turned his head to look at Father, and his eye caught sight of the mezuzah, the metal box that was fixed to the doorposts of all God-fearing Jews. Through the hole in the box Prodigal could see the words "El Shaddai" ("Almighty God") on the parchment containing the Shema, the declaration of God's mighty power and a call to worship Him alone.[1] Of course, Prodigal knew it by heart. He memorized it as a young boy and had recited it at many family and community gatherings. As he looked at it this time, though, he had a different feeling about it. All of a sudden he burst into a spontaneous song in which he recited portions of the Shema:

> *Yes! The Lord our God is one!*
> *Yes! I do love Him!*
> *With all my heart I do!*
> *With all my soul I do!*
> *With all my might I do!*
> *From now on these words will always be on my heart!*
> *From now on these words will always be on my lips!*

The second time through the Shema song Father and Phillip started clapping to the song's beat, and Prodigal, dressed in his new robe, started dancing and skipping down the side of the house, back and forth. As he skipped along the wall he dragged his hand along the house's sandy clay brick wall and drummed to the beat. It wasn't long before the others forgot their grievances against Prodigal and joined in on the fun. Even Mayor Joshua was singing and dancing to Prodigal's Shema song! He wasn't ready to celebrate Prodigal's return yet, but he loved the Shema!

Waiting at an Open Door

When Prodigal saw the home where he had grown up for the first time since he had left hastily for the far country of Antioch seven months ago, he exclaimed in joy, "I'm home! I'm home at last!" He ran toward the front door, which had been left wide open. Father always left it that way. To Prodigal it had always been like a "Welcome home" sign. It invited him back into the house. But Prodigal knew better than to go leaping through the doorway now, for his feet were filthy! Besides, even though Father had forgiven him and been so good to him, he didn't want to presume that Father would invite him back into the house. After all, given how he had sinned against his father, he didn't deserve to be brought back into the house. To bounce into the house now would be to disrespect the boundary his sin had put between him and his father.

As Prodigal waited at the doorway, he secretly hoped that he'd be let inside. Just a few short hours ago he would never have dared to have such a hope. And in his wildest dreams he would not have imagined what happened next. Father exclaimed to Phillip, "Quick! Bring the best robe and put it on Prodigal!" *What? Father's best robe?* Everyone was shocked at the command.

Father's robe was purple and covered with multicolored jewels and blue fringe. Father wore it in religious ceremonies just as his great-great-grandfather had. Prodigal was going to reenter his home as if he were righteous! As if he were a royal nobleman. As if he were an esteemed member of the village. As if he belonged in the family of Father. Indeed, he would enter as if he were partaking in a worship ceremony. Yes! That is Father's gift to his son.

Prodigal would have expected his father to say, "Go wash up at the lake, and get some clean clothes on, and then perhaps you can come inside." But, instead, Father had Prodigal dressed by a servant! And it's no accident that this robing ceremony took place right under the stone threshold. As the blood of the lamb cleansed Prodigal's ancestors of sin, spared them from the angel of death in Egypt, and led to their freedom from slavery in the mud pits of Egypt,[2] so also the robe of Father cleansed Prodigal's sins, spared him from social death, and freed him from slavery in a muddy pigsty!

It's no wonder Prodigal's view of himself changed. He put on Father's robe and realized, *I don't feel like a filthy sinner anymore. I feel righteous!* He stood up straighter and taller and thought, *I certainly don't look like a pig-herding slave anymore! I look like a nobleman!* He planted his feet firmly on the ground and rejoiced, *I don't belong in a pigsty; I belong in Father's house!*

We also can wear Father's best robe. The robe we can put on is Jesus Christ and His righteousness. Like Prodigal, we must first respect the boundary between the Father and ourselves. God is holy, pure, and perfect, and we are not. We dare not walk through the door to His abode unless we first put on the robe of righteousness given when we put our faith in Christ.[3] This royal robe covers the tattered and dirty clothes of our sinful nature and makes us brand-new creatures by cleansing our sin and empowering us to do good. And it's a free gift! It's not a righteousness that can be gained by measuring up to the requirements of the law, but one that we receive by putting faith in God's goodness to us in Christ.[4]

When we, like Prodigal, respect the boundary between God and ourselves and wait at the doorway of faith to put on Father's robe, then doors start opening for us just as they did for Prodigal—the doors to righteousness and cleansing from sin, to royalty and honor, to being an esteemed member of the body of Christ, and to belonging in our Father's house. Once inside, there is celebration and worship. Perhaps you'd like to walk through some of these doors too! Then follow Prodigal's example. As you learn how to put on Father's robe, you'll be amazed at how much better you feel about yourself.

Footsteps of Faith

1. Have you felt a boundary between yourself and God? Do you want to walk through the open door to his heart but feel afraid or unworthy? If so, then take some time this week to wait and pray at the doorway. Look at the tattered and dirtied clothes of your sins and the sins of others against you. Ask God to help you as you seek forgiveness for your sins and healing for your hurts. Then in faith put on the Father's special robe of righteousness, which covers and heals your shame so that you can hold your head high and draw near to God. (As you're doing this you might try wrapping yourself in a robe or a blanket.)

2. During the next week as you engage in your activities and routines ask yourself, "Am I wearing Father's robe?" When you're at home, at work, at play, or with friends, check if you are viewing yourself as righteous in Christ and acting accordingly.

3. The same doors that opened for Prodigal when he put on Father's robe can open for you. Which of the following doorways do you need to walk through?
- ☐ Believing that I am forgiven
- ☐ Feeling honorable and special
- ☐ Knowing that I'm valued by others
- ☐ Having a sense of belonging
- ☐ Being free to celebrate and to worship

4. Perhaps it's hard for you to trust that a father would want to open some of these doors for you. Which of these doors did your father help you to open? Which ones remained closed? Write "open" or "closed" in front of each door.

_____ Believing that I'm forgiven
_____ Feeling honorable and special
_____ Knowing that I'm valued by others
_____ Having a sense of belonging
_____ Being free to celebrate and to worship

Saying No and Setting Boundaries

Prodigal was proud to wear Father's robe and to represent him. The robe's soft linen wrapped around him like his father's embrace. Its purple color and multicolored jewels made Prodigal feel as though he was of extraordinary value. Its design reminded Prodigal that he was an esteemed member of the tribe of Judah. Its smell of incense gave Prodigal a holy feeling. Seeing Prodigal in Father's ceremonial robe perturbed Joshua and Rabbi, however, and they each tried to convince him to take it off. Joshua used guilt and intimidation, and Rabbi used the threat of rejection, but much to the surprise of them both, Prodigal stood firm in his boundaries, insisting to them, "No! I won't take it off!" Prodigal had not been that assertive before, but things had changed.

How did Prodigal develop such strong boundaries? Where did he get the courage to say no? Only a few months earlier he had allowed Elder to push him around, he had been manipulated financially by Timothy, and out of guilt he gave Alex whatever he wanted. But now he knew that Father was standing with him. Father proved this when he ran through the town to get to Prodigal before the mob, when he protected Prodigal by taking the blows from the gang of boys upon himself, and now when he gave Prodigal his own robe. Wearing Father's robe, Prodigal knew that he had been made righteous, was accepted, and would be protected. Through putting faith in Father's love for him, Prodigal was secure in his identity and strong in his boundaries.

Indeed, it takes a secure sense of who you are and a bold belief in what you stand for to do as Prodigal did and say no to someone who tries to cross your personal boundaries or to hurt you in some way. People who lack this security and boldness don't set the kind of firm and clear boundaries that Prodigal set with Joshua and Rabbi. Many people try in their own hesitant and fearful way to set a boundary, but when challenged they quickly back down. They're afraid of confrontation, easily manipulated by guilt, or unwilling to tolerate the rejection that will follow. I hear stories of this all the time. Consider the following cases of boundaries being crossed:

- The wife who is afraid to leave the house when her husband starts hitting her.
- The father who keeps dipping into his wallet to bail his seventeen-year-old daughter out when she can't pay her car insurance, can't afford to repair her car, doesn't have enough money for the trip she planned with her friends, or . . .
- The young woman who can't say no when a date makes a sexual advance.
- The mother who closes her ears to her ten-year-old daughter's complaint, "Uncle Eddie touches my private parts."
- The mother who says no to her six-year-old son's pleading for a candy bar and then gives in after he throws a tantrum.
- The employee who is pressured by his boss to work overtime but goes ahead and works late even though he had prior arrangements.
- The young man who spends Thanksgiving with his parents only because he doesn't want to hurt his mother's feelings.
- The husband who pretends not to notice when he overhears his wife criticizing him on the phone to her mother.

As these examples illustrate, it's a struggle for many people to set and maintain the clear and firm boundaries that will protect themselves or the children who are dependent upon them. But such boundaries are essential to developing a strong and secure sense of your separate identity. Boundaries define who you are. They say things such as

"I want this and not that."
"I feel _____."

"No, I don't like that."
"No, it's not appropriate for you to treat me that way."
"I'd like to share my thoughts on the subject."
"Yes, I would like to do that."

Statements such as those reflect who we are in a given moment. We all need the freedom to express our separateness and our unique personality, and to feel valued for our expression of ourselves. When you're not direct and clear in expressing yourself, you get into trouble. As the apostle James said, "Let your 'Yes' be yes, and your 'No' be no, or you will be condemned."[5] It doesn't work to beat around the bush and expect people to read your mind. If you want something, ask for it. (Of course, the other person may set his own boundary and say no.) If you don't want to do something, then decline the request.

Being honest and direct with our boundaries is important to God. Jesus illustrated this in a parable he told to the chief priests and the elders:

> There was a man who had two sons. He went to the first and said, "Son, go and work today in the vineyard."
> "I will not," he answered, but later he changed his mind and went.
> Then the father went to the other son and said the same thing. He answered, "I will, sir," but he did not go.
> Which of the two did what his father wanted?[6]

The religious leaders answered correctly in identifying that it was the first son who was in the right. Then Jesus went on to show them that the second son was a picture of them. They were passive-aggressive pretenders. They acted religious and cordial on the outside by saying yes to God, but on the inside they did as they pleased and thus were really saying no all along. Thus, Jesus said that the tax collectors and the prostitutes were entering the kingdom of God ahead of the religious elite because they said no to God at first but in the end changed their minds and said yes. And so it is that people who know how to say no also know how to say yes, but people who always say yes are insincere and can't be trusted.

Footsteps of Faith

1. Have you ever noticed in the Bible how frequently God defines for us His feelings, thoughts, desires, values, choices, and character? God's boundaries are clear; He makes His identity known. Over the next few days work at doing the same. On a sheet of paper write down these categories and fill them in with *your* feelings, thoughts, desires, values, and choices. Take several days to do this, returning to complete (or alter) the list after a time of reflection.

2. Perhaps you're someone who says yes too often. Sometime this week say no to someone just for the fun of it! For this to be a meaningful exercise you need to do it sincerely. In other words, be clear and direct with your no and don't back down from it. Note how it feels for you to say no. You may feel some of the following things, which usually inhibit you from setting boundaries:

- Afraid of rejection
- Worried about the other's feelings
- Intimidated
- Afraid of conflict
- Guilty
- Embarrassed
- Lonely
- Selfish

3. In what areas of your life are you struggling with boundaries? In what ways have your boundaries been crossed recently? This week make it your prayer that when

these situations arise God would help you find the courage and the strength to say no, to mean it, and to stick to it.

4. Did you receive from your father the kind of robe that Prodigal received from his? If not, you're probably struggling with your boundaries. Like Prodigal, you need a robe to wear: an encourager who wraps loving arms around you, valuing your separate identity and helping you to develop your boundaries. Sometime this week talk to a potential encourager about what you've learned about your boundaries.

Wearing Father's robe changed how Prodigal saw himself, and it gave him the courage to say no, protecting himself from being sinned against by Joshua and Rabbi. It also taught him to say no to temptation. When the gang of boys mocked Prodigal as though he were a king by bowing down before him and waving their hands up and down, Prodigal could have reacted negatively. He might have lost his temper and kicked them as they had tried to do to him earlier. He could have returned insult for insult and condemned them for their "bratty" behavior. Or he could have outsmarted them by accepting their mockery as if it were sincere and pridefully boasting of his greatness.

Instead, Prodigal was guided by wisdom and offered a righteous response to the gang of boys: "Get up, boys! Get up! You don't know what you are doing. I am like you. Apart from this robe of my father's I am nothing. Father is the king! He is the holy one! He is the one we ought to worship." Prodigal spoke the truth in love, showing the boys that they were confused about who to worship. He knew that his greatness came from Father, and so he remained dependent upon him.

Jesus also knew how it felt to encounter temptation. Immediately after He was baptized by John in the Jordan River He was led by the Spirit into the desert. There for forty days He fasted and prayed about his future ministry. During that time the devil tempted Jesus to turn stones to bread, to become a world dictator, and to jump off the top of the temple and into the arms of angels. Jesus had supernatural power, and He could have done each of these things. But Jesus resisted these temptations. He put His spiritual purpose before His physical appetite. He knew He was to be a savior of souls and not a world dictator. He refused to test God's mercy with vain pursuits. In each of these cases the way Jesus said no to sin was to refer back to Scripture, using the words of God as His guide to righteousness.[7]

In the Bible God provides us with many instructions to guide us in the way of righteousness and to help us resist temptations to sin. His words to us are not "Do what I want you to or I won't love you!" Nor are they "Do what you should or I will punish you in anger!" Instead, He says, "I love you, and I forgive you. Go in that knowledge and live rightly." And He says, "I created you. If you live according to my instructions, you will be fulfilled." God's Word is meant to show us who we are and to guide us into a life that is fulfilling and right.

Do you know who you are as a Christian? Do you maintain righteous boundaries to protect your identity and to resist temptation? Rosa lost sight of her righteousness when she discovered that her husband had multiple affairs in the eleven years that they had been married. When the shock wore off, Rosa entered our hospital program. Once she had understood the web of deception she had built around the incidents, the overwhelming truth of how she had been betrayed left her very depressed.

"I wasn't good enough to hold onto him." As she spoke, Rosa's eyes seemed to sag to the floor.

"How can you blame yourself?" blurted out Allison, another woman in the group. "If it was my husband, I'd never speak to him again!" Redirecting the group's focus back to Rosa's pain, I looked into Rosa's eyes and said, "It sounds like you're feeling really bad about yourself." She nodded and began to cry. Rosa needed a lot of tissues, listening, and hugs as she shared her tears with the group that day and in the days that followed.

A few days before she discharged from our program, Rosa began to feel the anger that Allison had correctly, but prematurely, identified. When Rosa got angry, she got very angry. And she let it be known in all the groups, including the Bible study group I did on anger. I was talking about the apostle Paul's concept of "Be angry and yet do not sin"[8] when she interrupted me. "What do you mean? Next time I see that adulterer I want to kick him in the groin! Or maybe I should cheat on him and show him how it feels! But no! I can't because God says, 'It is mine to avenge; I will repay.'"[9]

Rosa's rage was escalating, and I tried to contain it with calming words. "Rosa, it's OK to be angry, even at God. It seems you feel that God let this happen to you and now He's restricting your anger." The rest of group discussed some of David's angry words in the Psalms:

> How long will you hide your face from me? . . . How long will my enemy triumph over me?

> Awake, and rise to my defense! Contend for me, my God and Lord. Vindicate me in your righteousness.

> Break the arm of the wicked and evil man; call him to account for his wickedness.[10]

Hearing that David felt angry sometimes and that other members of the group also felt angry helped Rosa to not feel so alone with her anger. In the end, Rosa resisted her temptations to get revenge and trusted in God's justice.

Rosa repelled the badness that intruded upon her boundaries and threatened her righteous identity; she refused to accept that her husband's affairs were all her fault; and she resisted the temptation to seek revenge. She did this by working through her feelings of shame and anger over the series of betrayals and by setting protective boundaries, such as initiating a temporary separation while he got help in a sex addicts group and they went to marriage counseling.

*Footsteps
of Faith*

1. This week consider how you respond to temptation. The apostle John identified three ways that people "love the world" and sin. (He may have been referring back to the three kinds of temptations that the devil unsuccessfully brought to Jesus.) He indicates that each of these sins are symptomatic of having unmet needs for God's love.[11] Which of these three areas do you struggle with?

- ☐ Sinful cravings (physical desires and impulses)
- ☐ Lust of the eyes (jealousy, materialism, selfish ambition)
- ☐ Pride of life (self-sufficiency, boasting, superiority)

2. We all know that "two wrongs don't make a right," yet it's tempting to repay evil for evil. In which of the following ways do you respond when you've been sinned against?

- ☐ I feel hurt and may later become depressed.
- ☐ I get scared and try to avoid any further conflict.
- ☐ I feel bad about myself, as if I deserved to be mistreated.
- ☐ I rarely get angry, even when I've been offended.
- ☐ Sometimes I yell and say hurtful things.
- ☐ I lose my temper, and I might take it out in physical ways.
- ☐ I try to make the other person feel guilty for what happened.
- ☐ I detach from my feelings by engaging in the following compulsive behavior: _____.

☐ I confront the offender and try to speak the truth
in love.

☐ I set boundaries to protect myself.

3. As soon as you can, set aside some time for prayer.
Talk to God about any boundaries of righteousness that you
have crossed. Put on Father's robe of righteousness by putting faith in His forgiveness to you through Christ. To help
you with this you may want to get out your blanket or robe
again. Wrap yourself in it as you pray to your Father.

At the door to Father's house Prodigal noticed the holy Shema there in the mezuzah, the metal box affixed on the door. He had learned the Shema as a small boy and had recited it literally hundreds of times since. Seeing it this time, though, was like seeing it for the first time! He started to dance as he sang out from his heart:

Yes! The Lord our God is one!
Yes! I do love Him!
With all my heart I do!
With all my soul I do!
With all my might I do!
From now on these words will always be on my heart!
From now on these words will always be on my lips!

Soon the others were also singing and dancing to Prodigal's Shema song. Even the stiff and crotchety Joshua joined in! Prodigal was glad to be home, and he shared his joy with everyone. His joy was not as much about being physically home as it was about being spiritually home. For the first time his whole heart was at home with *El Shaddai*, the Mighty Father. Before, he felt obligated to respect the Shema and his father, but now he wanted to. Before, he rebelled against rules and traditions, but now he served his Lord and Father with gladness. Before, he sought the pleasures of sin and found himself in bondage, but now he pursued righteousness and found himself free. Prodigal was becoming a new man.

For some people, boundaries and laws are restrictive. A friend of mine, Sam, hitchhiked one summer several years ago from Southern California all the way to the East Coast and then back to Oregon. On his way he home he had been dropped off in northern California near the Oregon border.

Since it was illegal to hitchhike on the freeways in California, he walked the five or six miles from where he was dropped off to the sign that said "Welcome to Oregon." Relieved that he was finally free to hitchhike, he set his bags down just the other side of the sign and stuck his thumb out. Before long a California state police officer pulled over. Sam grinned at him as if to say, "Ha, ha! There's nothing you can do because I'm standing in Oregon—one foot out of the reach of your authority!"

Sam lost his grin though when the officer stepped out of his patrol car and told Sam that he was illegally hitchiking in California. Dumbfounded and a bit agitated, Sam replied in an insulting manner. "Sir, you need to have your eyes examined. Can't you see the sign?" The officer poked Sam's belt buckle and with a stern, cold voice said, "Young man, you have an attitude. And you're wrong. The state line is not where the sign is. It's twenty-five feet this way, and I have to give you a ticket!"

If Sam's attitude had been different, he probably wouldn't have received a ticket, but he had run into a hard-nosed police officer who was looking for a chance to show his authority. Sam needed to learn to respect authority. He had tried to respect a physical boundary without really respecting the authority behind it and ended up getting a ticket; his celebration of freedom was false and he got punished for it.

Sam needed to learn from Prodigal. Authority figures need to be respected, and boundaries aren't something to play around with. Because Prodigal respected Father's righteous authority and maintained clear boundaries, he was free to celebrate. And this is the purpose of boundaries. Boundaries between right and wrong are meant to free us to do what is good for us. Boundaries between ourselves and other people are meant to free us to be who we uniquely are. When put together, righteousness and separateness enable us to realize our divine potential as individuals.

When you understand boundaries this way, you'll want to be guided and disciplined by them. Even though God gives you complete freedom of choice to do as you decide is best,[12] you'll want to do what's right for you and for others because you'll realize that it's good for you. That is what David meant when he joyfully pronounced, "Delight yourself in the Lord and he will give you the desires of your heart."[13] And how different it is when you can serve God and do what is right because you want to and not just because you should.

So we can follow in Prodigal's steps of faith and put on Father's robe of righteousness. When we do, God writes His laws on our hearts such that we know that His righteousness is a gift, and we see a clear path before us. Moreover, we sense His way is good for us, and we become who we're meant to be. That spells f-r-e-e-d-o-m! Freedom from anxious striving to measure up, from chaotic confusion about what God's will is, from oppressive obligations to do more and more, and from joy-killing restrictions that hold us back. Now that's reason to celebrate!

Footsteps of Faith

1. Prodigal's Shema song depicted his increased love for the Scriptures. Do you love reading the Bible? Check the feelings below that describe how you feel when you open your Bible:

☐ Interest   ☐ Indifference
☐ Enjoyment   ☐ Boredom
☐ Peace   ☐ Restless anxiety
☐ Guidance   ☐ Confusion and lostness
☐ Hope   ☐ Despair
☐ Forgiveness   ☐ Guilt

☐ Acceptance ☐ Condemnation
☐ Comfort ☐ Distress
☐ Faith to keep going ☐ Discouragement

2. If you're feeling bored or discouraged spiritually, try reading Psalms 63, 119, and 84 this week. Notice how each of the writers express his longings for God and his love for His words. I've found it helpful to read passages like this prayerfully over and over until God whets my appetite for more of Him.

3. As we've seen in our story, Father loves to bless Prodigal. It pleases God to grant the deepest desires of our hearts.[14] In Psalm 22 David rejoices in a number of blessings he received from God. Which of the following blessings have you received?

☐ Strength ☐ Answered prayer
☐ Wealth ☐ Health
☐ Praise ☐ Intimacy
☐ Unfailing love

4. Perhaps you feel that many of your desires haven't come true. Whereas it's natural to celebrate when we experience God's blessings, it certainly isn't natural to rejoice when we're suffering; it requires tremendous faith. Take some time one day this week to write your own psalm to God. Express your desires to know His blessings.

NOTES

1. Deuteronomy 6:4–9.
2. Exodus 12:1–28.
3. Romans 3:21–24.
4. Romans 3:21; Ephesians 2:8–10.
5. James 5:12.

6. Luke 4:1–13.
7. Matthew 21:28–31.
8. Ephesians 4:26 NASB.
9. Romans 12:19.
10. Psalm 13:1*b*, 2*b*; 35:23–24; Psalm 10:15.
11. 1 John 2:15–17.
12. Joshua 24:15.
13. Psalm 37:4.
14. Psalm 21:2; 37:4.

"Put a ring on his finger."

Luke 15:22c

STEP 8

Accountability

Wearing Father's
Signet Ring

F rom now on these words will always be on my lips."

Yet another line of Prodigal's Shema song had resounded from the group for all to hear across the farmland and into the village of Nain.

"Amen!" exclaimed Father, trying to bring the singing and dancing to a close. "Everyone! Please give me your attention. Now that we've all rejoiced with Prodigal over his new righteousness I would like for you to listen to me. I have an important announcement to make."

"Oh, we were just starting to have fun," whined Sarah.

"I know. I know. I'm playing the party pooper," Father sympathized. "But there will be plenty of time to sing and dance later. So it's best that you save some of your energy anyway."

"But we were singing about the Shema," insisted Joshua. (He was still trying to overlook the fact that the real cause for rejoicing was that the "swine-smelling sinner" had been forgiven and was wearing Father's ceremonial robe!)

"Yes, the Lord is one!" everyone sang in unison. Then Rabbi Benjamin quickly added a pious and drawn out, "Ahhhhhh-men!"

"Indeed the Lord is one! Praise His holy name!" reiterated Father. "And it's because of His goodness that I speak to you now. Remember as we left the edge of town and I said I had still more blessings to give? Well, I have another gift for my son."

Prodigal swung his head around and looked at Father in amazement.

"Phillip?" Father turned to his servant.

"Yes, Father."

"Put my ring on Prodigal's finger." Father was holding up his right hand, displaying his signet ring.

"Not your signet ring, Father?"

A collective gasp came from the group of onlookers.

"Yes," Father replied. "Prodigal will have power of attorney over all my remaining estate."

Timothy raised his eyebrows and perked up his ears. The gang of boys whispered among themselves, plotting how they might steal the ring from Prodigal.

Phillip was greatly disturbed and continued his plea for restraint. "Father you mustn't do this! Elder will become like a wild pig, furious and fit to be tied. He's the legal owner of what remains of your estate. Besides, what if we lose everything? Last time you gave to Prodigal from the family estate it all went to the wind! Please don't do this, Father! We'll go broke!"

"I wouldn't take advantage of Prodigal," insisted Timothy.

"I bet you won't!" Phillip was looking into Timothy's sly eyes and remembering that fateful dawn when Timothy swindled the impulsive Prodigal and the whole family.

"Don't worry," offered the mayor. "I'll make sure every-thing is fair—as long as I'm given the right price!" Everyone laughed heartily. Everyone except Prodigal. He was lost in thought. *Maybe they're right. I can't handle that much re-sponsibility. What if I blow it again? And Elder... It'll be hard enough to face him as it is, but if he sees me wearing Father's ring.... But Abba wants to give me his ring! It's such an opportunity. I'd have a second chance! How could I turn this down? But how could I ever do all that would be re-quired of me?*

As the laughter died Sarah noticed that Prodigal hadn't been laughing. "What's the matter, Prodigal?" she said in a sarcastic tone as she elbowed him in the side. "You look sick. Why don't you wait to get sick until after you've spent your money and gorged yourself on chocolates and wine?"

Joshua, Timothy, and the gang of boys all started rolling with laughter again until Rabbi Benjamin interrupted them. "Stop this! Stop poking fun at Prodigal! Let's listen to what Father has to say."

"Thank you, Benjamin," replied Father. "I am giving my ring to my son because I trust him. He's learned his lesson, and he's ready for a second chance. He won't be foolish be-cause he knows how it feels to be on the brink of starvation. Besides, he's proven himself to be responsible by returning to me to confess his sins and to receive mercy and grace."

Then Father turned to look at Prodigal and spoke direct-ly to him. "Prodigal, we'll work together. I'll teach you all that I know." Prodigal nodded hesitatingly. He wasn't sure ex-actly what he was getting into, but he knew that it was both a huge responsibility and a tremendous opportunity, and he trusted that Father would help him as he promised.

Father looked for Phillip, who seemed to be hidden in the group of onlookers. He called out, "Phillip, are you ready? Come, take my ring and put it on Prodigal's finger."

"Father, only you can do this," pleaded Phillip.

"No, Phillip, I'm giving you the honor! In the past you've misused your peacemaker role by being a 'dodger of disagreements,' and it's torn you in two. But today I've been asking you to be a different kind of mediator. You have the privilege of being the 'bearer of blessings' by giving my gifts to Prodigal."

"Yes, Father!" Phillip replied. Immediately he went to Father and removed the ring from Father's hand and put it onto the fourth finger of Prodigal's outstretched right hand. Prodigal smiled as Phillip slid the ring onto his finger. He studied the ring with admiration. It was solid gold. The most special part of the ring was its face, which had Father's own personal engraved emblem and was encircled with little green emeralds. The emblem itself was unusual and represented a fantastic work of art. It was a long pole with a snake twisted around it.

Many times as a boy Prodigal had asked Father about the meaning of the emblem, but Father would only reply, "One day when you're ready I'll explain it to you, son." Whatever its mysterious meaning was, Prodigal knew that it was Father's own unique symbol. It was like his signature. He used it to seal legal documents by pressing it onto the parchment so that it left an impression of his unique emblem.

Prodigal flashed a proud and confident smile up at Father and said, "Thank you, Abba! I'll treasure this ring. I'll use it responsibly and in your best interests."

"You're welcome, son. I trust you and I will help you to use the ring well. On the first day after the Sabbath of each week I'll meet with you to discuss business and to get an accounting of how the farm is doing. And anytime you have questions you can come to me."

Prodigal nodded. He had a look of determination, as if he was ready to make good on his second chance. Then everyone gathered around Prodigal to admire his new ring. However, one person was still missing; noticeably absent was Elder.

WEEK 32
A Father's Encouragement

When Prodigal returned home to Nain, he did so with his head hung in shame. He had blown his inheritance big-time. He went to Antioch flying high on the wings of his fantasies of unending pleasure, monumental success, and widespread fame, but he crashed in a pigsty! His purple embroidered pouch, once full of clanking gold coins, now was empty. He returned home fully discouraged. The reception of condemnation, ridicule, abuse, and rejection that he received from the villagers certainly hadn't helped him to hold his chin up.

For Prodigal to continue his journey of recovery, he needed lots of encouragement. And that would have to come from Father. The gifts that Father had given already, including his best robe, were a start. But something more was needed, and Father gave it. He encouraged Prodigal in a way that no one would have expected: he gave his son his own signet ring! Phillip was impressed and fearful at the same time. *Wow! The fool who lost all of his inheritance now had power of attorney over what remained of the family resources. What will Elder say?*

Phillip worried that the tension between Elder and Prodigal would worsen once Prodigal had all that power. Furthermore, he didn't trust Prodigal to be accountable to manage the estate wisely; he was afraid that Prodigal would cost Phillip the shirt off his back and the bread on his table! Already, less than an hour after repenting of his sin and embracing Father, Phillip was reverting to his old behavior by taking matters into his own hands and trying to avoid conflicts and problems. Phillip didn't believe that Prodigal was up to the task; he didn't trust Father's judgment.

Of course, Phillip's lack of confidence in him, along with the sarcastic jesting of Sarah and Joshua, wasn't helping

Prodigal's confidence as he thought about the overwhelming task of managing the family's resources and property. But, although it was a struggle, in the end Prodigal listened to Father's *en*couragement, not everyone else's *dis*couragement. He went ahead and received the signet ring from his father and put his trust in his father's promise to teach and help him as he carried out his new responsibilities.

Like you and me and everyone we know, Prodigal was dramatically influenced by his father. Even absent fathers are always present in the back of their children's minds. Even small-in-stature fathers have a large influence upon those who call them "Dad." Even soft-spoken fathers have a loud voice in the ears of their sons and daughters. Even uneducated fathers teach their children more lessons—whether good or bad—than any amount of schooling could ever do. Almost everyone agrees that fathers have a critical influence upon the development of their children.

But what is it that children need from their fathers? Consider the following sample of tributes to an ideal father, which you can find at your local gift shop when searching for an appropriate Father's Day card:

- 'Dad, you've been such a strength to me over the years. It's because of your hand on my shoulder that I've become who I am today."
- "I could always count on you, Dad. Your loving support and careful guidance has made a big difference in my life."
- "Dear Father, I'm delighted to honor you today. It's the least I can do because you've honored me all of my life."
- "Thanks, Dad, for your wise words, your kind actions, your warm embrace, and, most of all, for your listening ears. I love you."
- "Dad, you were right. I didn't like being disciplined by you as a child, but now I see it did me good. You disciplined me in love and taught me the lessons I needed to learn. Thanks."

- "Dad, I admire you. You've been such an example to me of all that a man can be and for that I am eternally grateful."

Strength. Dependability. Loving support. Careful guidance. Honor. Wise words. Kind actions. Warm embraces. Listening ears. Discipline. An example. Add all of these characteristics together and they equal the single most important quality that children need from their fathers: encouragement. Children who are encouraged by their fathers can set sail for far lands, weather the stormy seas, and anchor down in the land of their dreams. A father who encourages his children is a father who deserves to be given tribute.

During the 1992 Summer Olympics from Barcelona, Spain, I watched on TV a father worthy of the highest tribute. His son, an English runner, was favored to win one of the middle-distance races; in fact, almost everyone wanted him to win because of his personal story. Four years earlier, in a different Olympic Games, he pulled his achilles tendon just before the race and was forced to withdraw from the event. Now after surgery, rehabilitation, training and more training, and four years of waiting, he was in the starting blocks.

The gun sounded and he got off to a great start. Almost halfway through the race he was in the lead. I was cheering for him with millions of other people. Then all of a sudden he fell to the ground! He had pulled his hamstring. Doctors ran out onto the track to attend to him, but he pushed them away, struggled back onto his feet, and started hopping his way toward the finish line. The race was long over, but now I was up out of my chair cheering for him to go on! Then I was surprised to see an older gentleman dressed in street clothes jump out of the stands, run up behind the wincing and grimacing English runner, and put his arm around his shoulder. Together they hobbled to the finish line.

Who was that man? The announcer answered my question: it was his father. I was still standing as I watched the two men slowly finish the race arm in arm, but now I was silent and a lump had gathered in my throat. That's a father who gave his son a gift of encouragement! That's a son who's become great!

Footsteps of Faith

1. Did your father give you his signet ring? Did he come alongside of you when you were struggling and give you the gift of encouragement you needed to finish the race? Which if any of the sample Father's Day tributes on page 230 could you in all sincerity give to your father? (Fathers, how are you doing at encouraging your children?)

_____

_____

2. Try to remember some examples of times when your father encouraged you, and write those down. Thank God for those gifts.

_____

_____

3. Perhaps you didn't receive much encouragement from your father. Think back on times in the past (especially when you were a child) when you were struggling and needed a father's help, but, for whatever reason, he wasn't there for you. Write those experiences down. Pray that God would help you to recover from those losses and to forgive your father.

_____

_____

_____

4. Set aside some time this week to pray about the empty places in your past and in your heart today where you need a father's encouragement. Talk to your heavenly Father about each discouraging memory and each pain in your heart. Imagine Him giving you His signet ring to empower you. Or picture Him helping you hobble to the finish line of the race you're running.

WEEK 33

Second Chances

Several villagers wondered about all the money Prodigal had lost in Antioch. *Had Father forgotten about Prodigal's waste of the family's precious resources. Had he neglected to hold his son accountable?* Remember, Prodigal changed his confession of sin at the last minute. He decided not to offer himself to his father as a servant who would save embarrassment by working off the debt he had incurred. Instead, he threw himself upon Father's grace and was welcomed home with gift after gift: compassion, forgiveness of sins, embraces and kisses, a purple robe, and a signet ring. But now we must ask, as the villagers did, "Doesn't Prodigal have to be held accountable?"

The answer is "no" and "yes." No, Prodigal isn't accountable for his debt because Father has forgiven it, but, yes, he is accountable for how he responds to Father's gifts of love.

Perhaps this is most clearly seen when Father gives Prodigal his signet ring. Prodigal is being given a second chance at the responsibility of handling money. And, as with all coins, there are two sides. On the first side is the inscription: "This is my gift to you." On the second side are the words: "Put this gift to good use or you will lose it."

Prodigal be wise with money? Timothy, Sarah, Joshua, and the gang of boys laughed hysterically at the thought, but Father knew that Prodigal was ready for this challenge. Sleeping alone in the streets, begging for food, working as a slave in a pigsty, these were the consequences of his past foolishness and also the lessons that trained him for his future. And Prodigal had already begun to demonstrate his new wisdom in the way he confessed his sins without minimizing them or trying to make up for them. Soon he would have the chance to manage the rest of Father's estate and benefit the entire family.

It isn't enough that we go to God to receive forgiveness for our sins; like Prodigal we also are accountable to change. Later we may repeat the same mistake two, three, four, twelve, or one hundred times. In fact, most of us will. We do struggle with sin, yet our struggles do not mean we're bad Christians.[1]

As wise old Solomon said, "Though a righteous man falls seven times, he rises again, but the wicked are brought down by calamity."[2] Our maturity is demonstrated more by our response to our mistakes—whether we get up again or give up—than by whether or how often we fall down. What gradually changes us is the process of confessing that we've fallen, asking for help, getting back up on our feet, and moving forward again. If each time we fall we learn from our mistakes, then over time we will fall less and less.

But I'm not falling less! you worry. Well, maybe you haven't learned all you need to learn yet. Solomon said that the righteous fall down *seven* times. Seven is the number of perfection and suggests that we fall down as many times as we need to in order to learn our lessons and mature toward the perfect image of Christ. Thus, after some time has passed (don't ask me how long; asking that question only slows down the process), we look back on our journey of healing and change to discover that even though we fell many times and took lots of backward steps, our overall progression was positive.

Ilene, a young mother, wanted a second chance. She was active in a twelve step recovery program called Overeaters Anonymous to help her overcome her problem of bulimia. With my help she identified the following destructive pattern. She'd give and give to her three children, her husband, and her church, all the while neglecting her own needs. Finally, late at night she'd sneak into the kitchen and do something for herself: she'd eat and eat and eat. Then she'd get angry at herself for eating so much and would take laxatives to get rid of all the food she ate. That made her sick to her stomach and very cranky the next day. Her kids got the brunt of her anger, as she'd often lose her temper at them, lecture them for minor trespasses, or nag them about doing this or not doing that.

In her recovery group Ilene, with her sponsor's help, worked through each of the twelve steps to recovery. These were difficult steps, but they held her accountable to continue working toward change. For instance, she had to repeat many times her fourth step of making an inventory both of her wrongdoings and her anger at how other people had wronged her. Each cycle of her binging and purging indicated that there were some more unresolved issues to address in her inventory. "Change is hard!" Ilene moaned to me one day. But, I pointed out, she was gradually improving.

As Ilene continued her journey of recovery, two of the most significant steps she came to were Steps 8 and 9: "We made a list of all persons we had harmed and became willing to make amends to them all. We made direct amends to such people wherever possible, except when to do so would injure them or others."[3]

"You mean I can make amends?" Ilene exclaimed. "Wow! I not only get second chances at change, but I can work to repair the damage I've created!" At the top of Ilene's amends list were her children. She knew that she had hurt them many times with her anger. After talking about it in therapy with me she decided to talk to her children. She asked each of them how they felt when she lost her temper at them, and then she listened. It was sad for her to hear how hurt they had felt, but she kept listening to their feelings and offering comfort. Then she admitted to her children that this was her problem and not their fault. She asked for their forgiveness and told them she was getting help for her temper problem and other issues because she didn't want to hurt them like that again.

Footsteps of Faith

1. Father gave Prodigal a second chance by giving him his signet ring. Do you regard God as being patient, tolerant, and quick to give you a second chance? Maybe you're struggling with a problem and need a second chance—a fresh start with a clean slate and a new perspective. If so, then you need to encounter the Father who is patient with your struggles, forgives your sins, and is powerful to help you change.

---

2. There is no better way to implement accountability in your life than to follow Ilene's example and write out amends. Perhaps you need to make amends to someone you've wronged. If so, then do the following four things as part of your amends.

(1) Make a list of people you've wronged and indicate how you hurt them.

(2) Seek to understand how your behavior has affected these people. If it's appropriate you might even ask them, "How did you feel when I did that? What impact has my behavior had on your life?"

(3) Write down how you feel about the damage you've caused.

(4) Purpose to change your problem behavior by seeking the help of at least one person you respect. Regular support and feedback from this person will help keep you accountable to continue your efforts to change.

3. When you were a child, did your parents make amends in this way to correct their problem behaviors? If they didn't hold themselves accountable for their behavior, there were probably some very large problems in your family then that weren't corrected or repaired. If this is true in your family now, you need to hold members accountable. This is the beginning of the forgiveness process. If there are problems in your family that have created strained relationships, consider talking to those you're at odds with, being careful to speak the truth in love. If you don't feel good about doing this, then talk to someone in confidence about the problem or write down on paper what you'd like to say.

WEEK 34

Empowered by the Father

Father encouraged Prodigal and gave him a second chance to prove himself trustworthy. Then he went a step further and began to empower his son to carry out his responsibilities. In the weeks and months ahead Father would take every opportunity he could find to teach his son about managing the farm and its resources. And Father had so much more to teach Prodigal about living as a godly man in a sinful world and about serving the Lord who loved him so much. Father would help Prodigal with other challenges, including Prodigal's relationship to Elder, whom Prodigal hadn't seen in seven months.

Wearing his new signet ring, Prodigal felt empowered and ready to face the challenges. He smiled with pride and confidence as he looked at his new ring. Having it on his finger was like having Father's arms embracing him. The gold in the ring reminded him of the wealth he had been entrusted to manage for Father. The green emeralds encircling the ring's face reminded him that in wearing this ring and in conducting his business affairs he didn't just represent himself, but also his father, his family, the community, and the whole tribe of Judah. The design on the ring's face (the long pole with a snake wrapped around it) left Prodigal wondering. He knew this symbol was important or it wouldn't be on the ring, but he had no idea what it meant.

When I became a father, I was concerned about how to empower my children from childhood to adulthood. Like most new fathers I had more than a few ideas about this. I looked back to my own childhood and the way that my father interacted with me and was thankful for some things and wanted to pass those blessings on to my children; some things I regretted, however, and wanted to be sure to do differently. Sorting that out was hard enough, but I had the additional complication of having a Ph.D. in psychology. It seemed I had studied or observed everything that could go wrong in a family.

I decided to simplify things by doing a brief study of what the Bible had to say to fathers about rearing their children. I expected to find a handful of verses, but was surprised to find a whole set of instructions. For instance, God instructs fathers, and parents in general, to empower their children by:

- Teaching when they're sitting down at home as well as when they're walking along life's road[4]
- Training them to become what they're meant to be[5]
- Disciplining them with love, care, and consistency[6]
- Being sure not to provoke them to anger[7]
- Investing financial resources in them[8]
- Securing their respect and obedience[9]
- Setting an example they can be proud of[10]
- Viewing them as a gift from God to be enjoyed for a season and then returned back to him[11]
- Guiding them through life toward a godly purpose like an archer shooting his arrow through the air toward the target[12]
- Nurturing them like a gardener who waters, fertilizes, and cares for a tender plant[13]
- Managing the family enviornment for their well-being[14]
- Respecting their great value[15]
- Learning from them and becoming like them[16]
- Always welcoming them and never hindering them[17]
- Being accountable for sins of commission or omission that cause them to stumble in any way[18]
- Never looking down on them[19]
- Seeking to find them whenever they are lost in any way[20]

Clearly this is a tall order for us parents to fulfill, but it is all part of helping a child to mature into adulthood physically, cognitively, emotionally, socially, financially, and spiritually. Obviously, no human father could ever do all of these things perfectly all the time. (Thankfully, our heavenly Father does, though it's difficult for us to experience His empowering love because we view His fatherly love through a poor mirror and know Him only in part.[21])

Even though fathers are inevitably imperfect, sin is still sin and a father's sins against his children have serious consequences.[22] Therefore, as a father I purposed to rely upon my heavenly Father, to do the best I could, to seek and listen to feedback from others on how I was doing, and to confess regularly my sins of commission and omission. Along the way I would attempt to make modifications in my fathering, all the while leaving the results of my fathering to God.

Footsteps of Faith

1. Father passed down to Prodigal his own ceremonial robe and his own signet ring. These were tangible objects that represented Father's love and empowered Prodigal to be like his father. I'll never forget when my grandfather gave me the opal ring he had worn proudly for years. I wear it every day as a reminder of his strong Christian witness and his influence on my life. Did you receive any sentimental gifts from your father or grandfather? If so, what were they and what did they mean to you?

_____

_____

_____

2. Were you empowered by your father to handle money wisely? Consider your father's example and instructions in

the following areas and how he influenced your handling of money. Check those areas below in which he encouraged you. In the other areas have you found encouragement elsewhere?

☐ Developing a good work ethic

☐ Learning how to save money

☐ Learning when to spend and when not to

☐ Being generous with others

☐ Leaning ways to earn money

☐ Learning how to invest money well

☐ Using money for enjoyment

☐ Discovering the value of tithing

3. Take some time this week to read carefully through this week's list of biblical instructions to parents. In which of these ways were you lovingly empowered for adult maturity by your father? Your mother? (Parents take inventory of yourselves also. Ask your spouse to help you be objective.)

_____

_____

_____

4. One day this week set aside time to pray about what you're learning. Thank God for the ways in which your parents empowered you. Then talk to Him about what you missed as a child and pray that as your heavenly Father He would help you in your journey of healing, forgiveness, and change. Lastly, ask God to forgive you for any ways in which you've passed on the pain of your childhood to others.

WEEK 35
Becoming a Good Steward

Phillip was a steward by trade; he had served his master dutifully and faithfully for years. Yet in one sense Phillip had missed the mark as a steward. He was a peacemaker, but he misused his gift by minimizing conflicts, avoiding confrontation, and sweeping problems under the carpet, all to maintain a superficial sense of peace. If you recall, Father confronted Phillip about his denial of truth and his lack of understanding about real love. Phillip's eyes weren't opened, though, until he watched Father give the repentant Prodigal a big hug and a kiss on the cheek. He wanted that too! He was ready to walk in truth and in love in order to know real reconciliation and perfect peace. So he called out to Father, and soon Father was embracing and kissing Phillip as he had Prodigal.

Phillip's change of heart only lasted about an hour, though, before he slipped back into his old ways again and tried to talk Father out of giving Prodigal his robe and his ring. Phillip was worried about what Elder and others would say, and he was afraid that Prodigal would waste his gifts again and bring trouble upon himself and the whole family. Phillip, as Father aptly pointed out, was a "dodger of disagreements." But Father encouraged Phillip, gave him a second chance, and empowered him to carry out his mission just as he had done for Prodigal. Phillip was given the honor of serving as the "bearer of blessings" to Prodigal: he dressed Prodigal in his robe, he put the ring on his finger, and when our story continues he will bear other blessings to Prodigal as well. As the "bearer of blessings" rather than the "dodger of disagreements" Phillip was using his gift of peacemaking well.

Phillip was a peacemaker, Prodigal was the manager of Father's estate, Joshua was a leader, Benjamin was a priest, Sarah was a storyteller, Timothy a businessman, Elder a labor supervisor, and the boys in the gang still had freedom and time to develop their hidden gifts. Not everyone was using his gifts well, but all had gifts. And so it is that God has given each of us an area of giftedenss to use in our service to the body of Christ.[23] Some have sensitive lips to proclaim clearly God's messages. Some have calloused hands to serve people in need. Others have a wise mind and are good at teaching. Still others have a strong arm for encouraging the downtrodden. Then there are those who have been financially blessed and are able to contribute to those in need. Others have broad shoulders to be leaders and to govern diligently. And last, but certainly not least, there are some who have huge hearts and are able to show mercy and cheerfulness to those in need.[24]

Whatever your gift is, you should discover it and use it faithfully to serve others. This truth is so important that Jesus told many different stories to illustrate this message. For instance, in the parable of the talents Jesus told a story about a master who entrusted his assets to three servants. He gave to each according to his ability: to the first he gave ten thousand dollars, to the second four thousand dollars, and to the third two thousand dollars.

After a long time the master returned to settle accounts with them and see how they had invested his property. The first two servants each had doubled their money and were rewarded for their faithfulness with even greater responsibilities. But the third servant had dug a hole and hid his master's money because he was afraid he would make a mistake and be judged. In response, the master took that servant's two thousand dollars and gave it to the first servant who had twenty thousand dollars. And the third servant spent the rest of his days in darkness, weeping by himself and gnashing his teeth in anger.[25]

The stewardship message is clear: our heavenly Father gives us gifts in talents, treasures, and time, and we are accountable to use these gifts to serve others wisely and faithfully. As we've already discussed, the Father doesn't just give us gifts, leave us on our own to develop them, and then hold us accountable for what we do. In between the giving and the accounting He encourages us to use our gifts, gives us many second chances when we fail, and trains us to use our gifts well. Those who do use their gifts well are entrusted with even more to manage. Those who don't lose even what they had to begin with.

Footsteps of Faith

1. Our time and treasures are two of the God-given gifts that we're accountable to use wisely. Answer these three questions:

(1) Are you enjoying your time and treasures?   _____
(2) Are you investing your time and treasures into others?   _____
(3) Are you doing worthwhile things with
your time and treasures?   _____

2. Talents are harder to quantify then time and treasures. This week identify your service gift(s) from the list below.[26] To do this ask yourself two questions: (1) What am I good at? and (2) What do I enjoy doing? (You may need a friend to help you answer these questions.) The areas in which you are effective and that you enjoy are your gifts.

☐ Hearing God's message and speaking it
☐ Doing practical things to serve people in need
☐ Teaching lessons that are helpful and interesting
☐ Encouraging those who are struggling

☐ Contributing financially to the needs of others
☐ Providing administrative leadership to a group of people
☐ Showing mercy to those who are hurting
☐ Another area: _____

3. Now that you've identified your gift(s), take account of your stewardship. Are you using your gift in a way that is fulfilling to you? (You won't be fulfilled if you're not using gifts that you enjoy or if you are trying to serve in areas that you don't enjoy.) Are you using your gift in a way that is encouraging to your family, friends, co-workers, and church? (If you're too aggressive or if you're too bashful in your service, then other people probably aren't benefiting.)

4. Perhaps you identify with the third servant in Jesus' parable of the talents in that your gift (or one of your gifts) is buried. Either you don't know what it is or you are afraid to try to use it. If so, then don't give up and walk away from your buried gift like the third servant did. You need help. Find someone who can serve you. No one can effectively serve and give to others except as they have first been served and given to.[27] Ask God to help you find the encouragement you need.

NOTES

1. If you need to remind yourself of this, then read about the apostle Paul's struggle with sin in Romans 7.
2. Proverbs 24:16.
3. From Alcoholics Anonymous's Twelve Steps.
4. Deuteronomy 6:7, 20; 21:19.
5. Proverbs 22:6.
6. Proverbs 13:4; 19:18; 22:15; 23:13.
7. Ephesians 6:4; Colossians 3:21.
8. 2 Corinthians 12:14*b*.

9. 1 Timothy 3:12.
10. Proverbs 17:6.
11. Psalm 127:3.
12. Psalm 127:4–5.
13. Psalm 128:3*b*.
14. 1 Timothy 3:4.
15. Matthew 18:1–3.
16. Matthew 18:3–4.
17. Matthew 18:5; 19:13–15.
18. Matthew 18:6–9.
19. Matthew 18:10.
20. Matthew 18:12–14.
21. 1 Corinthians 13:12.
22. Exodus 20:5.
23. Romans 12:4–6*a*.
24. These are the "service gifts" from Romans 12:6–8.
25. Matthew 25:14–30.
26. Romans 12:6–8.
27. Luke 6:38; 1 John 4:19.

"Put . . . sandals on his feet."

*Luke 15:22*d

STEP 9

Responsible Adulthood

Putting on New Shoes

Everyone was huddled around Prodigal, admiring his new ring, when Father interjected, "Phillip, it's time. Please put a pair of sandals on Prodigal's feet."

Phillip knew exactly what Father meant, and he hurried into the house. In fact, he responded to Father's request with such haste that he forgot to wipe his feet at the door. Probably no one would have noticed Phillip's oversight if Sarah hadn't remarked with a loud sigh, "Well! My servant would never be so rude as to rush into my house like that."

Phillip didn't hear Sarah's remark as he was already into the house and heading toward the chest in Father's private room. He opened the lid, dug underneath some garments, and, finding a pair of sandals in the bottom corner of the chest, he pulled them out.

Then Phillip scurried to the other side of the house and out to the courtyard. There he located a clay pot that was already filled with clean water, a fresh cotton towel, and finally a vial of frankincense. He placed the towel and vial next to the sandals, picked up the pot of water and used his right arm to brace it against his chest; then he carefully bent over and used his left hand to pick up the towel, sandals, and vial. Gingerly, but swiftly, Phillip made his way back toward the front door.

Prodigal could hardly wait for Phillip to return. Filled with excitement, he was humming and doing a little dance step, shuffling his feet, twisting his shoulders back and forth, and bobbing his head up and down, back and forth, and around and around. When Phillip returned, Prodigal spotted the sandals and smiled at his servant while admiring the fine sandals. He began to wriggle his toes in glee. The base of them was made of palm bark, which was firm on the bottom and soft on the inside, and the straps were made of fine, smooth leather.

Phillip put the pot of water down and the set the sandals and towel down next to it. He bent down to his knees and then he opened the vial of perfume and poured it into the water. It sent forth a pleasing aroma, which prompted Rabbi Benjamin to breathe in deeply, hesitate, and exhale. "Ahh, yes, the sweet smell of frankincense!"

Prodigal also took the aroma into his lungs as he put his left hand on Father's shoulder, lifted the hem of his robe with his other hand, and lifted up his right foot for Phillip to wash. The cool water refreshed Prodigal, and Phillip massaged Prodigal's foot as he cleaned it. Then Phillip dried Prodigal's foot with a soft cotton towel and slipped the foot into the sandal. Prodigal wiggled his toes again and slid his feet back and forth in the soft sandal. As Phillip began to wash Prodigal's other foot, Prodigal looked over at Father and beamed. He sang forth words of praise and devotion:

Oh, my Abba, I came to you as a barefoot slave,
With dirt from the pigsty under my toes,
With callouses from the desert on my tired soles,
With sweat from the hot sun on my feet.

But, Abba, you have welcomed me back as your son!
You have washed my dirty toes until they're clean;
You have massaged my tired soles back to life;
You have covered my smelly feet with frankincense.

Now, Abba, I want to show my gratitude to you;
I'll hold the wonders of your love in my heart;
I'll do for others what you've done for me:
I'll wash the feet of each and every one I meet.

The last line of Prodigal's discourse raised Joshua's eyebrows and left Rabbi Benjamin scratching his head. The perplexed rabbi leaned over and whispered to the mayor, "What does he mean, he'll 'wash the feet of each and every one he meets'? Surely he won't really wash people's feet!"

"Benjamin, I think he intends to wash our feet!" an astonished Joshua replied.

Footwashing was a job for the lowest servant in the pecking order. No one wanted that dirty job. However, Phillip had just proved the point that under the right circumstances someone might not only want that job, but think it to be a blessing. Sure enough, just as Phillip put the remaining sandal on Prodigal's other foot Prodigal tried to make good on his promise by reaching for the towel that was in Phillip's hands. Not sure what to do, Phillip looked up at Father and upon seeing Father nod in approval, Phillip conceded: he rose to his feet, gave the towel to Prodigal, and stepped aside. Prodigal turned around to face everyone behind him and bent down to his knees next to the water pot.

Immediately Sarah backed away from Prodigal, shuddered, made a face, and moaned, "Oh, that water is so dirty. It's hogwash!"

Rabbi Benjamin interjected, "But it smells so nice!" Everyone laughed. Then he stepped forward and lifted his foot to take up Prodigal on his offer. Prodigal began to wash the rabbi's feet. As he did so, Joshua, Timothy, and Phillip lined up behind Rabbi and waited their turn. Sarah hesitated, though. She didn't know what to do. She didn't want to be left out, but she was so nauseated by the dirty water. Finally, and with some prodding from Father, Sarah got in line behind Phillip. Father stood last in line since he was the host. The gang of boys weren't interested in all this fuss about feet; they were off to the side playing.

When Prodigal finished washing Father's feet, Father summoned, "Everyone, please come in. My home is your home. Make yourselves comfortable."

Sarah was the first to enter. She pushed on ahead of everyone, took off her sandals, entered the house, and exclaimed, "I love Father's house. It's the nicest home in Nain. In fact, it's the only one with a divan. (She would know, as she had been in every home in Nain many times to catch up on the gossip or pass on some more.)

"Yes, Sarah," Father replied from outside. "Everyone please have a seat on the divan. There's plenty of room for all of you."

Rabbi followed suit and walked in behind Sarah, sniffed a few times and mumbled, "Ooo. Hmm. Hmmmmm! Oh yes, it's the smell of myrrh that's here!"

"That's a fine nose that you have, Rabbi," commended Timothy as he walked inside and then started circling around the house inspecting the ornately decorated lamp stands, their lights shining from newly trimmed wicks.

Joshua was slow to enter as he had stopped at the mezuzah to recite the Shema again. This frustrated Prodigal who, up until then, had been so patient waiting for the guests to enter first. Prodigal was so excited to finally reenter his home he could hardly contain himself! Finally, his patience ran out, and he bumped into the mayor and helped him speed through to the end of the Shema: ". . . And thou shalt write them upon the posts of thy house, and on thy gates.

Amen!" And so Joshua and Prodigal entered, dropping their sandals next to the others just outside the front door.

Father was the last to enter the house. He motioned to Phillip, who had just entered in front of him. "Phillip, please get us all some pomegranate juice."

Phillip whisked into the kitchen, whistling as he went. He had always been a dutiful servant but now he was a happy servant. _I've been adopted by Father, and I'm his bearer of blessings!_ he smiled to himself, as he poured the juice in jars for everyone.

Prodigal was standing just inside the house, looking around, and reacquainting himself. "It's just like it was when I left Abba! And look! Over there it's my bed. I haven't slept on a bed in months!" Prodigal rushed over to the mattress that was rolled up and set in the corner. He unrolled it and plopped himself upon it. Laying on his back, he looked up at the beam of light coming through the small window high on the wall.

Phillip handed him his jar of pomegranate juice. Prodigal took a sip and concluded, "Ahh! The Lord is good. This is the life for me."

Prodigal stood at the door waiting . . . waiting. When he first ran down the cobblestone path toward the wide open front door he wanted to run inside, but he waited. When he had been dressed in Father's purple ceremonial robe he wanted to strut inside, but he waited. When he sang his Shema song he wanted to dance inside, but he waited. When he was given Father's signet ring he wanted to be escorted inside, but he waited. He waited for Father to invite him inside. Finally, Father did exactly that. He urged Phillip to get the sandals and put them on Prodigal's feet. The sandals were Prodigal's ticket to get into the door. Never mind the fact that he was dressed in a purple robe and wearing a gold ring. He couldn't enter the house without sandals on his feet.

Prodigal anxiously awaited Phillip's return with what would become his new sandals. (He had hocked his old sandals in Antioch for a loaf of bread during the famine.) He was so excited when he saw them that he wiggled his toes in glee. But before he could put them on, his feet needed to be washed. No one would put dirty, sweaty feet into a pair of brand-new sandals!

Phillip cleaned Prodigal's feet and slipped the sandals on. The soft inside lining of the palm bark soothed Prodigal's foot. The firm base of the bark protected Prodigal's feet from sharp rocks. The smooth leather straps wrapped around Prodigal's foot and gave him a secure feeling. Prodigal was no longer a barefoot slave who slept with swine. Now he was Father's sandaled son who slept in the house!

The sandals Father gave to Prodigal were a clear message to everyone, proclaiming, "Prodigal is my son. Accept him as you would me." In fact, each of Father's gifts have had a similar meaning. The robe meant, "Prodigal is righteous. Respect him as you would me." The ring meant,

"Prodigal is the manager of my estate. Do business with him as you would with me." Father was restoring Prodigal not only to himself but to the entire community. He wanted for his son to be at home in the house, in the fields, and in the village. This was a difficult message for villagers like Rabbi Benjamin, Mayor Joshua, Sarah, and Timothy to accept, but gradually they were making room for Prodigal in their hearts, as shown by their readiness to accept Father's invitation into his home. Soon they would recline inside and sip pomegranate juice with the one whom they had previously ostracized.

Ever since his pigsty prayer, Prodigal has been growing into a mature adult. Now he began to realize a critical aspect to adulthood: community. Community occurs when we put sandals on, leave home, and go out into the world to learn and relate with people. It's the experience we have when we open the door of our home to visitors.

We first learn about relationships during our childhood. Ideally, our childhood home provides not only a safe place for family members to love and care for each other, but it also offers opportunities for meaningful interaction with the outside world.

Everyone in the world is not safe and loving, of course. Making decisions about where it's safe to go and who is OK to let into the home can be challenging, even frightening, especially when we are children. Unfortunately, some parents overreact and, in an effort to protect their children and themselves, they establish rigid boundaries in their homes. The doors to these homes stay closed. The people inside are afraid to step outside and interact with the outside world, and they're embarrassed for the world outside to see what really goes on inside their four walls.

Carl grew up in a strict, religious home, and his parents limited his outside activities in an effort to protect him. "You'll get hurt out there!" they told him. "Out there" were drugs, sex, disease, sinful people, bad movies, and swearing, Carl was warned. His parents also sought to shelter him from disobedient children, rebellious adolescents, gangs, rapists, murderers, and "bad influences."

They protected Carl so much that he felt locked inside his house. They succeeded in sheltering their son from many of the bad things that exist in a sinful world, but they also kept Carl from experiencing friendships, school sports, learning opportunities, and fun activities. Eventually Carl grew up feeling he missed so much that once he was an adult, he was overly eager to enjoy his freedom. However, he was not equipped to make sound decisions about what people were safe and what activities were good for him. Consequently, he got into trouble.

Some children, however, *want* their home to stay locked —they are embarrassed about what their friends may see inside. An alcoholic mother, or a father who loses his temper, an obese grandmother living in the home, a mentally retarded brother, a father who abuses the children's mother, or a drug addict—children feel shame and fear about some family member and don't want their friends to see inside. They may have an unemployed father who sits around, a horribly cluttered and dirty house, a religiously fanatic mother, a grandfather with Alzheimers disease who says strange things, a mother who lectures her children in front of their friends, or a teenaged sister who has a baby but no husband. The list goes on. Whatever the problems in the home, they are buried in embarrassment.

Shame-based homes are inhospitable. Like the fear-restricted home where Carl grew up, these homes also lack a sense of community.

Perhaps like Prodigal you need to develop more of a sense of community by going out and interacting with the outside world and by becoming more hospitable in your home. If so, then put on a pair of Father's sandals and follow Prodigal's example as he grows into mature adulthood.

Footsteps of Faith

1. Did your father give you a pair of sandals such as Father gave to Prodigal? If so, then he would have communicated the thought to you, "I'm proud that you're my child," and he would have expressed to the world at large, "Accept my child just as you accept me."

2. This week meditate on what Jesus referred to as the second great commandment: "Love your neighbor as yourself."[1] Consider the importance of giving and receiving love to developing relationships outside and inside of your home.

3. As a child were you afraid to interact with the world outside? As an adult do you tend to isolate in your own little world? Try to identify some of the dangers that you've been afraid of as a child and now as an adult.

_____

_____

4. As a child were you ashamed for your friends to come into your home? As an adult are you hospitable? Note some of the things you've been ashamed of about your home as a child and as an adult.

_____

_____

5. One day this week get together with a friend to talk about what you've learned this week. Perhaps you could invite your friend over to your house or go to his or her house.

Have Your Feet Been Washed?

At Father's request Phillip washed Prodigal's feet. It certainly wasn't the first time that the family servant had washed a guest's feet, but never had he done it so willingly as now and never had it meant as much as this time. Phillip was once again the bearer of Father's blessing. He had the honor of welcoming Prodigal back into the home after seven months of living in sin in a foreign country far from home. Phillip knelt down, poured the vial of frankincense into the pot of water, and began washing Prodigal's feet.

Now to be sure these weren't your average, ordinary feet. Those would have been dirty enough. (Walking around in sandals on dusty dirt roads left everyone's feet quite dirty.) But these feet of Prodigal's were filthy! Dirt from the pigsty was imbedded under his toenails. Dried sweat, dust, sand, and little insects had been baked together by the hot desert sun into a layered mud cake, which became a sticky, smelly mess covering Prodigal's feet. Nonetheless, Phillip gladly washed Prodigal's feet in the cool, perfumed water, scrubbed off the dirt and caked mud, massaged the tired muscles, dried them with a soft cotton towel, and slipped the sandals on.

Now Prodigal's feet were clean, perfumed, and energized. Now he was a new man! Now he was accepted as a beloved son in spite of his past sins. Now he was an adult, not an adolescent. He could enter his home and enjoy the friendship of his father and his friends. And he had Father's generosity and Phillip's faithfulness to thank for this.

People who have traveled through the dirt of sin need to know that their feet can be washed, as Phillip cleaned Prodigal's feet. They know firsthand the shame of being left outside because their feet aren't clean. Anyone can be left standing outside the heavenly Father's house with dirty feet. You may find yourself left outside for one of two reasons—you've sinned or you've been sinned against.² In either case, Father wants to send a Phillip to you to wash your feet so that you can come inside his house as one of his beloved adult children. You can be forgiven. You can be healed. You belong in your Father's house.

Ron, age twenty-three, finally heard this message. He entered our day hospital program with dirty feet. He identified himself as a sex addict. In the last six years he had been involved sexually with more women than he could count. Many times his guilt had driven him to try to stop, but each time he succumbed to temptation again. He was powerless to overcome his compulsion. He was imprisoned by his shame. But now he wasn't alone anymore; he sat in a room full of people with dirty feet: an overweight woman, a recovering alcoholic, a man who was verbally abusive to his wife and children, a woman torn between her husband and the man she had an affair with, and a survivor of incest.

The group experience was helpful for Ron. Because he wasn't the only one with dirty feet, he felt less ashamed. And when he shared his pain and talked about his problem he discovered that the other group members wanted to understand his feelings, and they wanted to help him make changes because they too were hurting and needed help. The key to Ron's treatment, however, came the day he said to the group, "I've been too embarrassed to tell you something that happened to me as a boy." He looked at me and hesitated. He was becoming a little choked up but he continued, "I think it's somehow connected with sexual problems today. My first sexual experience was when I was eight years old. My older cousin forced me to have sex with her. I didn't enjoy it at first, but as I got older I learned to."

The dirt on Ron's feet wasn't just that of his own sins; it was also that of his cousin's and other's sins against him. In the weeks that Ron was in our program he learned a great deal about himself, and he began to experience healing for the shame that had imprisoned him and kept him from God. Upon his discharge from our program, Ron decided to continue his recovery by entering a Christian twelve step recovery program called Overcomers Outreach. There with the support and accountability of other people Ron regularly had his feet washed and also learned how to wash other people's feet. He experienced the truth of the Scripture, "Confess your sins to each other and pray for each other so that you may be healed."[3] And he received God's forgiveness for sin; that encouraged Ron to feel better about himself and to deepen his relationship with others and with God. He learned that he could experience intimacy and still maintain appropriate sexual boundaries. Ron was becoming a mature and responsible adult.

Footsteps of Faith

1. This week look at the dirt on your feet. What sins or injuries do you need to have washed off of your feet? Check any of the areas below that need to be cleaned up:

☐ Childhood trauma   ☐ Emotional neglect
☐ An unconfessed sin   ☐ An addiction
☐ Unresolved grief over   ☐ An injustice not
    a loss   forgiven
☐ Anger at God about   ☐ An issue you've
    unfairness   avoided
☐ A crisis   ☐ A compulsive behavior

2. Now that you've identified a general area where you need to work, take some time to get specific. Write down exactly what it is you're struggling with. You might try doing this in a letter to your heavenly Father.

3. What people in your life have washed your feet by forgiving your sins, healing your hurts, and accepting you into their hearts? Write down their names below, and then as you have time this week send a note or card to them that says "Thanks."

(1) _____

(2) _____

(3) _____

4. Hopefully at least one of the people you identified above is somebody with whom you have a current relationship. We all need a Phillip whom we can trust to go to when we need our feet washed. This week talk to someone about some of the things you identified in question one. Before you do, pray that God would give you discernment, courage, and the right opportunity.

WEEK 38
True Leaders Carry a Towel

Having his feet washed by Phillip moved Prodigal greatly, not so much because his feet were being washed as because he was being accepted back into the home as Father's beloved son. That is why he looked over at Father and sang:

Oh, my Abba, I came to you as a barefoot slave,
With dirt from the pigsty under my toes,
With callouses from the desert on my tired soles,
With sweat from the hot sun on my feet.

But, Abba, you have welcomed me back as your son!
You have washed my dirty toes until they're clean;
You have massaged my tired soles back to life;
You have covered my smelly feet with frankincense.

Now, Abba, I want to show my gratitude to you;
I'll hold the wonders of your love in my heart;
I'll do for others what you've done for me:
I'll wash the feet of each and every one I meet.

And to the astonishment of everyone but Father, Prodigal did exactly what he said he'd do: he assumed the position of a lowly servant by taking the towel in his hand, kneeling before his family and friends and enemies, and washing their dirty feet one at a time. Father wasn't surprised. He knew Prodigal had what it took to be a leader.

A leader? Yes, a leader! True leaders carry a towel. They're servants who wash other people's feet. Jesus Himself demonstrated this on the day before He was crucified. He was in the Upper Room with His disciples and was just about to start eating the long awaited passover meal when suddenly He got up from the table beside which He was reclining, went and picked up a towel and a basin of water, and bent to His knees to wash Peter's feet. Peter was appalled at the sight of His Lord and Master kneeling before him and insisted to Jesus, "No, You shall never wash my feet!"

Jesus answered Peter, "Unless I wash you, you have no part with me." At this Peter's tone changed, and he lifted his feet for Jesus to wash! Jesus washed Peter's feet and also the feet of the other eleven disciples who were reclining at the table. Then He explained to them the meaning of what He had just done. "You call me 'Teacher' and 'Lord,' and rightly so, for that is what I am. Now that I, your Lord and Teacher, have washed your feet, you also should wash one another's feet. I have set you an example that you should do as I have done for you."[4]

In doing the most menial and most humbling job of washing His disciples' feet, Jesus dramatically revealed perhaps the least noticed and least appreciated aspect of God's character: He stoops down to make us great![5] Yes! The One who flung the stars into the skies and holds the earth in His hand, the One who creates life in a mother's womb and makes the trees grow, the One who made the history that's written in the history books, the One who rules the kings of the world, the One who knows all that can be known and willingly forgives sins—this is the One who humbles Himself to serve us![6]

We who desire to have authority as adults and to be leaders of others must serve others as Jesus did. It's the meek who inherit the earth,[7] the humble who become great,[8] the last who become first,[9] the servant who becomes a leader.[10] Serving others means seeking the good of others before your own; looking out for others' interests as well as your own.[11]

However, let's not forget that we can only serve as we've been served, give as we've been given to, and love as we've been loved. The true gospel in miniature is this: "We love because he first loved us."[12] And God has many ways to show His love to us including, but not limited to, relationships,[13] nature,[14] historical circumstances,[15] and the Bible.[16] Truly, the more we experience God's love the more we want to share it with others.

In fact, if you're not serving others by sharing God's love with them, it puts into question the extent to which you have accepted God's love.[17] If you're not doing a good job of serving others in this way, then the answer is not just to force yourself and try harder, because that will only create more guilt, frustration, and emptiness. Instead, work at getting your needs met and, as you begin to receive, start helping others. This way you'll be serving not out of obligation or compulsion but out of a cheerful heart.[18]

This is the way it was for Prodigal. He had his feet washed by Phillip. He washed the feet of his family, his friends, and his enemies. And as we shall see, he will become a leader in the village.

Footsteps of Faith

1. Ask yourself this week if you carry a towel. Do you serve other people? Who do you serve and how do you serve them?

_____

_____

2. Perhaps you have some inhibitions about washing feet. Which of the following things holds you back from serving others?

    ☐ I don't want to get my hands dirty with other people's problems.

    ☐ Washing feet is a menial task, and I'm busy with more "important" things.

☐ Dirty feet smell! I don't want to smell bad. People won't want to associate with me if I become a foot washer.

☐ Washing feet takes more time than I have available.

☐ I'm too embarrassed to ask to have my feet washed, so why would I want to wash somebody else's feet?

☐ People should wash their own feet.

☐ My feet are so dirty it's hard to imagine being concerned about the dirt on other people's feet.

3. Last week you worked on getting your feet washed. Even though they're not totally clean (they won't be until you wade into the river of life in heaven), look at the feet of other people around you this week. Try to find someone who may need to—and want to—have their feet washed. Ask this person, "How are you, really?" and then listen and be supportive.

When Prodigal left his father's house he was a rebellious adolescent; many called him a disobedient, immature, and insecure little punk, and for good reason. He thought he knew what was best for himself, and so he did as he pleased and ignored the advice of others. When he reentered the house, he was returning as an adult, to *his own* house. Of course, it was still Father's house, but it was also Prodigal's house. Prodigal was the distinguished adult wearing the purple robe. Prodigal was the powerful man wearing the signet ring. As the beloved adult son, Prodigal wore sandals, could come and go as he pleased, and gladly sipped pomegranate juice as he talked with Father, Phillip, and the visitors.

These were all signs that Prodigal was at home now; he belonged there. Previously Prodigal didn't know his father adult-to-adult; he did not know how to live as an adult in Father's house. He had known how to be a child in the home, but not an adult.

Ever since Phillip saw Father hug Prodigal he had been trying to follow Prodigal's example. Now, however, obvious changes are occurring in Phillip. He's finding himself at home in Father's house in a new way. Instead of serving Father out of duty, he serves because he wants to. Instead of working with a glum face, he can whistle as he works. Instead of being a "dodger of disagreements," he is learning to be a "bearer of blessings." Instead of trusting only in his own abilities, he is learning to trust in Father's goodness to him. Like Prodigal, Phillip is growing up on the inside and becoming a more mature and responsible adult.

The others from the village are also beginning to grow up on the inside. Rabbi Benjamin and Joshua haven't argued in a while. Sarah has stopped slandering, and Timothy has stopped mocking. And, most important, each of them now allows Prodigal to wash his feet. They too enter into Father's house and sit down on the divan to drink pomegranate juice and converse with everyone, including Prodigal. There are some exceptions, though. The gang of boys all stay outside; they aren't ready to enter Father's house. And Elder is busy working in the fields somewhere; he is out of touch with Father's house and the real meaning of adult responsibility.

How old are you on the inside? Often people are confused at first when I ask them that question, but after they think about it they understand that I'm referring to their inner child, the underdeveloped or immature part of their emotional self. I get all sorts of answers to my question:

- "I'm a five-year-old boy who doesn't know his daddy," said a depressed pastor.
- "I'm a teenage girl who is using her attractiveness to get attention from men," replied a single woman in her late twenties.
- A woman who had been sexually abused as a child answered, "I'm an eight-year-old girl who is afraid of her uncle."
- "I don't know how old I am inside, I don't remember my childhood," admitted a middle-aged man. "I guess I was emotionally detached as a child."
- An overweight woman replied, "I'm a girl who stays in her room because she doesn't want to hear people call her fatty."
- "I'm a twelve-year-old child who has to decide whether or not to live with her mother or her father," explained a woman.

If you don't know your age on the inside, then answer this question: "How do you feel when you're alone with your mother and or your father in their house?" You may feel belittled, afraid, guilty, insecure, controlled, inadequate, or lectured at. Or do you feel pampered, protected, or emotionally checked out? Any of these feelings suggests that you may be younger than you think on the inside.

Whatever you're age on the inside, you will be making progress toward adulthood when you begin to relate with your parents on an adult-to-adult basis rather than a child-to-adult (or adult-to-child) basis. That means accepting the fact that you're responsible for yourself; others aren't responsible *for* you (though they may be responsible *to* you). So to be a responsible adult you need to make sure that you don't ask or even allow your parents to have responsibility for you. If they try to tell you how to live your life, then tell them and show them that you can (and *do*) make your own decisions. If you're in financial trouble, try to work through the crunch without asking your parents to help. If you don't agree with their opinions on a subject, say so in a kind way.

Footsteps of Faith

1. Answer my question, "How old are you on the inside?" Indicate your inner age in the following blank. _____

2. Do you need to grow up on the inside? Perhaps you feel like a child when you're alone with your mother and or your father, especially if it's in their house. If you experience any of the feelings below when you're with your parents, you're probably in a child position. In the blanks print (F) if you feel that way with your father and/or an (M) if you feel that way with your mother.

Belittled	_____	Afraid	_____	Guilty	_____
Controlled	_____	Lectured	_____	Inadequate	_____
Rescued	_____	Insecure	_____	Protected	_____
Emotionally checked out	_____				

3. Perhaps you need to follow Prodigal's example and take some steps toward responsible adulthood. The apostle Paul referred to this process when he exhorted us to put childish talking, thinking, and reasoning behind us and step into adulthood.[19] Which of the following childish ways do you need to put behind you?

☐ Whining or complaining to get my way
☐ Hinting when I need something rather than just asking for it
☐ Letting people rescue me from trouble
☐ Allowing people to make decisions for me
☐ Being afraid to disagree and state my own opinion
☐ Yielding to people to avoid conflict with them
☐ Being rebellious toward authority
☐ Showing passive-aggressive behavior
☐ Blaming other people when things go wrong

4. Some people avoid being in a child role by getting into a parent role in their relationships with other adults. They take responsibility for other people's well-being and yet may fail to take adult responsibility for themselves. If this pattern describes you, then you're hiding from the undeveloped and childlike parts of your soul. Do you exhibit any of the following symptoms of needing to be in a one-up, position (the parent role) over others? (Check any that apply.)

☐ Seeking out relationships with needy people
☐ Rescuing other people from trouble
☐ Making other people's decisions for them
☐ Telling other people what they should believe
☐ Blaming yourself for others people's mistakes
☐ Trying to fix other people's problems for them

5. Moving into responsible adulthood includes transferring dependence from your earthly father to your heavenly Father. The key to this transition is forgiveness. Review Ap-

pendix 1, "Blessings and Curses from a Father," and identify any blessings you missed or curses you received. Pray that God would help you to forgive your earthly father for those sins of commission or omission. Then look for the blessings you need from your heavenly Father, who loves you perfectly.

NOTES

1. Matthew 22:39.
2. John 13:10–11; Matthew 10:14.
3. James 5:16
4. For a complete account of when Jesus washed his disciples feet read John 13:1–17.
5. Psalm 18:35*b*.
6. Philippians 2:6–7.
7. Matthew 5:5.
8. Proverbs 29:23; Matthew 18:4; Luke 18:14.
9. Matthew 20:16.
10. Philippians 2:6–11.
11. 1 Corinthians 10:24; Philippians 2:4.
12. 1 John 4:19.
13. 1 John 4:7.
14. Psalm 19:1–6.
15. Ecclesiastes 7:14; Hebrews 12:7.
16. Psalm 19:7–11; 119:103.
17. 1 John 1:9; 3:17; 4:8.
18. 2 Corinthians 9:6–15.
19. 1 Corinthians 13:11.

"'Bring the fattened calf and kill it. Let's have a feast and celebrate. For this son of mine was dead and is alive again; he was lost and is found.' So they began to celebrate."

Luke 15:23–24

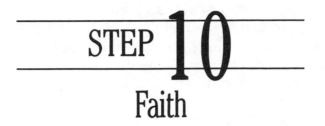

STEP 10

Faith

Celebrating in Father's House

Everyone was still relaxing in Father's house, refreshing themselves with the pomegranate juice. Father finished his juice and set his jar down on the table. It made such a loud clank that Rabbi Benjamin, who had nodded off, let out a startled snort. Everyone laughed, as the rabbi rubbed his face and blinked his eyes.

Then Father stood up from his chair and, looking at Phillip, announced, "Phillip, sound the shofar [ram's horn]! It's time to get the fattened calf and kill it! Gather the other servants and make preparations. We're going to have a feast and celebrate together. Everyone is invited to come and honor Prodigal."

Then Father turned toward Prodigal and continued, "For this son of mine was dead and is alive again; he was lost and is found."

Joshua glanced over at Prodigal and then looked back at Father and cracked, "Hey, that beats boiled onions!"

"I'll say it does!" Rabbi Benjamin laughed.

"Wow! I haven't eaten a fattened calf in years! And now during a famine! I've never encountered such generosity!" exclaimed Timothy.

"Me neither." chimed Sarah.

"Well, you'll all eat fattened calf with me tonight!" Father repeated. Then he spoke to each of his guests on the divan, beginning with Sarah. "Go spread the news, Sarah! Tell all your friends and everyone in the village who you can find. Timothy, go find us some musicians and dancers. Pay them whatever is fair and put it on our account. Prodigal will be sure that you're paid tomorrow.

Joshua, make sure the village elders are invited to come. And Benjamin, bring your candelabra and incense. Now hurry along, all of you! Phillip will have the fattened calf butchered and roasting on the fire pit before you reach town. It'll be ready by sundown!"

No one needed to be told twice. Faster than you could say, "Oh, Abraham, father of our faith," everyone leaped from his seat. Sarah was the first one to the door. She was so excited that she mistakenly put on Joshua's sandals, but not wanting to waste time correcting her mistake, she just went ahead and flopped her way out the door and down the cobblestone path toward the village. As she ran she proclaimed over and over, "Father's throwing a party tonight! Father's throwing a party tonight!" This got the attention of the gang of boys who were playing on the stone watchtower in the vineyard. They all yelled, "Yippee!" as they jumped off; landing in tumbling rolls on the ground, they playfully piled on top of one another.

Joshua was chasing fast behind Sarah in his bare feet. He was carrying Sarah's sandals and hollering, "Slow down, Sarah! You have my sandals!" Rabbi Benjamin and Timothy thought this was hysterical, and they were laughing so hard that they could not run straight. They were bent over and holding their stomachs as they tried to run. They ran wildly, back and forth, all over the place—everywhere, in fact, but on the cobblestone path.

Just then Phillip blew on the shofar, "Hewh ooooooo! Hewh oooooooooo!" The sheep nearby jumped and baahed wildly at the sound. "Yes, baah aaah! Baah aaah! It is a wonderful day today!" Phillip burst out in joy as the sheep bleated and bumped into each other and scurried around in fright. He was excited to be chosen to round up the fattened calf. For months he had been feeding this select calf choice grain in anticipation of just such a celebration as this one today. Now that day had finally come.

Meanwhile, Prodigal remained in the house with Father. It was the first time they had been alone since Prodigal returned home. "Abba, I don't know what to say. You've done so much for me already. I—."

"Son, you don't need to say anything. I've been waiting so long for this day I can't contain my joy. I'm so glad to have you home with me. I want to stand on top of a mountain and shout out my love for you!"

"Oh, Abba!" Prodigal bounced to his feet and hugged his father.

"Tonight is your night, Prodigal," Father was patting his son affectionately on the back. "You just enjoy yourself. Relax. I will see that the servants take care that everything is ready." Father hugged Prodigal tight and then released him and walked to the kitchen.

Prodigal went outside into the courtyard. He found Phillip humming a made-up tune and standing by the fire. Now and again Phillip turned the roasting calf, by twisting the spit that stretched across the open fire.

Phillip noticed that Prodigal's head had dropped and his shoulders were sagging. This seemed quite odd, inasmuch as he was the guest of honor for the night's great feast. "What's the matter, Prodigal?" he asked.

"Oh, I'm just wondering where Elder is. Hasn't he come in from the fields yet?"

"No," Phillip replied. "He's probably still over in the olive orchard on the west slope. This morning . . . er, yes, I guess it was this morning! It's hard to believe that was the same day as today. It seems the whole world has changed since then! Anyway, he told me he was taking some servants over there. I guess they have quite a few olives to harvest. You know Elder. He's probably trying to push the servants to get two days' work done in one. I'm sure he doesn't even know you're home yet."

"That's what I'm worried about!"

"Oh, Prodigal. Let Father take care of Elder. He's always handled him well in the past. Besides Elder has to accept you back. Look at you! You're dressed in Father's ceremonial robe. You have the signet ring on your finger. There's sandals on your feet. And you're the guest of honor for what is sure to be the greatest feast in recent memory! What's more, according to the custom, Elder will be the one to serve you the fatty portion of the calf!"

"Oh, I hope Father doesn't ask him to do that! He'll be upset enough as it is!"

"Relax, Prodigal. Father will take care of everything. Look, he's got you to this point! Did you ever imagine that you'd be welcomed home like this?"

"I sure didn't! In fact, Phillip, sometime I'll have to tell you about some of the nightmares I had about returning home. They were terrible! But, about Father's welcome, you're right. I'll never forget seeing him run down the village street to get to me before the mob of villagers—and the way he protected me from the gang of boys and their sticks. I know I can trust Father. And thanks to him the mayor, the rabbi, Timothy, and Sarah have all started warming up to me. Maybe in time Elder will do the same."

"Now you're talking!" Phillip was pleased to have put Prodigal at ease. Motioning toward the sycamore tree that

Prodigal liked, Phillip said, "Why don't you go sit in the shade under your tree and rest while I finish the preparations. You've got quite a night ahead of you."

"Thanks, Phillip." Prodigal went over to the huge tree. _Another thing I missed about home_, he thought as he sat down in its welcome shade. Sitting there on the ground, he pulled out the embroidered pouch in his pocket. Once it was full of gold coins, but now there was just a rock in there. Prodigal pulled out the rock and felt it with his fingers. _This rock is worth more to me than all the gold in the world! It got me home!_ Prodigal's eye caught a rock on the ground near him. He compared it with his special rock. He smiled as he got an idea. _Yes, that will be a great way to show everyone how Abba's love has changed me and can change them too._ He began to search for other rocks on the ground near him. He filled his pouch with as many rocks as he could stuff in there and then tied it shut.

Later that evening the guests started arriving. Sarah and some of the ladies from the village came first. And Joshua came with a couple of the village elders. Then there was Rabbi Benjamin and his family, each member carrying a candelabrum to provide extra light in the courtyard that night. Timothy brought his family and some men from the town along with the singers and dancers he hired.

Soon people were everywhere on Father's property. They were milling about inside the house, in the courtyard, and on the roof too. In fact, the roof was the center attraction. Music descended from the rooftop, and those standing there cheered each melody. Whistles of the flute, delightful, harmonious plucks of the harp and lyre, toots from the trumpet, beats of the drum, and occasional cymbal clangs. The men, wearing village regalia, danced and clapped and sang joyously in deep baritone voices. Now and again various women sang out in their soprano voices.

Prodigal stood in the courtyard taking it all in. As he surveyed the sight, Sarah would bring different people to him to show them his robe and his ring. The were making such a fuss over him that Prodigal joked, "What is this, Sarah? You'd think I was Moses come back from the dead!"

It was almost nightfall now and everyone was anxious to start eating. Father was getting concerned. He found Phillip, who was humming the tune he made up earlier and interrupted him, "Didn't you sound the ram's horn?"

"Oh, yes, Father. That had to be over three hours ago by now."

"Elder must have heard it. Sarah said her friend from the other end of Nain heard it! I don't know why he hasn't come yet. Our guests are getting hungry, but you know the custom. Elder is the one who should serve our guests. Prodigal certainly can't. He's the guest of honor! But I don't know how much longer I can hold up the party. You know, this is getting quite embarrassing. Everybody knows why we're waiting. Hmmm. What shall I do? I know! Phillip, you're my son too, why don't you go ahead and bring out the wine and the cheese. Oh, and get the grapes you harvested early this morning. You serve the guests. But we'll hold the calf and the rest of the meal a little longer. Hopefully Elder will be back soon."

"Yes, Father. Pray to Yahweh he gets home soon."

Phillip brought out the grapes and cheese for people to snack on. Then he located the best wine and poured drinks in gold goblets and served some to everyone. Then, since Elder wasn't there to propose the first toast, Phillip went ahead. He shouted to be sure he was heard over the music, "Everyone! I'd like to propose a toast to our guest of honor. Prodigal, I'm glad you made it back home! May you be happy in Father's house all the days of your life!"

Everyone said "Amen!" and clanged their goblets and took a drink. "Hmmmmm, hmm! Father you always have made good wine," complimented Mayor Joshua in his unmistakable gravel-sounding voice. "Why, I don't think Noah himself made better wine than this! Well, since I have the attention of all of you, I'd like to propose a toast. "Prodigal, all I can say is that it's a good thing you're not my son!" Everyone laughed and Joshua continued, "But since you're Father's son and he's accepted you back, I will too!"

And there was another chorus of "Amens," clanging goblets, and sips.

Rabbi Benjamin was the next to give a toast. "Son, I see you in the light of the candelabra. Father's robe becomes you; it has covered your sins. I hope you'll wear it to the synagogue this Sabbath—just don't bring any swine with you!"

This brought hearty, good-natured laughter from everyone, along with another series of "Amens," clanging goblets, and sips of wine.

Timothy couldn't resist keeping the ball of laughter rolling and he toasted, "Prodigal, I'll give you two farthings for that ring you're wearing! No, seriously. I pledge to do business fairly with you. I hope you'll visit me again."

Hearty laughter interspersed with "Amen" resounded from the group along with the clanging of goblets and sipping sounds.

Father addressed the group next. He started to speak and got choked up for a moment. He cleared his throat. "Ehm, hmm. I'm so glad all of you came to celebrate my son's return with me. This is a wonderful day." Father turned to Prodigal. "I never doubted you'd come back. You're a man after my own heart! Welcome home, son."

Again the toast was sealed with amens, clangs, and sips.

Finally Prodigal addressed the group. "Don't worry, I'm not going to toast myself! I did enough of that in Antioch!" This brought more hearty laughter from everyone. Then Prodigal continued. "My toast is to all of you. Thank you for honoring me tonight. Your presence and your kind words are Yahweh's blessing to me."

After everyone had said their amens, clanged their goblets, and taken additional drinks of wine, Father said, "Phillip, I heard you humming a song earlier. Why don't you share it with us."

"Well, I didn't quite finish working on it."

"Oh, c'mon, Phillip!" a number of voices pleaded. "You're the best ballad singer in the village," reassured Rabbi Benjamin.

"OK, I'll sing it, but only if the musicians help me out." So Phillip sang his song with the musicians catching on to it as he went along. Soon people were clapping out the beat.

> *O yes, what a wonderful day!*
> *Prodigal is home safe and sound!*
> *So let's sing praise to Yahweh.*
> *So let's laugh and dance round and round.*
>
> *O yes, look at Father's great son:*
> *He's the one in the purple robe,*
> *He's the one with a signet ring,*
> *He's the one with sandals on his feet.*

"Hey, everyone. Join me on the chorus! Let's sing out!" And join him they did. Father led the way. He was clapping and dancing and singing out. In fact, he got so excited that he jumped up onto the table and started dancing. What a sight it was to behold. There was Father holding a cluster of grapes in each hand as he danced round and round on top of the table. Everyone loved it! They were cheering him on and clapping and dancing and singing right along with him.

> *O yes, what a wonderful day!*
> *Prodigal is home safe and sound!*
> *So let's sing praise to Yahweh.*
> *So let's laugh and dance round and round.*
>
> *O yes, give thanks to our honored guest,*
> *Because of him we drink the wine,*

Because of him we eat the calf,
Because of him we know Father.

O yes, what a wonderful day!
Prodigal is home safe and sound!
So let's sing praise to Yahweh!
So let's laugh and dance round and round!

Everyone clapped loudly as Phillip's song ended. Prodigal clapped loudest of all. He particularly liked the words, not only because the song was in honor of him, but also because the last verse—*so let's laugh and dance round and round*—reminded him of his old mouse song. So when the clapping died down he exclaimed, "Hey, everyone! I want to teach you all a song I sang as a child! I thought about this song when I was in the pigsty, and it helped get me back home. Are the musicians ready? How about the dancers? Now watch me, everyone. There's some dance motions to this one. Are you ready? OK, everyone follow along with me."

Why, even if I were a mouse
I'd live in my father's house!
Why run in circles round and round
And live alone on the bare ground?
Inside my father has bread to spare!
And smiles and hugs to share!

Prodigal's silly mouse song was a big hit. Everyone caught on to the words and to the dance motions as they must have sung six or seven choruses together. What a happy scene it was. Everyone soon was dancing in circles and hugging one another. It was the perfect picture of celebration and community. *Almost* perfect, that is. Although no one was thinking about it at the moment, there was someone missing out on the party.

WEEK 40

Faith Is Conscious Contact with God

"For this son of mine was dead and is alive again; he was lost and is found." Father's words sounded out like church bells, high at the top of a steeple. They rang true and loud, and their message was clear: "Hear ye, hear ye! Prodigal has been raised to new life; he has been found with new faith! Come one, come all! You too can have new life; you too can find new faith."

Prodigal's faith met Father's love; Prodigal's needs met Father's heart; Prodigal made conscious contact with God.

Father's announcement was like a coronation, a celebration of Prodigal's steps of faith that brought the son into Father's house. But faith isn't easy. And it never leaves you standing still. One minute Prodigal is captivated by Father's love; he exclaims, "Oh, Abba!" and bounces to his feet to give Father a hug. Then next minute he is doubting Father's love; his head drops, his shoulders sag, and he worries about Elder's response. Indeed, Prodigal's faith will soon be challenged by his older brother. But after receiving some encouragement from Phillip and holding Father's rock in his hand, Prodigal is ready to celebrate with the village and to face Elder. Prodigal has regained his conscious contact with God.

No one, except Jesus, has been able to maintain unbroken, conscious contact with God. We are sinful. We are easily distracted. We fail to see the light of God's love. Like the moon, we have our shining moments of reflecting the Sun and radiating light and love, but we have our dark moments of being lost in space and hiding from light and love.

So the best we can do is to keep checking and rechecking ourselves and finding friends with whom we check in often. The question we need to answer is: "What are you experiencing right now?" When we answer this question truthfully—whether the answer be joy or grief, security or fear, peace or anger, love or hate, clarity or confusion, trust or mistrust, fullness or emptiness—then we make conscious contact[1] with our personal self inside. Then God's love can find us, and faith will have happened.

Faith happened for Alicia when she stopped folding her tissues. Week after week whenever she started to talk to me about a sad or difficult subject, Alicia would take out a tissue, fold it up neatly, and carefully blot out her tears before they formed. Alicia was seeking help for her depression, but we couldn't treat the core of her depression, years of sadness that hadn't been grieved, losses that hadn't been counted, emptiness that hadn't been filled, anger that hadn't been acknowledged. Finally we were able to help when she was ready to take the most gigantic step of her life and walk off the ledge she was standing on and into the deep, dark void in front of her.

You see, Alicia had another problem besides depression. Control. She needed to be in control of her feelings—and her needs, and her therapy, her image, and her food—all of the time. She also wanted to control her house, her work, and her children. Perhaps the only thing she couldn't seem to control was her husband. He had learned how to keep her arm's length in order to avoid her control.

It's no wonder Alicia needed to have such a high degree of control all the time. She grew up in one of those homes where the only thing that was clear were three rules: "Don't feel. Don't talk. Don't trust." So she didn't. Until the day she stopped folding her tissues!

That day she sat down on my couch, pulled out nine tissues in rapid succession, held them all in a wadded mess in her hands, and started crying. The tears came, and she did not blot them out. She did not worry about her makeup. The tears poured down her cheeks. Some found the wad of tissues, some found her dress, others found the cushion on my couch. All found my eyes and ears. I'd been waiting for many weeks for an opportunity to provide her with a meaningful sense of comfort.

God had been waiting a lot longer than that. His bottle was dry. His book had no record in it. "What bottle? What book?" you ask. God has a bottle for you and a bottle for me that He uses to catch each of our tears. He has a book for you and a book for me that he uses to record every one of our tears.[2] And don't worry because God's bottle and book are very large. Your tears—and all your experiences—are precious to God. He wants to know you. He wants to send other Christian believers to know and help you.

When you make conscious contact with your personal self and let a messenger of God inside your soul, then faith has happened. You're "walking in the Spirit."[3] You're in an attitude of constant prayer and are resting in God's love for you.[4] Then like Alicia and King David of old you'll be crying to God, to all the angels in heaven, to all the saints in the great cloud of witnesses, and your tears will be tears of joy that exclaim, "You have collected my tears and preserved them in your bottle! You have recorded every one in your book."[5]

Footsteps of Faith

1. Consider the obstacles that stand between you and conscious contact with God. Which of the following do you need to hurdle? This week pray to God about these areas.

- [ ] Feeling so discouraged that it's hard even to try
- [ ] Worrying about unresolved conflicts with others
- [ ] Wanting always to maintain control
- [ ] Having a short attention span
- [ ] Feeling unworthy of love

☐ Being overwhelmed by intense feelings inside
☐ Fearing rejection if I take a risk to trust God
☐ Being so focused on helping other people that it's
   hard to find time and energy for my own needs

2. Perhaps you would like to feel more connected with God than you do right now. There are countless ways that conscious contact with God happens. The method you use is far less important than the attitude of your heart. In fact, usually the contact "just happens." It spontaneously sneaks up on you, and all of a sudden you're aware that God is in your midst. Nonetheless, there are some spiritual disciplines that may help you if you're feeling distant from God, apathetic, or bored in your walk with Him. Try to implement some of the following suggestions this week:

(1) Read several psalms. Look for ones that express how you feel and observe how the writer works through his issues. Here are some categories of psalms (with chapters in parentheses) that exemplify those feelings: sad psalms (3, 7, 13, 25, 44, 74, 79–80), anxious psalms (6, 13, 22, 69, 88, 102), angry psalms (5, 7, 9, 10, 13, 16, 21, 28, 31–36, 40–41, 52, and others), guilty psalms (6, 25, 32, 39, 40, 51, 102, 130), yearning psalms (42, 63, 143), trusting psalms (3, 16, 20, 23, 27, 31, 34, 42, 61–62, 91, 121), praising psalms (96, 98, 100, 103, 107, 136, 145, 148–50).

(2) On a sheet of paper write your own psalms. Simply tell God how you feel and what you need from Him.

(3) Read Jesus' parables in the gospels. Put yourself in each story and ask God to speak to your struggles and your needs.

(4) Take one day this week to fast. During mealtime get alone, be quiet, pray, listen.

3. Life is a journey of steps we take in faith through different stages. The parable of the prodigal son is one metaphor of that journey. Another one is Psalm 23. Consider the following poem. Where are you in the journey? Wherever you are, seek to make conscious contact with God.

The Twelve Steps of the Twenty-third Psalm

The Lord alone is the Shepherd I need,
For without Him I can't manage my life.

In His greener pastures my soul does feed;
In him I trust and lie down without strife.

I drink from the still waters of His love,
Then I look close to see me as He can.

When I fall I call for help from above,
And he restores me to my feet again.

He guides me to the path that's right for me;
To all the other paths I must say "no."

Though the path goes through a long dark valley,
I won't fear since he's there to help me grow.

With his rod he disciplines me wisely
And helps me set boundaries that protect.

With his staff he always guides me safely
And inspects me when I pass under it.

He leads me up to a mountain plateau;
There are enemies there I must forgive.

His oil heals and anoints so I can go;
His cup for me o'erflows so I can give.

My steps back home I know I can retrace
Because He follows and has made me new.

In life's journey I look to Shepherd's face,
And he guides me to home all the way through.[6]

"Phillip, sound the shofar! It's time to kill the fattened calf. Gather the other servants and make preparations. We're going to have a feast and celebrate together! Everyone is invited to come and honor Prodigal!" It wasn't every day that somebody sounded a shofar. It had to be big news. And it was—a big party, complete with fattened calf. Such meat was a luxury reserved for the wealthy. Some villagers had never eaten it before. And that wasn't all. There would be more food and a celebration with music, singing, and dancing—and everyone in the village was invited. All this was to honor Prodigal's return home.

Why such a fuss over one young man who just hours earlier returned home in shame with tattered clothes, empty pockets, bare feet, and a bloated stomach? Because Father was restoring Prodigal to the community. The robe, the ring, the sandals, and the feast were all Father's way of telling the villagers, "This is my beloved son. He represents me, so treat him as you would me." How could they not? Mayor Joshua, Rabbi Benjamin, and the village elders couldn't disrespect a man in a purple, ceremonial robe of the tribe of Judah. Timothy and the business community of Nain couldn't disrespect a man wearing the gold signet ring that gave him access to the largest estate in the village. Nor could Sarah and the rest of the villagers disrespect a man who offered them fattened calf!

Everyone saw the value of Father's gifts. Father forgave Joshua for his harsh misuse of the law and respected him as the leader of the village elders. He forgave Rabbi Benjamin his blindness to grace and asked him to share light and incense with everyone. He forgave Timothy for his dishonesty and trusted him to be fair next time. He forgave Sarah for her slandering and encouraged her to become a messenger of good news. The same grace that Father bestowed on Prodigal he was now sharing with everyone. And it was uniting the whole village and bringing everyone to life.

The signs of life abounded. Sarah ran down the cobblestone path in Joshua's oversized, flopping sandals as she heralded the good news of the feast to come. Joshua chased after her in bare feet, and Rabbi Benjamin and Timothy doubled over in laughter at the sight. The boys jumped down from the watchtower in the vineyard and rolled around on the ground. Meanwhile Phillip sounded the shofar and sang to the sheep. Here were the beginnings of a village reunion that would be remembered forever.

Some people have reunion memories that they wish they could forget. Reunions aren't always happy occasions. Just because families get together at Christmas and say grace at the dinner table doesn't mean that people feel loved by one another. Just because everyone from the class of '79 shows up doesn't mean they all have a good time. Often it's the opposite. People feel more hurt and more disappointed by what happens (or doesn't happen) at reunions than in perhaps any other life experience. More suicides happen in the beginning of January than any other time of year because the reunions with family and friends at the holidays were depressing and lonely.

For reunions even to come close to measuring up to expectations and fulfilling anticipations, the needs of everyone must be considered, and lots of grace must be spread around. Now that's a tall order, one that becomes even taller the more people there are in the family. The more people, the more unresolved hurts and disappointments existing from the past, the more expectations that haven't been communicated, and the more interpersonal conflicts that aren't being addressed.

How wonderful it would be if our reunions of family and friends could begin to approximate the reunion that Father is holding for the village of Nain. Yet even this reunion isn't turning out as planned. Elder is missing. And as we shall see later, this will cause an upheaval at the reunion. (Has there ever been a reunion without at least one "incident"?) But keep following our story, because Father's response to Elder will shock you (and may bring you to tears).

In spite of the problems that Elder is causing, from beginning to end this reunion is a true reunion. The same theme weaves through the whole party: reconciliation. Father is reconciling to himself and to the community everyone who receives his grace in faith.

Footsteps of Faith

1. What thoughts come to mind when you think about going to a family reunion? Check all boxes that apply.

☐ I hope I'm not disappointed again.
☐ Will I feel alone?
☐ Will I get my feelings hurt?
☐ How will I handle it if that issue comes up again?
☐ How will I keep everyone happy?
☐ Will all that I invest in this be appreciated this time?
☐ I'm not going to go if so-and-so will be there.
☐ I hope I don't eat too much.
☐ Will I feel inadequate compared to so-and-so?
☐ I don't want to go but I have to.
☐ It sounds like fun. I'm looking forward to it!
☐ What an opportunity to reconnect with so-and-so.
☐ Family times like this are what make life meaningful.

2. What have your reunion experiences been like? What have you enjoyed about these? What things do you wish were different?

_____

_____

_____

3. Meditate on 2 Corinthians 5:14-21. This passage is all about God's reconciliation in Christ. It's message is simple. Christ died to save you from your sins and He wants to re-create you into a "new creation." Put your faith in His love for you and then become an "ambassador" of God's love to others. Reunions are reunions when the spirit of this passage is in all hearts.

Father's house was packed with people from the village; the crowd overflowed into the courtyard and onto the roof. The night was young, but dusk had come. Rabbi Benjamin's candelabra were scattered around, casting light inside the house and out. The sweet smell of incense filled the air. People were talking and laughing, and they enjoyed an abundance of wine, cheese, and fruit. Sounds of music from the roof were carried into the countryside: flute whistles, harmonious plucks of the harp and lyre, trumpet toots, and occasional cymbal clangs. Men in village regalia were dancing and clapping. Everyone had come to celebrate Prodigal's return.

Everyone except Elder. Elder's absence at the party created a major problem for Father. According to the customs, the oldest son would host a party like this. In his absence the next oldest son could step in, but in this case that was Prodigal, the guest of honor. Elder was the one who should greet the guests as they arrived, pour the wine, give the first toast, serve the food, and bring the choicest piece of meat to the guest of honor. But he wasn't there!

The guests were all present and hungry, and there was no one to serve them. But what could Father do? This was quite an embarrassment for him. He couldn't hold up the party indefinitely. He chose to remedy the situation by having Phillip, his head servant, faithful friend, and adopted son take Elder's place.

Where was Elder, anyway? Phillip had blown the shofar hours ago. People as far as the other side of Nain heard the announcement. Elder must have heard it. For that matter he must have heard the music coming from the party. Where was he? Why hadn't he come?

Elder was busy working in the olive orchards, putting in another long day of work. Like a taskmaster, he was pushing the servants beyond their limits to get more work done in less time. This was Elder's way. He was only treating the servants as he treated himself. He worked and worked and then maybe he'd relax and play. He produced and achieved, and then maybe he could hold his head high. He solved all his problems the same way: just work harder.

Do you live with a taskmaster like Elder? Perhaps your father, your mother, your spouse—or perhaps yourself! George Brett, baseball star for the Kansas City Royals, once lived with a strong taskmaster, his father. In 1980 George Brett hit for an average of .390. In the previous forty years of major league baseball only one other player had hit for a better average. That one season alone will probably put Brett into baseball's Hall of Fame. Guess what George's father had to say about it? "If you would have got five more hits you would have hit .400!"[7]

A taskmaster like that has a very clear message: "You've got to try harder. You've got to work more. You've got to do better. You've got to get it right. Never be content with yourself."

If there's a voice inside your head that sounds like this taskmaster, then you're not doing much celebrating in life, and you're not experiencing God's grace. You're under "the yoke of bondage."[8] You're like the ox who's yoked to a heavy plow or the slave who's yoked to a ruthless master. This yoke of bondage is a deadly disease. It's like a cancer that spreads through your whole body. It only takes a little bit of it to kill you.[9] It cuts you off from the grace of God that saves spirits, heals hearts, and satisfies souls. The theological name for it is legalism. The psychological name for it is perfectionism. It's the pressure you feel to justify your goodness and to prove your worth.

Maybe, like George Brett, you've inherited this problem from your father, as shown by trying to measure up to his standards and please him. Or maybe like Elder you have this burden but are not sure why. In either case you need to find a cure. And there is only one: faith in God's grace.[10]

Like the father of Prodigal and Elder, God loves you unconditionally, and He freely gives you His good gifts. Do you experience God like this? Until he returned home from the pigsty, Prodigal did not. Elder still had not. Many Christians don't. All perfectionists don't.[11]

Intellectually believing that God is unconditionally loving and graciously giving is one thing. Experiencing it is quite another. In the research study I did on church-going Christians' images of God, I found that 88 percent of those surveyed admitted that they sometimes felt as if God were pushing them to measure up to His high demands.[12]

If you have a distorted image of God pushing you to try harder, work more, do better, or get it right, then you need to leave the fields where you're working with Elder and join Father's party for Prodigal.

Footsteps of Faith

1. Do you have Elder's problem? Do you struggle with perfectionism? Take the following survey[13] and see. Simply put a check mark in front of those statements that are mostly true of you.

    ☐ I often put things off because I don't have time to do them perfectly.
    ☐ I expect the best of myself at all times.
    ☐ I generally think I could have done it better.
    ☐ I get upset when things don't go as planned.
    ☐ Other people can't understand my desire to do things right.

☐ I am often disappointed in the quality of other people's work.

☐ I feel my standards should be the highest possible, allowing for clarity of direction and standard of performance.

☐ If anything I do is considered average, I'm unhappy.

☐ I think less of myself if I repeat a mistake.

☐ I avoid tasks because I'm afraid to fail.

☐ I don't experience enough pleasure in my life.

☐ My expectations for myself influence me more than my faith.

2. One day this week take some time to read and meditate on God's grace as described in Galatians 5. The chapter begins with: "Plant your feet firmly therefore within the freedom that Christ has won for us, and do not let yourselves be caught again in the shackles of slavery" (v. 1, Phillips).

3. Another time this week prayerfully meditate on the image of the heavenly Father that Jesus portrayed in the parable of the prodigal son. Review the Father's "Gifts of Grace" on page 10 and the steps of faith Prodigal took in response to them, beginning with humility and climaxing in ministry. Pray that God would help you also to take these steps of faith, responding to the Father's grace as Prodigal did.

Faith in the Father Leads to Celebration

Father welcomed Prodigal home. Everyone respected Father. Everyone welcomed Prodigal home.

The key to that progression is that everyone respected Father. Without Father's help, Prodigal never would have even made it into town, let alone through town and to home. The "welcome home, Prodigal" party initially was shunned at the edge of town. Only condemnation, rejection, ridicule, sharp criticism, and beatings marked Prodigal's return. But at his Father's house Prodigal found forgiveness, warm acceptance, friendly laughter.

Eventually others would join the celebration, even offering congratulatory toasts. Indeed, in this one action-filled day Father's expressions of grace brought dramatic changes in each of the villagers. Mayor Joshua had mellowed so much when it came to enforcing his rules that he accepted Prodigal back into the community. Rabbi Benjamin had a new respect for the righteousness that comes through being forgiven of sins. Timothy had a new sense of fairness, and Sarah was passing on good news instead of bad news. Everyone had come to a new faith in Father; the whole village celebrated Father's love for Prodigal and for them.

It was a time for merrymaking, light-hearted laughter, singing songs, and dancing in circles. Father himself led the celebration. Phillip sang his song of praise to Yahweh and tribute to Prodigal. Prodigal sang his silly mouse song, which really wasn't so silly when you consider that it came from a small boy who loved his daddy. Perhaps the highlight of the evening was seeing Father dancing in circles on the tabletop and holding clusters of grapes above his head in each hand!

Faith in God's goodness leads to spontaneous celebration. Indeed, God is a good God. He sent Jesus to proclaim His favor toward us. Jesus did this by sharing good news with the poor, freedom for the prisoners, recovery of sight for the blind, and healing for the oppressed.[13] How much we need that good news today! We need to have our impoverished souls blessed with the wealth of God's grace, to be freed from our compulsions, to have our eyes opened to see what is true, and to be healed of that which oppresses us. When we recognize and receive God's shining graciousness, we cannot help but rejoice.

The joy of the Lord is our strength.[14] It keeps us going, particularly during the long, hard journey of emotional recovery and spiritual growth. Working through our pains and our issues and seeking to grow closer to God require more energy and persistence than we have within ourselves. We need to tap into another power source. When by faith we connect with God, we feel joy. Without joy we tend to get bogged down in the process of change and growth, becoming discouraged, tired, and unable to move forward. Those of us who are lacking in joy need to learn not to take ourselves too seriously and not to live our lives too intensely. We all need moments of spontaneous laughter, hilarious joy, and ridiculous fun in our life journeys in order to keep fighting the good fight of faith.

Jesus certainly lived on earth with a sense of joy. At times He even had so much fun that the stuffy Pharisees accused Him of being a drunkard and a glutton.[16] Other times when other people were trying to get work done He would be playing with children.[17] Sometimes when He rebuked someone He used a subtle sense of humor to lighten the heaviness of His words and was able to do so without compromising the integrity of His rebuke.[18] Most of the time He taught, He did so with stories; many were funny or had unexpected twists, and all created an easy context in which to apply a challenging message. Many of the things Jesus said and did contained elements of surprise, and the unexpected outcome probably brought laughter to others.[19]

One thing that gives me maximum laughter is playing with children. Usually it's just little things, things that nonetheless make me laugh and help me not take life too seriously. For instance, many times I've played "get you" with my little boy David or my niece Elizabeth (and, occasionally, with both). I'll chase one of them around the house exclaiming, "I'm gonna get you!" hide behind a corner, sneak up from behind, and tackle the little bundle with laughter, hugs, and tickles.

Once, when David was about one and a half years old, we were all in the family room when he suddenly began dancing. I made a surprised expression, and he started giggling with delight. From that day forward he did his little dance step if he wanted some attention—and he got it!

The highlight of David's first birthday party was his one-year-birthday cake. We wisely had decided to make two cakes for this occasion—one for David and one for everyone else. We gave David his cake and let him dig in. And did he ever dig in. We gave him free rein to do whatever he wanted with that cake. (This drove some of the neat and tidy parents of other little children who were at the party crazy.) Within minutes he had chocolate cake oozing between his fingers, smeared all over his face, stuck in his hair, mashed onto his clothes, and thrown all over the table!

It takes a childlike faith and a reckless abandonment of inhibition to celebrate and enjoy the Father's blessings. And it is this freedom to rejoice in God that keeps your life going in the right direction.

Footsteps of Faith

1. Perhaps the biggest enemy to joy is anxiety.[20] When you're troubled about something but trying to repress your troubled feelings (that's what creates anxiety), there's no room

for joy, gratitude, or peace. That's because whenever you're trying not to feel "bad" you will detach yourself from your emotions and thus lose positive feelings too. Take some time this week to reflect upon whatever you're anxious about. Then you'll be in a better place to be surprised by joy!

2. Do something spontaneous this week. When a fun idea pops into your mind just go do it! Maybe go visit the local zoo (talk to those animals), order pizza late at night, do something romantic with your spouse, take your kids some place new, do something crazy with a friend, or . . ?

3. Read Psalm 150, one of the "Praise the Lord!" psalms. As you read it, listen with your imagination and hear the saints singing out, "Praise the Lord!" Hear the trumpets, the harps and the lyres, the tambourine, the flute, and the clashing of cymbals.

NOTES

1. Step 11 of Alcoholic's Anonymous is: "We sought through prayer and meditation to improve our conscious contact with God as we understood Him, praying only for the knowledge of His will for us and the power to carry that out."
2. Psalm 56:8.
3. Galatians 5:16.
4. 1 Thessalonians 5:17; Hebrews 4:11.
5. Psalm 56:8 TLB.
6. This poem reflects the allegory I wrote to illustrate the journey of faith and healing in Psalm 23. See *A Walk with Your Shepherd* (Chicago: Moody, 1991).
7. Craig Horst, "Tribulations Take Toll on Brett's Season," *Midland* (Texas) *Reporter*, June 25, 1992, sec. B, p. 1.
8. Galatians 5:1 KJV.
9. Galatians 5:9.
10. Galatians 5:5.

11. A research survey by David Stoop (of people attending his seminars on personality types) found that 84 percent of the people polled admitted to having perfectionistic tendencies. See _Hope for the Perfectionist_ (Nashville: Nelson, 1990).

12. William Gaultiere, "The Development and Preliminary Validation of a Measure of God's Image," doctoral dissertation, U.S. International University, 1989. The survey received responses from 595 adults.

13. Stoop, _Hope for the Perfectionist_, 27.

14. Luke 4:18–19.

15. Nehemiah 8:10.

16. Matthew 11:19.

17. Matthew 19:13–15.

18. For example read Matthew 19:16–26. Speaking of the tempatations of wealth, Jesus tells His disciples that it's easier for a camel to go through the eye of needle than for a rich man to enter the kingdom of God. The image of the ungainly, strange-looking beast trying to pass through the opening of a needle was both absurd and amusing. Or read Jesus' rebuke of the pharisees in Matthew 23. One of the things He tells them is that in their legalism they strain out a gnat and swallow a camel (v. 24). That wild contrast probably brought chuckles to the non-Pharisees in the crowd.

19. For example, read Matthew 18:22. Wouldn't you laugh in amazement if Jesus cursed a fig tree and it withered? And what about Jesus' teaching that faith the size of a tiny mustard seed can move mountains!

20. Philippians 4:4–7.

"Meanwhile, the older son was in the field. When he came near the house, he heard music and dancing. So he called one of the servants and asked him what was going on. 'Your brother has come,' he replied, 'and your father has killed the fattened calf because he has him back safe and sound.'

"The older brother became angry and refused to go in. So his father went out and pleaded with him. But he answered his father, 'Look! All these years I've been slaving for you and never disobeyed your orders. Yet you never gave me even a young goat so I could celebrate with my friends. But when this son of yours who has squandered your property with prostitutes comes home, you kill the fattened calf for him!'

"'My son,' the father said, 'you are always with me, and everything I have is yours. But we had to celebrate and be glad, because this brother of yours was dead and is alive again; he was lost and is found.'"

Luke 15:25–32

STEP 11

Forgiveness

Forgiving Your Brother

Excited but tired, Father stopped dancing to rest. He looked out at all his guests and was pleased by what he saw. Prodigal and Timothy were still dancing in silly circles like dizzy mice. Joshua, Rabbi Benjamin, and some of the other men were clapping to the music. Sarah and her friends were talking. Phillip was serving wine with a smile. Everyone was having a happy time.

"Phillip!" Father called out. "When you have a moment I need to speak with you."

Phillip refilled Joshua's goblet with wine and then skipped over. "Yes, Father."

"We can't wait any longer for Elder. It's been dark for nearly an hour. He must have gone off with a friend or who knows what. Anyway, it's long past time for the feast. Please make arrangements for the rabbi, the mayor, Timothy, Prodigal, and myself to eat in the dining room. The others can eat out in the courtyard where there is more room."

"Yes, Father. I'm sorry it's turned out this way."

"Me too, Phillip. Me too. For months I've waited for this day thinking that at last I would have my family together. Perhaps it was not meant to be."

Phillip made the arrangements for everyone to eat. Even the musicians and the dancers were invited to come down into the courtyard and eat. Everyone was very hungry, so they made haste. The music, the dancing, the singing, the talking all died down quickly. Then things got quiet, very quiet—too quiet. There was an eerie shift in mood. From gay celebration, the setting changed to tense silence. Like the calm before a storm when the birds stop chirping, the crowd seemed to sense gathering dark clouds. They noticed that Elder still hadn't arrived, even though the hour was late. *What does this mean? Something bad is about to happen*, many concluded.

Father didn't know what else to do but to continue. He invited everyone to sit down, and then he asked Rabbi Benjamin to say the blessing. The rabbi prayed, "Blessed are Thou, Jehovah our God, King of the world, who causes to come forth bread from the earth. Bless this food we ask and bless Prodigal, whom we're honoring tonight." And everyone said, "Amen."

Meanwhile, Elder was finally heading toward home. Trailing behind him were the three servants he had brought with him to the olive orchards. All wore signs of a long, hard day of work; covered in dirt and breathing heavy, they dragged weary feet. Elder and the servants each carried a huge basket overflowing with olives as they trudged toward home.

Elder lifted his head and turned his ears. "What's that noise?"

"Oh, didn't you hear the music?" answered one of the servants. "It started more than an hour ago. If you listened closely you could hear it while we were working."

"I didn't hear it!"

"Master, surely you heard the sounding of the shofar that announced a gathering. It went forth a few hours ago."

"Don't talk down to me, you slothful servant! If you had been working harder you wouldn't have heard anything either."

When the house was within view Elder could see people on the roof playing music and dancing. Then all of a sudden the music stopped. Everyone on the roof disappeared from Elder's vision, as the guests filed down the stairs into the courtyard in back.

Elder was anxious to find out what was going on. He quickened his pace as he headed toward home. When he reached the front gate he found the gang of boys doing their rendition of the stick dance out in front of the house. "Hey, you! What's going on here?" he shouted at the boy nearest him.

The boys had been anticipating Elder's return and had prepared for it. Now the boy closest to Elder picked up the stick from the ground, and, using it like the conductor of a boy's chorus, he led the gang in reply.

> _Elder, Elder, Oh where have you been?_
> _Elder, Elder, Oh where have you been?_
> _Off in the fields working so hard again!_
> _Not in the house serving the guests then!_
> _Your brother has come home to stay._
> _He's back safe and sound we say._
> _So your Father has killed the fattened calf_
> _And all but you are here to dance and laugh!_
> _Elder, Elder, Oh where have you been?_
> _Elder, Elder, Oh where—_

"Stop! Stop!" Elder was red in the face as he screamed at the boys. "How dare you taunt me that way!" He grabbed the stick-baton from the boy's hand and began swinging it wildly in the air and chasing the boys. In seconds they scattered like scared chickens.

Phillip, along with everyone else at the party, heard the raucous sounds. He ran outside to look and discovered the angered Elder. "Elder! Where have you been?" he exclaimed.

"Another lazy servant with the same ignorant question! Where do you think I've been? Can't you see I've been working? Let me ask you some questions. What's this I hear about Prodigal?"

"Yes, Elder! He's home!"

"I thought he was dead," Elder replied in a disappointed voice.

"No, he's alive! He's here! And he's the guest of honor tonight!"

"Prodigal? He's the guest of honor at this ridiculous extravaganza? Well, did he come home riding on a camel and followed by an entourage of servants carrying gold, cloth, and spices?"

"No, I'm afraid not. He was barefoot, in tattered clothes, and his pockets were empty. He spent everything in Antioch."

"Oh? So he visited the prostitutes in the Temple of Daphne, did he? I'm glad to know that he enjoyed himself while he destroyed the family honor and wasted our hard-earned money."

"Elder! You don't know that to be true! Antioch brought Prodigal more than pleasure. He ended up hiring himself out to tend pigs so he wouldn't starve. At one point Prodigal slept near a pigsty."

"Just as I thought!" Elder was smiling with delight. "Didn't I tell Father that this would happen? I knew a lazy fool like him couldn't survive long without begging for food! So why didn't Father send him back to the pigsty where he belongs?"

"The pigsty? Elder! Father was so glad to have Prodigal back home. Why, his tears of joyous relief flowed like the first rain after a drought! Surely you knew that Father missed Prodigal all these weeks and months. Couldn't you tell that his heart has been heavy ever since Prodigal left? Why do you think he spent so much time over in the vineyard Prodigal loves?"

"Yeah, yeah. Enough of the sentimentality! What did Father do to Prodigal? He must have beat him half to death!"

"No, Elder. You should have seen the reception Father gave—"

"Hey, wait a minute," Elder interrupted. "Why are you calling him 'Father'? You're just a lowly servant! He's not your father!"

"He told me to call him 'Father.' And your brother calls him 'Abba.'"

"'Abba?' Oh, isn't that cute? The 'Baby Beggar' wants his 'Abba!' He's a filthy fool if you ask me! I can't believe this! What's going on around here anyway? Oh, never mind. Get back to your story. Did they beat the filthy fool?'"

"Well, Father gave Prodigal an incredible reception. I wouldn't have believed it, but I saw it myself. I was with Father when he spotted your brother way off in the distance. He _ran_ out to greet him! Across the farmland and through the village he ran—exposing his undergarments, kicking up dirt, sweating and panting—all because he wanted to get to Prodigal before the villagers did. You know how upset everyone was at him. Well, the mayor had the gang of boys ready to beat him to death!"

"As they should have! Well, did they beat him?"

"Well, they tried to."

"Tried to? What do you mean? Prodigal is a wimp! He couldn't defend himself if his life depended upon it! What are you saying, Phillip?"

"Elder! If you'd stop interrupting me, then I could finish the story! Well, when Prodigal returned he confessed his sins to Father and Father forgave him. But we all were listening, and when everyone found out that not only had Prodigal lost all of his inheritance but he had been feeding swine, well that was the straw that broke the camel's back! They knew he had disgraced the village name, but no one knew just how badly. At that point their insults turned to an all-out attack. The gang swarmed on top of Prodigal, kicking and beating him and pounding him with their sticks."

"Good! Good! And Father stood in approval?"

"No, Elder! You keep interrupting me!"

"OK! Get to the end. What did Father do?"

"When Mayor Joshua finally called the boys off Prodigal, we discovered that it wasn't Prodigal they had beaten. It was Father! Father had gotten in between the gang of boys and Prodigal and had taken their beating upon himself!"

"He *what*?"

"Father covered Prodigal with his own body. He was the one who got beaten. He was quite bruised and banged up, but he's OK. Prodigal wasn't touched, though!"

"I don't believe you, Phillip! You've gone mad! My father is honorable. He's a man of law and righteousness. He would't close his eyes to such sin! And he certainly wouldn't let himself be beaten to spare a filthy fool like Prodigal."

"Yes, Elder, he did. And more."

"More! What do you mean?"

"Father gave to Prodigal his purple robe, new shoes—and the ring!"

"What? The signet ring? This must stop! That means he has access to *my* property! That lazy lunk! He doesn't deserve it. I worked hard for that property. He's good-for-nothing! He'll waste my wealth the way he did his! Then we'll *all* be feeding pigs!"

"Father trusts him, Elder. Now you must get control of yourself. You need to come in and serve the guests. I've been taking your place all this time. It's been a terrible embarrassment to your father. You've insulted him horribly."

"Oh, *he's* embarrassed! He's insulted! How do you think *I* feel! For months I've been ridiculed and mocked because the brother of Elder is a filthy fool. Now Father turns him into 'Heaven's Hero' in front of everyone and spends my money to do it! No! I won't go in. Just leave me alone. You've already started without me anyway, so just continue."

"But Elder, we've saved the fattened calf for you!"

"Oh yes, the boys mentioned that. The fattened calf for the 'Filthy Fool!' It's swine's flesh as far as I'm concerned!" Elder raised his stick over his head and screamed at Phillip, "No! I'm not going in there! Now leave me alone before I take my anger out on you!"

Phillip's eyes popped out of his head. He covered his head with his hands, turned, and ran back to the house. Once inside, he moved quietly to Father's side and whispered in his ear, "Elder is back and he—"

"Go ahead and speak up, Phillip. We heard everything through the window."

"You did?" Phillip blushed. He glanced nervously around the room. He looked out the back door and saw a group of onlookers. Among them was Sarah smiling with delight as she eavesdropped and Timothy rubbing his hands together as he plotted how he might profit from this situation. Quickly, Phillip looked back at Father. "I'm so sor—"

"It's OK, Phillip. We're all family here."

"What do you want me to do now, Father?"

Prodigal stood up abruptly and started heading for the door. Father reached over and grabbed him by the arm, "No, son! Sit back down."

"But Abba," Prodigal replied. "I'm the one he's angry at. Maybe if I go and apologize—"

"No. That'll only make things worse. He nearly killed you after you asked for your inheritance. He's my son. I'll go out and talk to him."

"Please spare yourself this embarrassment," pleaded Joshua. "I'm the mayor of the town. Why not let me go out and set the matter straight. I'll make sure he honors you. And if he won't, then I'll send him away, and he will learn his lesson."

"Oh Joshua, what good will that do? If I punish him and force him to respect me, I will have a slave and not a son. And what good will it do when he doesn't even understand his wrong?"

"Yes, he would only serve you resentfully," agreed Rabbi Benjamin. "Why don't you forgive him like you did Prodigal? Allow me to help you. I can spare you the shame of going out to your defiant son. I will go out as the town priest and proclaim your forgiveness to him."

"Benjamin, you don't understand. Of course I'll forgive him. I always have and I always will. But what good is that when he doesn't see his sin? He is blind to the rebellion, the pride, and the greed that are in his heart. He hears not the insults he hurls at his brother and at me. He thinks only of his own piety and of what his 'rights' are."

"Yes," Joshua looked over at Father in agreement and then reminded him, "Even though the law gives him as the eldest son access to two-thirds of your estate, it's still your property while you're alive. And so now you must assert your authority and set down the law, or justice will be mocked."

Rabbi Benjamin stood up from his chair and pointed his finger at Joshua, "Don't you know, Joshua, that in the Psalms David, speaking of Yahweh, said, 'He does not treat us as our sins deserve'?"[1]

"But Benjamin," Joshua stood to face the rabbi and smiled with delight at the opportunity to beat him at his own game, "haven't you read in your Psalms where David also said of Yahweh, 'He will judge the world in righteousness; he will govern the peoples with justice'?"[2]

"Joshua, you are a hard and ruthless mayor!"

"Perhaps, but you, Benjamin, are a soft and weak rabbi!"

"Settle down! You're both right, and you're both wrong." Father stepped between the two arguing village leaders, who were nose to nose and about to get into a scuffle. "I thought that I had settled the differences between the two of you once and for all. Didn't you understand what I did for Prodigal? Do you still not see that justice and mercy are one? Once more I will show you my love. I will go out and talk to Elder. Both of you, please sit down at the table."

"No, please don't go, Father! Let me go! Just tell me what to say," pleaded Phillip.

"Phillip, you've already tried to smooth out this conflict. I am the only one who can address this problem. But first I have one more thing to tell everyone before I go out to talk with Elder." Father stood up from his chair and lamented, "I waited for seven months for Prodigal to come home. But now my other son refuses to join us. I've waited the night out, but Elder refuses to join us. I wanted so much to do this with my two sons on either side of me, but that wasn't meant to be."

Father picked up the loaf of bread in front of him, broke it in two, passed half to his left and half to his right, and said, "This bread is the bread of my fellowship for all of you." Then Father picked up the jar of wine, set it in the center of the table, and said, "This wine is the fruit of my labor and is for all of you. Drink and be happy."

"Now, all of you, please eat and drink at my banquet table while I go and talk to Elder." Father walked out of the house to find his other son. Those he left behind were stunned. And confused. No one said a word. But each stayed in his place and quietly ate his bread and drank his wine. And listened.

Sarah, who was out in the courtyard, was the only one who moved. On tiptoes she walked lightly to the side of the house and peered around front to see what would happen. She spotted Elder a short distance from the front of the house. He had his back turned to the party. He was leaning against the fence in front and twirling the stick around in his hand. Then she saw Father walk out to him. She listened.

"Elder, my son. It looks like you've been working hard. You must be exhausted. Please come in and dine with me. I want you to share in our celebration. The fattened calf is hot off the fire and waiting for you!"

309

Elder, with his back still turned to Father, replied, "You think I'm going to go in there and take in my fingers the choice pieces of meat and hand them with a smile to that baby beggar? Never!"

"Dear son, please don't talk about him that way. Why don't you come join us? Everyone wants to see you. Even Prodigal is concerned about you."

"I bet! I bet he is! That thief! What does he want to take from me now! That's my money that paid for his party. And no one even consulted me. This isn't fair!"

"What do you mean, son? Tell me."

Elder turned around, looked straight at his father, and raised both his arms emphatically, "Look! All these years I've been slaving for you and never disobeyed your orders. Yet you never gave me even a young goat so I could celebrate with my friends. But when this son of yours who has squandered your property with prostitutes comes home, you kill the fattened calf for him!"

"Elder! Why do you speak of prostitutes? You shame yourself with such evil thoughts. You just got home. You don't know how Prodigal lost his money."

"Yes, his money and *yours* too! And now you give him the signet ring so he has access to *my* money! You didn't protect my interests before, so how can I trust you to do so now? I can't! You're giving this filthy fool a hero's welcome!"

"But dear son, what you don't see is that you are always with me and everything I have is yours to enjoy. You work and work and you follow the law but you don't enjoy all the good that I have to offer to you."

"Well, somebody has to work around here!"

"No. Your heart is wrong. You work to justify yourself, to prove yourself worthy, to show yourself better than others. Then you point your finger at others' sins. But all the time you fail to look at the darkness in your own soul."

"Darkness in *my* soul? What's in the filthy fool's soul? Horse dung?"

"Elder, if you would come join our celebration, then you would see Prodigal. He's changed! He was lost and now he's found. He was depressed and now he beams with love. Before he thought only of his own appetites, but now he thinks of others. He was dead and now he is alive again!"

"I wish he *were* dead!"

"Elder! He's your brother!"

"No! No, he's not! And you're not my father! You have destroyed the honor of this home! You have perverted justice! You have brought disgrace upon me." Suddenly, Elder raised the stick in his hand above his head and with a look of hatred in his eyes and veins popping out of his neck, he screamed, "I hate you!" He lunged toward Father and struck Father's head with a stick.

Father fell to the ground. Elder stared and blinked his swollen eyes as his father lay motionless.

"Oh!" Sarah screeched. "Elder has hit Father in the head!"

It happened so suddenly. Everyone had been listening, but no one thought that Elder could do such a terrible thing. Inside the house there arose a frenzied and panicked commotion. Chairs fell to the ground, tables skidded across the stone floor, and pottery broke into pieces. The chaos continued—wine splashing, bread rolling, feet scurrying, bodies bumping. People scrambled over one another trying to get outside, to the scene of argument.

"Stop, Elder! Stop this evil!" Joshua yelled out the window as he ran toward the front door. Prodigal was right on his heels, as were Phillip, Timothy, and Rabbi Benjamin. They blasted through the door and ran to Father's side near the sycamore tree. Father's body was lying limp on the ground. He was on his back, and his arms had flailed outward. His head rested to the side of the rock his head had struck.

Everyone stood staring at Father's body—dazed with disbelief and frozen by fear. Elder looked at the stick in his hand. His hand started to tremble uncontrollably—he dropped the stick to the ground. His lips quivered; he began to hyperventilate and cry hysterically. Overcome with guilt, he looked over at the others, many of whom stared in horror. Between gulps of air and sobs he stuttered, "Wha-wha-what have I-I done?" He had a ghastly look on his face as he started slowly backing away from Father's body.

Elder grabbed his forehead with both hands, flung his head backwards, screamed, "Oh, God!" And yet he could not truly call upon God. Instead, overcome with guilt, he turned around abruptly and fled running and screaming.

No one else moved. They didn't know what to do. They watched Elder run off into the distance. Prodigal felt compassion for his brother. He wanted Elder to know the forgiveness and new life that Father was offering him. Prodigal thought to run after his brother in order to console him and to explain Father's forgiveness to him. But then he thought better of it, as he was unsure of Father's condition. He knew he couldn't leave his father's side.

He looked down at Father again. He called to him, "Abba! Abba! Are you OK?" Tears started to form in his eyes. He knelt down beside his father, kissed him on the cheek, and gently stroked his forehead and face, as he thought to himself, *How much Abba must love Elder*. Prodigal noticed the wound on the side of his father's head and saw that it had stopped bleeding. He touched father's face again. It was warm, and little drops of perspiration had formed on his forehead. *He must have been knocked unconscious,* Prodigal thought hopefully. Then he leaned over his father's body, put his ear against Father's chest, and listened for a heartbeat.

"Meanwhile, the older son was in the field."[3] Wait a minute! Read Jesus' words again. "Meanwhile, the older son was in the field." In just eight words Jesus spoke volumes! Let's be sure we don't read past those words without stopping to think about what's been going on here. Elder has been working so hard in the fields that he's missed everything! The freedom to make choices. The patient prayers in the vineyard day after day. The footrace. The eyes of compassion. The bodily sacrifice. The affectionate embrace and the kind kisses. The robe. The ring. The shoes. The music and the dancing and the fattened calf. Father's love.

"Life is work and work is hard" say the Germans—and Elder too. Elder was working while his brother and the others who believed in Father's love were being showered with one blessing after another. Even the gang of boys could see the foolishness of this. They taunted him,

Elder, Elder, Oh where have you been?
Elder, Elder, Oh where have you been?
Off in the fields working so hard again!
Not in the house serving the guests then!
Your brother has come home to stay.
He's back safe and sound we say.
So your Father has killed the fattened calf
And all but you are here to dance and laugh!
Elder, Elder, Oh where have you been?
Elder, Elder, Oh where have you been.

Elder was enraged. But they were right. What did Elder have to show for his long, hard day of work? A dirty body. Tired muscles. Calloused hands. A big head. Dull ears. A long face. An empty stomach. A hard heart. Another workday ended in darkness, and three resentful slaves trailing behind him. Yet to Elder it was all worth it because he carried home with him four huge baskets overflowing with olives.

What do you think? Are four baskets overflowing with olives worth all that? Many people today think they are. They give up their lives to work. They miss hours of sleep, days of sunshine, hugs from their spouses, meals with their families, time with their kids, fun with their friends, and worship with God to work.

The "work" I'm referring to isn't just what you may do to earn a living. Work can also include things like yard work, house work, church work, child care, errands, helping a friend in need, and all sorts of other projects and commitments. For many people today the American dream has become a fast-paced, do-it-all, have-it-all frenzy that has destroyed their quality of life. In fact one study found that the average American adult spends half of his weekend time (fourteen hours) doing chores. Even worse, most of these busy people report feeling no more energetic at the end of a weekend than they do on Friday.[4]

But work doesn't have to be work! For some, work is play. (For others play is work!) What do I mean? Simply that whatever things you do because you *should* do them are work. The things that you do because you *want* to do them are play.

In other words, work and play are better defined by the attitudes you bring to an activity than by the activities themselves. Activities that are motivated by a sense of obligation, a feeling of compulsion, a pressure to measure up to an expectation, or a burden to please someone are work. Clearly this kind of work is no fun! Instead, it is exhausting and troublesome for the worker. It leads to bondage, bitterness, and burnout. On the other hand, activities that are motivated by a love that seeks to share itself and by a freedom that wants to enjoy the experience are play. These attitudes can make work fun. In the end they lead to celebration.

Elder's motivation in his work was all wrong. He put the cart before the horse; obedience before love. Work is righteous when obedience is driven by love, not when love is driven by obedience.[5] Like the Pharisees and teachers of the law who were among those listening when Jesus told His parable, Elder mistakenly thought he had to earn Father's favor, and he pridefully believed he could. He was a blasphemer of grace who tried to measure up to the standards of righteousness by his own efforts. He was like a machine that worked and worked without rest and enjoyment. He was like a textbook that had much knowledge but little heart.

On the outside Elder was busy and proud. On the inside he was empty and insecure. By focusing on the outside he distracted himself from the inside; by engrossing himself in his work he avoided his need for love. As a result Elder missed out. All the gifts that Father offered to Prodigal were available to Elder if he'd open his heart. But Elder was in his own world while he worked in the olive orchards. So much so that he didn't even hear the announcement of the shofar nor the music coming from the celebration.

The party went on without Elder, but his absence was an insult to Father. Father had to ask Phillip to welcome and serve the guests in Elder's absence. Father waited and waited to serve dinner, hoping that Elder would arrive, but the longer he waited the more he stretched the patience of his guests.

Elder's absence was also an insult to Prodigal. Prodigal was the guest of honor at this village party, and everyone else was there to celebrate his safe return home and his new life. Everyone knew that Prodigal's only brother was missing and wouldn't want to be there anyway. Elder's disdain for Prodigal was common knowledge in the village. But Prodigal anxiously awaited his brother's return from the fields, eager to reconcile with the one who had been his enemy.

There are many like Elder in our world and in our churches. According to a recent survey, 68 percent of Americans believe that the Christian faith has all the answers to leading a successful life.[6] Yet the majority of those people haven't received into their hearts the joyous new life in Christ that they profess to believe in. They haven't taken Prodigal's healing journey; they are too busy living their own experiences to respond to the invitation to the Great Banquet.[7]

Footsteps of Faith

1. Consider some of your important commitments and responsibilities, whether on the job, at home, or in the community. Which of the following motives tend to squeeze out the fulfillment and enjoyment God intends for you in your work? Check all that apply.

- ☐ A sense of obligation to fulfill responsibilities
- ☐ Feelings of guilt if you don't do all you "should"
- ☐ The need to complete a task even if you're quite tired
- ☐ A compulsive drive to feel significant and worthwhile
- ☐ An insatiable appetite to achieve status or recognition
- ☐ Pressures to measure up to others' expectations
- ☐ The burden to please others in need
- ☐ Escaping from unresolved relational conflicts
- ☐ Distracting yourself from uncomfortable feelings (i.e., boredom, inadequacy, depression, loneliness)

2. Do you identify with Elder? Have you been slaving away in the olive orchard while others are laughing, singing, and dancing at the party? If you have checked four or more

boxes above, you probably are a lot like Elder. If so, you need to make some changes, because you're on a path toward getting burned out, having a breakdown, or blowing up! This week pray that God would help you to learn to enjoy His goodness to you. Then look for opportunities to have some fun!

3. In many of his parables, including the parable of the prodigal son, Jesus presented the kingdom of God as being like a great feast and celebration. For instance, read the parable of the great banquet in Luke 14:15–24, in which four kinds of people are invited to a great celebration. The first three groups give their excuses as to why they can't come. One, like Elder, is busy working in the field. The second has bought some new oxen and wants to try them out. The third is newly married and is worried about what his spouse will say. But a fourth group is invited and they come. This group includes the poor, the crippled, the blind, and the lame. Which of the four groups are you in? Check the appropriate box; then realize that Jesus wants you to join Him at His banquet.

- ☐ The workers who are too busy with their projects
- ☐ The wealthy who are too distracted by their possessions
- ☐ The people-pleasers who are too worried about what others think
- ☐ The poor, crippled, blind, and lame who know they need God and are waiting for His invitation

If ever there exists an example of sibling rivalry, it is Elder and Prodigal. Maybe it is because they are so different.[8] Elder is a perfectionistic performer; Prodigal, a sloppy sluggard. Elder obeys Father to the letter. Prodigal does as he pleases. Elder works arduously. Prodigal plays foolishly. Elder bosses the servants around. Prodigal takes orders from the servants. Elder thinks he has proved to everyone how great he is. Meanwhile, Prodigal wishes he could one day prove himself to be great. It's no wonder that Elder arrogantly looks down upon his lazy younger brother and that Prodigal envies his older brother's success!

The heated conflict between them boils over when Prodigal demands his inheritance to do with as he wished. Elder would have killed his spoiled brat of a brother if Father hadn't stepped in and divided his inheritance between them. The brothers got what they wanted: Elder stayed to work in the fields and manage his two-thirds share of the family resources, and Prodigal ran off to the far country to do as he pleased with his one-third share. Then the sibling rivalry simmered under the surface for a while.

When Prodigal finally returns home he is a new man. His encounter with Father and the amazing gifts of love have changed him. He no longer envies his older brother. Nor does he hate Elder or want to compete with him. Instead, he wants to share Father's love and forgiveness with him. Nonetheless, because Elder hasn't changed his arrogant ways, it doesn't take long for his old hostilities against Prodigal to bring things back to a boiling point.

When Elder hears the news from Phillip of Prodigal's return as a beggar and the grand reception he received from Father, he is furious. *I've slaved away working for the family without recognition. My brother blows a third of the family* _estate and the whole village is honoring him! Instead, Prodigal should have been beaten and sent back to the pigsty! It isn't fair._ Elder wondered what has gotten into Father. Perhaps most frustrating of all to Elder was his own perceived loss. _They're spending_ my _money without even consulting me!_

Elder—as was typical for him—took matters into his own hands. He decided that he would bring about justice since Father didn't seem worried about it. He would take his anger out on his wicked brother! But when Father humbles himself and goes out to plead with Elder, it becomes clear that Elder has no understanding of true justice. He judges his father and his brother falsely and fails to look at the sin in his own life. Even after Father's sacrifice Elder doesn't understand that he is in the wrong and needs to seek forgiveness.

Prodigal's response to the old sibling rivalry was different. He had a change of heart and was prepared to humble himself and reconcile with his brother. But this wasn't enough to heal the sibling rivalry. Elder had to change too, and he didn't. Indeed it requires the involvement of both estranged parties to solve a conflict. In this case Prodigal could only deal with his part, and he did. Already he's confessed to Father his sins against Elder and forgiven Elder's sins against him. His heart is now swelling with love for his older brother, and he hopes to communicate this to him. Later in our story, after Father deals with Elder, we'll see how Prodigal plans to deal with Elder.

The sibling rivalry between Elder and Prodigal reminds me of successive phone calls I fielded during a local radio show. The focus of the program was comparing the pathway to healing in Psalm 23 with the twelve steps to recovery in Alcoholic's Anonymous. The first caller arrogantly blurted out over the air, "I don't believe the twelve steps really help anyone. AA is full of dry drunks who smoke and swear! There's nothing Christian about those groups." I asked the caller if he'd ever been to a twelve step meeting, and he said no.

The next caller called to reply. "You know people like that just don't understand. I struggled with bulimia and depression for eighteen years. People in my church put me down for not having more faith. They said I needed to read the Bible and pray and then God would deliver me. Well, I'm calling to say that God delivered me, but not the way those people said. He used the support of people in Overeater's Anonymous and the accountability of working and reworking the twelve steps. It's taken two years, and sometimes I still struggle, but now my life is so much better. It's sad, but I found more of God's grace in that group than in my church. But, thank God, recently I found a new church with a recovery ministry."

A stern Christian brother who was anti-recovery. A wounded and bound up Christian sister who was searching for help in a recovery group. Another sibling rivalry. The first caller was like Elder. Arrogantly looking down on those with struggles and blinded by his own hostility and prejudice, he focused on the specks in others' eyes when all the while there was a log in his own eye. He needed grace and he didn't know it and he didn't find it. The second caller was like Prodigal returning home and beginning a journey of healing. She needed grace and she knew it and she found it.

Meanwhile, Father is brokenhearted because he wants all his children to get along and because the world remains lost, waiting for Christians to be an example of how to love one another.[9]

Footsteps of Faith

1. Is there a family member or friend with whom you're at odds? Have you done your part to deal with that conflict

and to resolve it? This week pray that God would guide you in this matter.

2. Perhaps you identify with Prodigal. Have you ever been picked on and mistreated by a sibling or friend? How did you handle the situation? Did you talk to your father about it? If so, how did he respond? If not, why didn't you?

_____

_____

_____

3. Consider the sibling rivalry between Elder and Prodigal before Father divided his property between them. Elder arrogantly looked down upon his younger brother and felt superior. Prodigal enviously looked up at his older brother and felt inferior. Arrogance and envy are the seeds of all the relational rivalries that kill community. Have either or both of these seeds germinated in your soul?

4. Sometime this week read 1 Corinthians 12:12–26. Here we learn that we need each other. The parts of the body are one. The body doesn't function well if a foot that feels dirty, ugly, and smelly envies a hand that's been washed, covered in jewels, and lotioned. Where can the hands travel without feet? Nor does it make sense for the eye that's proud to be the window to the soul to arrogantly look down upon the hand because it's not looked at nearly as often. What doors can eyes open without hands?

When You Relapse into Old Patterns

In a moment of crisis, the truth of our hidden weaknesses and vulnerabilities often surfaces. Elder's return from working in the fields and subsequent refusal to participate in the party was an example of this. It was a crisis that unleashed the forces of hell upon Father's house.

It seemed everyone reverted back to his or her worst behavior. The gang of boys was once again taunting and mocking someone in an unfortunate position. Phillip couldn't stop pleading and trying to smooth over the conflict. Sarah feasted on the juicy morsels of gossip. Timothy plotted for selfish profit. Prodigal started to act impulsively on his heroic fantasies. The mayor and the rabbi got into another skirmish as Joshua got strict about justice and Benjamin became blinded by soft love. Meanwhile, Elder was still outside steaming with jealous anger and would soon go mad with murderous rage.

Father was understandably frustrated. Everyone had so quickly forgotten his display of sacrificial love. It was just a few hours ago that he humbly gave himself for Prodigal, stepped between the hostile gang and his sinful son, and took upon himself the just punishment due his son. They all had seen this and received his love and forgiveness into their hearts. Yet no one wanted to let Father show his loving forgiveness to his other son who had finally returned home.

But this didn't stop Father. He humbled himself and went out to Elder. He took the initiative to show his love to his son. He sacrificed himself for his son. He offered the forgiveness of sins for everyone who would believe in him.

When a crisis brings out the worst in you—when you relapse into old and destructive patterns for any reason—there is one thing you must do to get back on your feet: do some more forgiveness work. Confess your sins and seek

God's forgiveness. Confess the sins of others against you and share God's forgiveness with them.

How many times will you have to do this? Peter thought seven times was enough, since that was the answer that Solomon gave in one of his proverbs.[10] Jesus showed Peter that he missed the whole point and told him that he'd need to forgive seventy multiplied by seven times. And he didn't mean 490! Given the symbolic significance of those numbers he probably meant maturity (eldership) multiplied by perfection![11] However you add up the numbers, though, Jesus' point is clear: Mature Christians and leaders in the church will be seeking and offering forgiveness again and again and again.

A young man named Jason, who was a college pastor, learned this the hard way. He relapsed into his old sexual compulsions after his girlfriend broke up with him. It began when a friend talked him into watching an X-rated video with him. Soon he was back into his old patterns of compulsively indulging in X-rated videos, phone sex, and pornography. When he got hold of himself he entered our hospital program for help.

One day the light turned on for Jason. We were in a men's group, and another patient named Steve was talking about his relationship with his father. "I'll never forget the game I hit my first home run. I was so excited. As I rounded third base I looked into the stands. I saw my mother standing and clapping, but I didn't look at her long. I kept searching for my father. He wasn't there. He had missed another game."

I looked over at Jason, and he was crying. Later, I asked Jason what his tears were about. "I identified with Steve's story. My father never went to any of my games either. That's probably why I stopped playing ball. I just lost interest. I never felt close to him. I don't think I was important to him. But my Mom was a big support . . ."

Like so many men I meet, Jason (and Steve) had a distant relationship with his father and a close relationship with his mother. In fact, Jason tried to be everything to his mother that his father wasn't: warm, sensitive, responsive. His mother loved the boy he was, but he'd never become a man without his father or some other man to relate to.

Now at age twenty-seven things were the same, not only with his parents, but even in his social circle. Relationships with other men felt stiff and forced, but he was usually pretty comfortable talking with women.

Jason was trying to get his masculinity affirmed from the women in his life because he didn't know how to trust another man. It wasn't working. The crisis of the breakup with his girlfriend and his subsequent relapse into sexual sin made that clear.

What did Jason need? Relationships with other men, for starters. And he needed the ability to set and maintain boundaries with intrusive women and with his own sexual temptation; forgiveness for his sexual sins; and help forgiving his father for the countless ways that his masculinity hadn't been affirmed by him. In short, he needed the Father in his life.

Footsteps of Faith

1. Does a crisis sometimes bring out the worst in you? When something bad happens to you or you find yourself in a difficult place for some reason, do you sometimes relapse into old, destructive behavior patterns? Perhaps you struggle with some of the responses below. Mark any that apply.

    ☐ I get depressed. Sometimes very depressed.
    ☐ I feel anxious, as though I need to do something but I'm not sure what.
    ☐ I become panicked and look for someone to make things better.

☐ I help other people who are troubled.
☐ I try to take control of the situation.
☐ I get perfectionistic.
☐ I blame myself for how I could have avoided the situation or made things better somehow.
☐ I isolate from people around me.
☐ I eat too much.
☐ I stop eating and don't take care of my needs.
☐ I give into a compulsive behavior _____.
☐ I'm amazingly strong in a crisis. Probably I cope by detaching from my feelings.
☐ In a crisis I _____.

2. Relapsing into old patterns reminds us of our need for forgiveness. This week consider if you need to do some more forgiveness work. What sins do you need to confess and receive forgiveness for? What sins that have been committed against you do you need to forgive?

_____

_____

3. Do you identify with Jason and Steve? Did you have an overly close relationship with your father? If so, consider how that has affected you and pray that God would help you forgive your parents and resolve any problems caused by your response.

4. Read the parable of the unmerciful servant in Matthew 18:23–35. Pray that God would help you to avoid making the mistake that the unmerciful servant made. He was forgiven by the king for a debt of several million dollars but he refused to forgive a fellow servant who owed him just a few dollars. The unmerciful servant hadn't truly received the king's gracious forgiveness; otherwise he would have forgiven his friend just as the king had forgiven him.

Broken Bread and Poured Wine

Despite Father's invitation and Phillip's pleading, Elder wouldn't come into the house to join the feast. So Father began the banquet without him, breaking the bread and serving the wine for his guests. Yet beginning the feast without both his sons at his side broke Father's heart. He had waited for Prodigal, who finally returned home; now Elder stood close by, yet refused to enter the house.

Then Father did what no Eastern patriarch would ever do, especially in front of a house full of guests. He went out to his obstinate son and urged him to join the celebration. Father humiliated himself and sacrificed his honor to show his love to Elder. He offered listening ears, a compassionate heart, the fattened calf, the welcome of the village, all of his possessions, and all of his love. He also offered Elder the opportunity to confess his sins and the way to new life.

Elder refused. To him it wasn't fair that Prodigal be loved and forgiven by Father without having earned it. He despised his wicked brother, and he refused to share the house with him. He hated his generous father, and he refused to serve him anymore. Blinded by jealousy and pride and consumed with rage, he took matters into his own hands; he raised the stick and cracked his father in the head.

When Jesus told the parable of the prodigal son, one of the groups of people He was speaking to were the Pharisees, teachers of the law, and other religious leaders. In the character of Elder He gave them a mirror to look into. Like Elder they arrogantly looked down upon the sinful Prodigals—the tax collectors, beggars, prostitutes, drunkards, and other "sinners." They also were too proud to see the darkness in their own souls. They refused to see that God was a gracious Father; to them He was a strict judge. They hated Jesus for claiming that He was the Father in the flesh.

Later the Pharisees would spearhead the false legal charges against Jesus. They stirred up the people against Him and pressured Pilate to crucify Jesus. Thus we can determine the missing conclusion to the parable of the prodigal son—Elder would physically reject the Father's love, even as the religious leaders would spurn the heavenly Father's love, sentencing His Son to death. Upon hearing the parable, the religious elders sneered with hatred at Jesus,[12] and then just a weeks later they had Him killed.[13]

In truth, Jesus' death was known and foreseen by His Father. The Father God willingly gave His only Son for us. God felt the agony of allowing His beloved Son to suffer and die a humiliating and tortuous death.

Recently I heard the true story of how a mother and her four-year-old daughter survived the earthquake that hit former Soviet Armenia. Their fifth floor apartment shook violently for several seconds, and then, without warning, the structure crumbled. Suddenly mother and daughter fell into the basement, and the four floors above collapsed around them. Trapped together underneath the debris, they cried for help until they could cry no more.

Eight days passed, but no one had come. In the blackness around her, the mother finally lost track of time. She and her daughter lost the feeling in their fingers and toes, as the outside cold chilled them. With gnawing hunger pains and dehydrated bodies, they tried to hold on and survive together. "Mommy, I'm so thirsty! Mommy, I'm so thirsty!" the little girl kept crying.

But the mother couldn't move out of the debris to find her daughter any water. Time wore on. Nothing changed, and she began hallucinating. She tried to sleep but couldn't because something always awakened her: the cold, body aches, hunger, thirst, night terrors, or her daughter's repeated cries, "Mommy, I'm so thirsty!" The mother gave up hope; she began to wait for death in the debris she was entombed in.

Then she had an idea on how she might help her little girl to survive. She felt around on the floor near her with her numb fingers and found a piece of shattered glass. She sliced open her left index finger and gave it to her girl to suck. The drops of blood gave warmth and had nutrients, but they weren't enough. "Please, Mommy. Some more. I'm so thirsty!" The mother slit another finger and another. She kept her daughter alive. Finally, the mother and child were rescued. Mother was in critical condition, extremely anemic. She had been willing to die so her daughter might live.

Beneath the rubble of a fallen world we were trapped in sin and death. Jesus Christ entered the cold, dark basement of our existence and died on a cross so that we could survive and be saved. Before His death, He suffered extreme pain. Jesus gave all He had so that we could live; upon His death a soldier pierced His side with a sword and His own blood poured out for us. It is relationship with Him that we hunger for and His loving forgiveness that we thirst for.[14] We can draw close to the Father God and be forgiven of our sins if we accept the wine of His Son's blood and the bread of His Son's flesh.[15]

Footsteps of Faith

1. Perhaps at various points in our journey you've identified with Elder. If so, then take this opportunity to do what Elder was too proud to do—confess your sins. Which of the following sins of Elder's listed in Appendix 2 do you need to confess so that you can join the celebration of Father's love for you? (This list is a modification of Appendix 2.)

- ☐ Pride
- ☐ Identity in work
- ☐ "Punish them, Father."
- ☐ Trust in own abilities

☐ Self-aggrandizing   ☐ Hiding sin
☐ Emotional distance ☐ Legalistic /
   from Father   perfectionistic
☐ Rigid boundaries   ☐ Overly accountable
☐ Compulsive   ☐ Depressed / repressed rage
☐ Arrogant   ☐ Driven to achieve

2. To join the celebration you need to follow Prodigal's example and take the same twelve steps of faith that he took. (These are described in Appendix 2.) Consider how much Prodigal changed when he left the far country and entered Father's house. Acknowledge the ways in which you're like Prodigal in the far country and pray that God would help you to change.

3. Look for an opportunity to celebrate Communion this week. When you eat the bread and drink the wine consider the missing conclusion to the parable of the prodigal son— think about how the Father, in Jesus Christ, humbled Himself and sought you out to invite you to celebrate His love and forgiveness.

"I hate you!" Crack! Thump! "Oh! Elder hit Father in the head!" These were the horrifying words and sounds that Prodigal and the others heard cascading in from outside the front of the house.

And from inside the house, at the dinner table, horrible sounds replied: Boom! Boom! . . . Boom! Ehrrrrrrrr! Crash-sh-sh-sh! Splashhhhh! Thumpty-thump-thump-thump. Stomp-stomp-stomp-stomp. . . . Stomp! Bump! Bump! "Stop, Elder! Stop this evil!"

Joshua, Prodigal and the others ran out of the house. Sarah and those who were in the courtyard came from the other direction. Everyone swarmed to Father's side. There they stood and stared at his body on the ground.

Elder hadn't moved. He too stared at Father. He looked at the stick in his hand. He looked at the others. Waves of fear and guilt overtook him. His hand started to tremble uncontrollably until the stick dropped to the ground. He began to hyperventilate and cry hysterically. He stuttered, "Wha-what-what-at have I done?" He couldn't bear to face the sight another second—he backed away, turned around, and ran away screaming in agony.

Prodigal started to run after him but stopped himself. He wanted his brother to know Father's forgiveness just as he did, but Elder had rejected Father's offer of forgiveness and new life because he didn't want to face his sin. Prodigal looked back at his father. He called out to him, "Abba! Abba! Are you OK?" With tears in his eyes he knelt beside him, kissed him, and gently stroked his face as he thought to himself, *How much Abba loves Elder.* Then he leaned over and listened for Father's heartbeat.

Father loved Elder so much that he humiliated himself in front of everyone at the party and went out and begged his son to join the celebration. Not only that but he exposed himself to a dangerous and risky situation. He knew how angry Elder was because he had heard him yelling at the gang of boys and arguing with Phillip. But he wanted his other son to know forgiveness and new life also. So he went out and faced his explosive and arrogant son, but he was struck in the head.

So also the Father God paid a great price to offer us forgiveness—the life of His only Son Jesus Christ. First, He let His Son don mortal clothes and feel pain. Then He suffered the agony of watching His dear and beloved Son being crucified. What did the Father see? What did He feel on that day of trial and death? Look through the Father's eyes and feel with His heart as you consider the pain that Jesus endured when He was crucified.

Anticipating the cup of suffering He was about to drink, Jesus prayed, "Father, if you are willing, take this cup from me; yet not my will but yours be done."[16] Exhausted from anguish, He sweat drops of blood.[17] Suddenly He was surrounded by men with swords and clubs. All of His disciples abandoned Him. The soldiers brought Jesus to an unlawful nighttime trial before the religious leaders of the Sanhedrin, who slandered Him with false accusations.[18] The palace guards mocked Him, beat Him, blindfolded Him, spit on Him, and struck Him in the face.[19]

The next day Jesus was brought before Pilate. Though Pilate found Jesus innocent, he was afraid of the people who called for Jesus' death; so he gave them their wish and ordered that Jesus be scourged and then crucified.[20]

Jesus was stripped of His clothing. His hands were tied to a post above His head. A Roman soldier held a flagrum, a whip made of heavy strips of leather, each with pieces of lead attached to it. Again and again and again Jesus was whipped across His shoulders, back, and thighs. Cutting into skin, the flagrum brought excruciating pain. Blood oozed from His back; muscles tore. The soldiers put a purple robe on Jesus, and it stuck to His raw and bloody flesh. They pressed a crown of thorns onto His head, and sharp pain seared Jesus' scalp and blood dripped down His face and neck. Again and again the soldiers struck Jesus in the head with a staff and spit upon Him. They feel to their knees in mocking worship.

At Golgotha, site of the crucifixion, a Roman soldier hammered a heavy, square wrought iron nail through each of Jesus' wrists and through the arches of Jesus' feet and into the cross. Nerves were severed. Blood spurted. Intense pain shot through His whole body. Jesus looked at those who tortured Him and prayed, "Father forgive them, for they do not know what they are doing."[21]

Then Jesus—the Son of God—was left to hang and die a slow, torturous, and humiliating death. On the cross He hung. His body sagged. Muscles cramped, knotted up, and throbbed. His chest rose and fell in pain; He could hardly breathe. Each little breath of air meant pushing His body up and created acute pain in His feet and hands and searing up and down His whole body. His shoulders and back rubbed against the rough wood and filled with sharp splinters. Onlookers mocked Him.

He cried out, "My God, my God, why have you forsaken me?"[22] He was all alone with the punishment for the sin of the world upon Himself. And the Father, who had lost His own Son in order that the Son might redeem mankind, turned away. He could not behold the sins covering His Son. However, the Father still loved the Son and the people that Jesus came to save, and later the Father would crown Christ with glory.

At this point the pain in Jesus' chest became crushing. His heart struggled to pump heavy, thick, sluggish blood to His body tissues. Eventually, refusing a wine drenched sop, He spoke one final time. "It is finished,"[23] He declared simply. Then He used up His last breath: "Father, into your hands I commit my spirit."[24]

It was for the joy of seeing you and me forgiven of our sins and restored to intimate relationship with Himself that Jesus endured all this pain. He was successful in conquering sin and death; He rose from the dead and now sits at the right hand of the throne of the Father in heaven. There He is preparing a home for those who believe in Him.[25]

Footsteps of Faith

1. Father forgave Prodigal, and Prodigal forgave Elder. This is the way it is supposed to work. In the apostle Paul's words, "Forgive whatever grievances you may have against one another. Forgive as the Lord forgave you."[26] Are you having trouble forgiving anyone? Part of the solution might be to consider your own sinfulness and God's gracious forgiveness to you.

2. Perhaps one of the people you're struggling to forgive is your father. How can you forgive him? The following seven steps can enable you to forgive your father:

    1) Encounter the heavenly Father and His perfect love.
    2) Contrast your father with the heavenly Father. (See Appendix 1: "Blessings and Curses from a Father".)
    3) Confront the truth of your father's sins—both committed and omitted acts—that affected you.
    4) Work through your anger at your father.
    5) Grieve what you lost or missed out on from your father.
    6) Let go of your expectation that your father make up for his past sins or become the father you think he should be.

7) Put your faith in your heavenly Father, seeking to know and rely upon His perfect love for you.

3. This week reflect on how Christ suffered a tortuous death to bring you forgiveness for your sins. Thank God for His love for you.

NOTES

1. Psalm 103:10.
2. Psalm 8:8.
3. Luke 15:25*a*.
4. Jack Smith, "Worn Out by His Wife's Weekend," *Los Angeles Times*, July 25, 1989, Sec. IV, p. 1.
5. John 14:23.
6. George Barna, *The Barna Report: 1992-93* (Ventura: Regal, 1992), 256.
7. Matthew 22:1–14.
8. For a list of differences between the two brothers, see Appendix 2.
9. John 13:35.
10. Proverbs 24:16.
11. Matthew 18:21–22.
12. Luke 16:14.
13. Luke 22:52–53; 22:66–23:25, 35.
14. John 6:35.
15. John 6:53–58.
16. Luke 22:42.
17. Luke 22:44–45.
18. Matthew 26:57–66.
19. Luke 22:63–65.
20. Mark 15:15.
21. Luke 23:34.
22. Matthew 27:45.
23. John 19:30.
24. Luke 23:46.
25. Hebrews 12:2; John 14:2-3.
26. Colossians 3:13.

"Therefore go and make disciples in all the nations ... and be sure of this—that I am with you always, even to the end of the world."

Matthew 28:19–20 (TLB)

STEP 12

Ministry

Spreading the Good News

H is heart is beating! He's alive! He's alive!" Prodigal exclaimed from his knees as he looked up at the crowd gathered around.

"Praise the Lord! His mercy endures forever!" sang the rabbi. Others echoed his thanksgiving as they called to one another, "Hallelujah! Yahweh lives—and Father does too! Thank the Lord!"

"He must have been knocked unconscious," Prodigal concluded. "Phillip, run get us some water and a cloth for his face."

In short order Phillip returned to Father's side with a jar of water and cotton cloth and handed them to Prodigal. Prodigal dipped the cloth into the cool water and gently wiped his father's face. Then he carefully blotted the bloody wound on the side of his head.

"Oww!"

"Father!" Prodigal pulled his hand back from the wound.

"Oh! He's coming to!" Sarah and her friends gasped in unison.

Father blinked and opened his eyes. He squinted in the moonlight to look at the crowd of onlookers surrounding him. Then, seeing their concern, he smiled. "Did you save me some fattened calf?"

"Ah ha, ha! Ha! He must be OK. He still has a sense of humor!" Timothy looked over his shoulder and reported to those who were behind him.

Phillip took Father's question seriously. "Father," he explained, "we didn't even finish the bread and the wine. Why I hadn't even served the fattened calf yet when we all heard Sarah scream out that Elder had hit you in the head."

"Oh, yes. That's why I have this splitting headache. And this rock. Oww!" Father placed his hand against his throbbing head and looked at the crowd gathered around him again. One at a time he glanced at each face. Suddenly he sat up and said, "Where's Elder? Elder, my son, step forward! I can't see you. Elder, are you—"

"Father, I'm afraid he ran away into the fields," Prodigal answered softly. "When he saw you hit the ground and not get up again and not even move or speak a word he was deeply shaken. He couldn't believe what he had done. He seemed overwhelmed with guilt. He dropped the stick here" —Prodigal picked up the stick and handed it to Father—"and then he fled. We didn't know what—."

"Why didn't anyone stop him? Didn't you say anything to him? What if he hurts himself?"

"I'm sorry, Father. I—I was shocked by all that had happened, and I was worried about you."

"Father, we were all worried about you," Phillip added. "And Elder, well, he had just hit you in the head. We didn't know what he'd do to—."

"Well, I know what I wanted to do to him!" Joshua interrupted. "That boy needs to be taught a lesson! In all my life I've never seen such a display of absolute disrespect for tradition and outright rebellion against a father's authority!"

Prodigal looked at Joshua, and started to reprimand. "You weren't at the dinner table on the fateful night this past winter when I demanded to have the money due me when Father died."

...when Father died. The words landed with a loud thud in everyone's hearts. A silence followed for a couple seconds, but it seemed much longer.

Finally Phillip broke the quiet and spoke what almost everyone was thinking, "Father, you could have been killed! Why did you go out to Elder? You knew how enraged he was. We tried to tell you not to go out there."

"Oh, don't worry about me, Phillip. I've got a headache all right, but I'll be OK. Maybe you'd feel better if I stood up." Father reached out his hand to Phillip. "Please help me back onto my feet."

Father stood up straight. "See? I'll be fine.

"Everyone, the issue here isn't my health, it's Elder. Don't you understand my love for him? Don't you see why I had to go out to him personally and invite him to join the celebration?" Father took hold of Prodigal's left hand, held it up for everyone to see. "Look closely at the emblem on this ring, and then you will understand."

Everyone crowded around Prodigal and gazed intently at the ring on his finger. In order to see, those in back—the elders from the village, the families of Rabbi Benjamin and Timothy, the musicians and dancers—all had to stand on their tiptoes and peer over the others' shoulders or squeeze their heads between bodies.

There was a chattering of admiring "Oooo's" and "Wow's" mixed in with perplexed "Hmmm's." Many were seeing the ring for the first time. As most were gaping and scratching their heads, Rabbi Benjamin was stroking his long gray beard. One by one, beginning with Prodigal, people began to give the rabbi their attention. It was clear that he was about to say something profound.

"Yes. I see it now. This is Moses' pole with the snake wrapped around it. When our forefathers were wandering in the desert and spoke against God and Moses, the Lord sent venomous snakes to bite them. Later, when the people repented, the Lord had Moses make that bronze snake and put it on a long pole. Whenever someone was bitten by a snake Moses would lift up the pole, and if the snake-bitten person looked up at the pole he lived."[1]

Phillip raised his eyebrows, shrugged his shoulders, threw up his hands, and looked at Father. "But what does Moses have to do with this?"

"There aren't any venomous snakes around here, are there?" Timothy questioned. Sarah and the other ladies shrieked at the thought of it.

Prodigal's eyes lit up; he cleared his throat and spoke. "No, it's not about snakes. It's about being delivered from evil. Just as Moses brought his pole to the snake-bitten sinners to heal them, so also Father gave himself to Elder to forgive his sin."

"What?" Phillip shook his head in confusion. The others looked equally perplexed. Even Rabbi Benjamin was confused by the connection Prodigal was making between Moses and Father.

"Don't you see?" Prodigal questioned emphatically. "Father risked his life by going outside to Elder to plead with him that he join the celebration. He was willing to suffer public humiliation, physical pain, and even to risk his life in order to restore Elder to himself. Elder has been snake-bitten by sin, as have we all. Along with him we need to look up and see Father's mercy and accept his forgiveness in order to have new life."

Prodigal looked around at a sea of blank faces. "You must understand." Prodigal paused and then took another direction in his effort to convince them of Father's great mercy. "Remember when I approached the edge of town weighed down by the burden of my sin and carrying the stench of the pigsty with me? You all were in the village mocking me as I walked toward you. Sarah, you were leading the mockery, remember? And you were the first to turn your attention away from me to see Father running through town, exposing his undergarments, sweating, and kicking up dust. You pointed your finger at him and laughed. But Father took my shame upon himself and gave me a wonderful welcome home.

"And what about the attack from the gang of boys? I'm 'the fool who brought shame upon Nain!' I'm the one they tried to beat up. Mayor, you gave the boys the go-ahead to attack me. They came after me, screaming obscenities, pounding with their sticks, punching with their fists, and kicking with their feet. But Father stepped in between them and me. He took upon himself the beating I deserved. He risked his life to save me.

"Rabbi, surely you understand the importance of sacrifice? Look at how Father sacrificed himself for me! It's because of his mercy upon me that we had this celebration tonight. Just as he offered his love and forgiveness to me so he did to Elder—he still does—and so he does to all of you!

"And many of you have seen and embraced that love during the party—laughing and loving together, without rivalry or selfishness. Yes, like Moses and the people of Israel, we were in danger of dying because of our sins. But Father was willing to suffer ridicule, pain, or (in the case of Elder) even death that we might live. By Father's example, you are beginning to turn to Yahweh in love. Mayor, you have learned to show mercy and forgive me because Father has. Rabbi, you are learning the need for discipline and being accountable, because Father let me receive the consequences of my sins yet accepted me when I came back to him.

"Look at how Father desires to bring each of us to wholeness through his love. He has shown us the power of forgiveness that Yahweh has for us, and it is God's love that can deliver us from our fears and selfishness. Sarah, surely you can recognize the power of my father's good words to transform me and the excitement of having a restored life!"

Prodigal turned to Timothy. "You of all people, Timothy, must be able to see this banquet and the gifts I have received as a demonstration of Father's love. Even a merchant such as you would need a few hours to add up the cost of all the gifts that Father has given me today. And the money behind these gifts is a mere shadow of their true value. Father has given all that he has and all that he is to me and to all of you who came to celebrate with me."

Everyone was spellbound by Prodigal's incredible discourse. His message was clear. No one said a word. But Father's face spoke loudly—he was smiling and nodding in approval.

Prodigal continued. "If we believe that these things are true then we must go and tell others. We need to show others that just as we have been changed by Father's grace and Yahweh's mercy, so can they.

First, we must find Elder and convince him of Father's forgiveness. Then we must go beyond our village of Nain and even beyond Galilee. We need to go to Antioch, that city of pleasure where everyone lives for themselves. We need to go to the world! Now who will join me? If you're with me, then come stand next to me here under the sycamore tree."

Immediately Phillip bounded over to his brother and embraced him. Joshua followed behind him, and before the reserved mayor realized what was happening Phillip had embraced him. Rabbi Benjamin stepped forward saying, "You can always count me in on the Lord's work!" Sarah, who had been whispering to two of her friends, grabbed them each by the arm and blurted out enthusiastically, "Hey, don't leave us out!"

Timothy was struggling with his decision more than the others. Twice he started to step forward only to be pulled back by his wife and children who clearly did not want him to leave his home and business to go on a mission. But he remembered God's love shown through Father—a love that had forgiven his unjust business dealings. Finally, with insistence and tears he pulled himself away, promising to be back as soon as he could. His family was crying as they huddled together and tried to console one another. "I will be back," Timothy promised. "I love you still, but I love my Lord too.

Rabbi Benjamin's family was used to such sacrifices. His oldest son would take over the priestly duties in Nain while he was gone. Now most of the villagers began to walk away in groups; it was late and it had been a long evening. The musicians and dancers had performed well, and now it was time to go back home. The village elders all went back to their homes as did Sarah's other friends.

But Prodigal and his friends stood under the sycamore tree, unable or unwilling to move. Finally Prodigal spoke. "Listen to my plan. First thing in the morning all of you go up to Antioch. Find a man named Demetrius, a rich man in a country villa, and tell him that I sent you. Tell him everything that you have observed. Explain to him what I just told you. He will listen to you and help you. Tell as many people as you can find in Antioch about Father's grace and then move on until you reach Rome and beyond! We must tell as many people as possible so that they too can find new life!"

"Prodigal, why are you telling us to do all this? Won't you be leading us?" questioned Joshua.

"No, first I need to go back to Elder and try to win him over. I have decided that I alone must earn Elder's respect and attention.

"No! It isn't safe! He might still be angry at you. I won't let you go," insisted the mayor.

"Joshua, he's my brother and I love him. And now that my heart is overflowing with Father's love, I shall give it to Elder. I must finish the work that Father began this evening."

"If you must go, then you need to bring at least one of us with you," bargained Joshua.

"The only one who might be able to help me is you, Joshua! You're the only one here who Elder respects because you stand for the law."

"I will go with you, then."

"Good," Prodigal concluded. "Then Phillip, Rabbi Benjamin, Timothy, and Sarah and her friends will go to Antioch."

"Wait a minute!" Phillip cautioned. "What about Father? Somebody needs to stay and look after him. Maybe I should stay and take care of him. Besides, I'm a slave! If anyone finds out I've left my master I could be thrown in jail."

"Phillip, I told you I was OK. You don't need to worry about me," Father reassured his faithful servant. "I have other servants who can nurse me back to health and help me run the affairs of the farm. And as far as your freedom goes I meant it when I adopted you as my son earlier today and I will give you the legal papers to prove it."

"You will?" Phillip was shocked. "You mean I'm free? I'm *really* your son, and you're *really* my father?"

"Yes, of course, Phillip! I meant what I said." Father looked proudly over at Prodigal. "My son, you are living up to the true meaning of your name—you are generously spending my love to you on others." Then Father announced to the crowd, "Now everyone listen to the rest of Prodigal's plan."

"I have something to give each of you that you'll need." Prodigal continued "I never told you how I found my way back home from the pigsty."

Prodigal pulled his gold embroidered purple pouch out of the pocket of his robe. He untied the pouch and pulled out his smooth stone. He looked with admiration at his father and then looked back at the others. "See this rock? This is like the stones that Father and I used to skip on the lake when I was a boy. He secretly slipped it into this pouch just before I left for Antioch. When I ran out of gold in my pouch I found this rock. Then I remembered Father's love for me and I came home.

"I have here in this pouch other rocks that I found underneath this very tree we're standing under right now with Father. I want to give each of you a rock as a reminder of Father and his love for you. I hope it will mean as much to you as it has to me. Hold it in your hand when you're scared and alone. Hold it in your heart when you doubt. Hold it in your pocket no matter where you are, and remember that Father is always thinking of you.

"Joshua and I will find Elder, and, hopefully, we will be able to persuade him of Father's mercy; then we will join up with you in Antioch. If not, then we will see you at the banquet in heaven. Then we can finally eat the fattened calf together!"

They joined hands together in a circle, and Father prayed his blessing upon each of them and for the missions they were embarking upon.

Show Us the Father

The sacred celebration had been ruined by sacrilegious sabotage. Tranquillity had turned into terror. Happiness to havoc. Father's love had drawn them together but now Elder's outbreak of rage against Father had brought an abrupt ending to the party. Now everyone was huddled around Father's body that lay on the ground. Everyone wondered the same thing, *Is he alive?*

Prodigal, who was kneeling beside his father's body with his ear against Father's chest, answered, "His heart is beating! He's alive! He's alive!" Prodigal gently wiped Father's face and head with a damp cloth and Father regained consciousness. He was wounded and he had a splitting headache, but he would recover.

Of course, everyone was singing praises that Father was alive and well. But he could have died. This bothered everyone, especially Phillip. He said, "Father, you could have been killed! Why did you go out to Elder? You knew how enraged he was."

Father's signet ring, which he had given to Prodigal, had the answer; the emblem on the face of the ring, depicting Moses' pole with the bronze snake wrapped around it, told the story. Just as Moses went to those who had been bitten by the venomous snakes and lifted up his pole with the bronze snake so that those who looked upon it were healed, so also Father went out to each of his sons who had been poisoned by sin, and to the villagers as well, and he displayed his forgiveness. All except Elder trusted his message of love; they found deliverance from sin. The ring portrayed God's salvation for sinners—His desire to accept and restore the lost. This is the very heart of the parable of the prodigal son.

The apostle John explained our heavenly Father's forgiveness this way, as he declared the gospel of forgiveness of sin and new life:

> Just as Moses lifted up the snake in the desert, so the Son of Man must be lifted up, that everyone who believes in him may have eternal life. For God so loved the world that he gave his one and only Son, that whoever believes in him shall not perish but have eternal life.[2]

Later in His ministry on earth, Jesus Himself explained this gospel to His disciples: "I am the way and the truth and the life. No one comes to the Father except through me."[3] But one of Jesus' disciples, Philip, was unsure how to return to the Father. He responded to Jesus' statement with the plea, "Lord, show us the Father and that will be enough for us."[4]

"Show us the Father." The cries are heard everywhere. People are seeking the love and restoration that only the heavenly Father can give. A devastated boy after his father walked out of the home for good; the man in prison who wanders into the chapel; the woman who has been jilted by another lover; a city gang spraying a parked police car with graffiti; a teenage girl weeping at her father's funeral; a widow in the back pew of the church; the frustrated mother who is trying to manage three young children; the children whose busy father neglects spending time with—we all long to see the Father.

We cannot be fulfilled until we come to know the Father personally, deeply, and truly. Jesus revealed the Father and made it possible for us to know Him. He was the exact image of the Father; He was one with Him. To know Jesus is to know the Father.

Yet Philip didn't understand. In frustration Jesus answered his "Show us the Father" plea: "Don't you know me, Philip, even after I have been among you such a long time? Anyone who has seen me has seen the Father."[5]

Many people who read the parable of the prodigal son don't understand either. They may see a loving father but fail to see that he sacrifices himself for both of his sons. Think about it. He ran through the village so that he could get to Prodigal before the mob, enduring the scorn, ridicule, and abuse that his foolish son deserved. He left the dinner table to go out and plead with Elder that he join the celebration and received upon himself the public humiliation and the physical punishment that his obstinate son deserved.

Therefore in Jesus' parable we see a picture of the Father God's sacrificial love and forgiveness that was expressed to its fullest extent later, when the Father suffered the anguish of seeing His only Son crucified for the sins of the world.

Footsteps of Faith

1. Are you looking for the Father? Where are you in your journey of returning to the Father? Sometime this week take some time to write down your story of how you've come to know the Father personally. What people have revealed Him to you? In what ways have they revealed Him to you? What injuries needed to be healed and what adversities had to be overcome for you to find the Father? What is still ahead for you in your journey? (It may help you to answer these questions if you reflect on Appendix 1, "Blessings and Curses from a Father.")

2. Find someone else who is looking for the Father and share your story with him or her. Then listen to this person's story.

Wow! Look at Prodigal now! See how he's changed! Before he was lost in his own world. Now he is concerned about the needs of others. Before he indulged himself to satisfy his own appetites. Now he determines to do what is right. Before he lived in resentment. Now he forgives. Before he ran away in fear. Now he faces challenges with courage. Before he shamed his name, wasting Father's inheritance. Now he lives up to his name, spending Father's lavish love on others.

It's this new Prodigal who looks for Elder in order to reach him with Father's love. Like Father, Prodigal is willing to risk his life to save Elder from sin.[6] Prodigal had known how it felt to live without Father's love, and now he knew what it was like to discover that love. He was determined to do what he could to reach his brother so that through him Father's love might reach Elder. He picked Joshua the village mayor to go with him on his mission because Joshua was a man of the law like Elder, but, unlike Elder, had discovered that the purpose of the law was to point out our need for grace. Together they sought to convince Elder that he needed Father's grace.

Is this not the situation we find ourselves in today? There are literally millions of people like Elder in our world. They believe in God, they try to live a righteous life, they do many good things for other people. Whether Jewish, Muslim, "Christian," or some other faith, they try to practice their religion in their own way, but they don't have true relationship with the Father through faith in Christ. They are working hard in Father's fields, but they haven't entered his house; they are so close to the Father but so far away.

They are like the Pharisees, scribes, and other religious leaders of Jesus' day. Jesus described these people as having the following characteristics:[7]

- Piety displayed for others to see
- Pride in religious accomplishments
- Seeking to have power and control over others
- Rigid convictions and rules they preach but they and others cannot live up to
- Converting others to legalism
- Teaching others even though they are blind themselves
- "Straining a gnat and swallowing a camel," that is, legalistically following certain details of the law yet missing the heart of the law: justice, mercy, and faithfulness
- Cleaning up their image but not confessing sins of the heart
- Hypocrisy—they are whitewashed tombs, which look beautiful on the outside but are full of dead man's bones on the inside

Yet Jesus loved them with the Father's love. In his parable of the prodigal son Jesus showed the religious leaders who sneered at Him that the Father loves them too, just as He loves the tax collectors and "sinners." But they, like Elder, missed His love because they refused to see themselves as being equated with the sinful Prodigals of the world. Now it's only by receiving the Prodigals they despise—listening to their message and learning from their lives—that the Elders among us can be saved.

People like Elder are hard to reach. They are proud and stubborn. And even though they are quick to preach at others they don't like to be preached at themselves. Thus, the best witness to them is one that is modeled in loving relationship over time. Then as your relationship develops, look for opportunities to share pieces of your own story of encountering God's love. "And be prepared to give the reason for the hope that you have. But do this with gentleness and respect."[8]

The other problem with ministering to people like Elder is that they are dangerous. They are often powerful people who can be critical, judgmental, controlling, and vengeful. Thus it's important that when you're with people like this you be able to protect yourself with appropriate boundaries. Clearly it's a scary thing to try to present the Father's love to people like Elder. Nonetheless, once we've taken Prodigal's journey home to the Father, when we've received His love into our hearts, when we've put our faith in His sacrifice, then we must go to the Elders of the world. His love compels us.

So Jesus says to us, "My command is this: Love each other as I have loved you. Greater love has no one than this, that one lay down his life for his friends."[9] This is what Prodigal did. He and Mayor Joshua went to Elder to share the love of the Father with him. They risked their lives to try to save Elder's soul. They met the challenge of looking for ways to share the Father's grace with someone who didn't think he needed it. Their mission needed much care.

And so does ours.

Footsteps of Faith

1. Do you know anyone like Elder? (Perhaps you see some of him in the mirror!) This week ask God to put an Elder in your life on your heart.

2. Sometime this week meditate on Jesus' famous prayer for unity in John 17:20–26. Notice the progression of unity. The Father is in Jesus. Jesus is in the Father. Jesus is in us. We are to be in each other. We are to be in the world of those who are lost.

3. Seek to make Jesus' prayer for unity true in your life. Pray that the Father would be present in you and in your relationships in this way and that He would help you to reach an Elder who is lost with the message of Father's love.

WEEK 51
Back to Antioch

It was in Antioch that Father's prayers found Prodigal. There in the pigsty of his master Demetrius Prodigal began his return to the Father. Now that Prodigal had found the salvation he needed, he wanted to share the good news with everyone he knew. Demetrius, Alex, and the other citizens of Antioch needed Father's love too. From Antioch, Father's followers would try to reach the entire Roman Empire and beyond with Father's love.

So Phillip, Rabbi Benjamin, Timothy, and Sarah and her two friends went to spread the good news of Father's forgiveness to Antioch. Meanwhile Prodigal and Joshua would try to reach Elder with the message of grace. If they were successful in their mission, then they would catch up with Phillip and the others later.

This mission to Antioch was no small challenge. Antioch was the third greatest city in the world next to Rome and Alexandria. And as we saw earlier in our story it was a city of vast wickedness. One would think it to be the last place to receive openly the message of love and righteousness.

Furthermore going to Antioch was not a small sacrifice for those who went. Timothy especially had to count the cost. He left behind him a broken-hearted family and a profitable business. Leaving Nain was a risky proposition for Phillip too. Even with his legal papers granting him freedom, Phillip was just a common servant. It would have been safer and easier for him to return to his old life of serving in Father's house and fields. That way he knew his needs would be provided for. But Phillip had to wonder whether he could survive outside his master's house.

The others made sacrifices too. Rabbi Benjamin had to walk away from his prominent position as the priest of Nain and leave his family behind. Sarah and her two friends left their other friends (who thought they were crazy for believing in Father and devoting their lives to this mission). For all, their commitment was a sign of how much their lives had changed by encountering Father's love. Most villagers, in fact, were not willing to leave their daily lives and offer Father's grace to others far away.

When Jesus sent His disciples to "go and make disciples of all nations" they had to make great sacrifices. They left their homes, families, businesses, and communities to follow Him. Jesus promised them that by forsaking all and following Him they would receive a hundred times as much, as well as eternal life.[10]

One of the first places the disciples went was to Antioch. In fact it was in Antioch that the disciples were first called _Christians_.[11] This title probably began as a jesting nickname, referring to the followers of Christ scornfully as "those Christ-folk." It was from Antioch that Paul set out on his missionary journeys, spreading the good news of Christ's death and resurrection throughout the Roman Empire.

As believers in Christ we too are to respond to Jesus' Great Commission to "go and make disciples in all nations." What does this mean? How do we carry out the Great Commission? The most obvious example is to become a missionary in a foreign country. But there are countless other places and ways to heed Jesus' exhortation.

From refurbishing a house for a poor family in an inner city slum to visiting a sick man in a suburban hospital, we can bring the message of God's love through our actions, coupled with declaring God's provision of forgiveness through Jesus. We can declare the gospel in many other ways. From passing out the gospel of John to people in a park to going to live and minister in a third world country. From visiting an orphan to visiting a murderer in prison. From teaching Sunday school children to talking with the elderly in a retirement home. From counseling the fatherless to counseling fathers.

Whatever we do and wherever we go, the idea is that we be ambassadors of the Father's love.[12]

In ministry, our motive while serving is much more important than our specific action or place of service. There are three main kinds of givers: cheerful givers, obligated givers, and compulsive givers.[13]

The way to be a cheerful giver is to share with others from the abundance of God's grace to us (which often comes through people in the body of Christ).[14] This means that we share comfort with those who are in need by sharing the overflow of the comfort we ourselves have personally received.[15] Cheerful givers give freely because they want to and they have something to give.

In contrast, obligated givers help others because they believe they "should." They become enslaved by their sense of duty and commitment. People with this motive feel guilty if they don't meet the other person's needs. So they give and give to avoid the guilt and in order to feel significant. They need to discover their freedom of choice to do what they want and learn when to say yes and when to say no to some commitments. Also they need to feel valued apart from what they do for others, so that they can be motivated by love (because they want to) instead of compulsion (because they must).

Compulsive givers are no more cheerful than obligated givers. They try to fill up others' love tanks when their own tank is on empty. They become enslaved by their sensitivity to the needs and problems of others. People who give to others what they wish they had received themselves are projecting their own needs onto those they're trying to help. They become oversensitive to the needs of others and comparatively insensitive to their own needs. They need to focus more appropriately on their own needs so that they do not give from an empty tank; in short, they must learn when to say yes and when to say no to the needs of others.

Both obligated and compulsive givers are prone to resentment unless they address their hidden motives, and they're prone to burn out unless they address their unmet needs. To become cheerful givers they must let go of expectations that their giving be appreciated or returned and they must learn how to get their own needs met.

Ministry is always a sacrifice, but it can be very rewarding if like Prodigal and his friends you have the attitude of a cheerful giver.

Footsteps of Faith

1. Have you gone back to your Antioch? (Your Antioch is wherever you were when the Father's seeking love drew you to himself.) Have you gone back to help others who are seeking help with the kinds of struggles you've been helped through?[16] When you're ready, look for the opportunity to help someone as you've been helped and you'll find it very fulfilling.

2. What kind of a giver are you most like? Ask a friend who knows you to explain what kind of giver he or she thinks you are.

☐ Cheerful giver
☐ Obligated giver
☐ Compulsive giver

3. Depending upon what kind of givers your parents and others you've relied upon were and what kind of a giver you are, it may not feel good for you to receive help. Perhaps you feel some of the following things. Try to sort out where

these feelings are coming from. Check any of the following that apply.

- ☐ It seems I'm a burden to the helper.
- ☐ I feel obligated to do something good in return.
- ☐ I try to show my appreciation, but I can't show enough.
- ☐ I don't feel deserving of the attention I receive.
- ☐ I feel like I "made" the other person do too much for me.
- ☐ I feel like the help is more for the helper than it is for me.
- ☐ Help comes with expectations that I improve.
- ☐ It's embarrassing to even need help.
- ☐ It's scary to need help because it may not last.
- ☐ My relationship with the helper is so up and down that it's confusing.

4. Pray that God could enable you to become a cheerful giver who overflows with the Father's love to those in need.

Hold onto Your Rock

Before Prodigal parted company with those who were going up to Antioch, he gave them a gift. This was an important gift. They couldn't make it on their journey without it. It was something they needed to hold onto and never lose or they would lose heart when times became difficult.

Everyone was surprised by the object Prodigal gave them. He pulled his purple pouch out of his robe, untied it, and pulled out the smooth, sparkling, skipping stone that Father had given him. He explained to the others the happy memories of how Father and he used to skip stones on the lake near home. He told them that Father had slipped this stone in his pouch before he left home seven months ago, and that he found this stone when he ran out of gold in Antioch. It was by looking at this stone and considering the memories of Father's love it rekindled that Prodigal found the faith to return home.

Then Prodigal gave a rock to each of his friends, just as Father had given to him. The rocks came from underneath the sycamore tree at home. The same tree where Prodigal sat to plot his rebellion and where Elder stood when he struck Father now became the tree where Prodigal and Father's followers would receive their commission to declare Father's grace to others. Their rocks would remind them of Father's love when they felt alone and give courage when they were afraid. When in doubt, they would look to the rocks and be strengthened in faith.

After Jesus rose from the dead and right before He ascended back into heaven to sit at the right hand of the Father He gave each of His disciples a spiritual rock—the Holy Spirit. The Spirit gave the power to live the Christian life and to minister to others. It was a reminder of all that Jesus gave to

357

them. It was a deposit guaranteeing the inheritance Jesus promised them in heaven.[17]

For the first disciples, the rock was a breath of air. Jesus breathed on His disciples, and the Spirit of the Father was imparted in them, and they were empowered to go forward in their faith and to share that faith with others.[18]

I pray that you've breathed in the Spirit of the Father in this journey we've taken together. If you have any doubts, then find yourself a rock. Hold your rock as you prayerfully meditate on Jesus' beloved parable. Hold your rock when you're with those who love you. Then you'll grow in your sense that the Spirit of the Father is with you.

 *Footsteps of Faith*

1. Peter, one of the first disciples, got hold of a rock of faith when he confirmed that Jesus was the Son of God and the Savior of the world. It's upon that rock, that confession, that the church is being built.[19] Have you grasped that rock? If you have, you received the Holy Spirit.[20] Let Him empower you to share God's love[21] with the Elders of the world who still need to return to the Father.

2. Take a moment of prayer now. Get alone in a quiet place, get comfortable, and then breathe. Deeply and slowly exhale your worries and troubles. Trust the Spirit of the Father and His Son, Jesus Christ. It's in the Spirit of God that we live, move, and have our being.[22] Keep in step with Him as you continue your life's journey, and it will be well with your soul.

Notes

1. Numbers 21:6–9.
2. John 3:14–16.
3. John 14:6.
4. John 14:8.
5. John 14:9.
6. I'm referring to my dramatic interpretation of Jesus' parable at this point. Remember, Jesus didn't finish His story. We don't know for sure how Elder responded to Father's last words. And we don't know for sure what Prodigal did at this point either. But we do know that just a few weeks after telling this parable Jesus went to the cross. And after He rose from the dead He gave us the Great Commission to reach the other Prodigals and Elders of the world.
7. Matthew 23.
8. 1 Peter 3:15.
9. John 15:12–13.
10. Matthew 19:29.
11. Acts 11:26.
12. 2 Corinthians 5:20.
13. 2 Corinthians 9:7.
14. 2 Corinthians 9:8.
15. 2 Corinthians 1:3–5.
16. Those familiar with twelve step recovery programs will recognize this principle as step 12: "Having had a spiritual awakening as the result of these steps, we tried to carry this message to others, and to practice these principles in all our affairs."
17. 2 Corinthians 5:5.
18. John 20:22.
19. Matthew 16:16–18.
20. 1 Corinthians 12:13; Ephesians 1:13–14.
21. Romans 5:5.
22. Acts 17:28.

Afterword

Closing the Curtain

As we close the curtain to this moving story of a father's love and a son's repentance and restoration, I invite you to look back on the journey. Truly this is a healing journey we've taken together. Read again the Father's gifts of grace to Prodigal and to us (p. 10). Consider Prodigal's steps of faith that show us the way to return to the heavenly Father and to receive His love in our own lives. Where are you in the journey?

Take a moment to meditate on the following poem I wrote to summarize the prodigal son's journey of healing. "A Prodigal's Journey" (next page) reminds us of our need for the Father's love for lasting wholeness in our own lives.

A Prodigal's Journey

"I want to do it my way!" Prodigal demanded of Father one day;
He took one-third of Father's estate and he ran far away.

Fame, fortune, fun were his but fled in famine;
Once a nobleman, now suddenly a humbled beggar feeding swine.

But thank God that dirty, smelly pigsties open eyes!
The sinner saw himself as low and his God as Most High.

He faced his nightmares and crossed the desert toward home
And what did he find but Father running out to greet him!

Father reached his son before the hostile village mob did.
Prodigal looked deep into Father's eyes of compassion and cried.

In front of all he stood and offered his confession of guilt,
But not the one he rehearsed because he couldn't repay his debt.

The villagers hurled insults, threw fists, and kicked feet;
But Father took it all upon himself and embraced his son sweet.

Father gave his own righteous robe to cover his son's shame.
Then Prodigal said no to sin and held his boundaries firm.

Father gave his son his signet ring and thus the rest of the estate.
With a second chance to be a good steward Prodigal could hardly wait.

Father gave his barefoot son new sandals to wear;
They welcomed him home as an adult and were full of Father's care.

Father got out the fattened calf and threw a party in Prodigal's honor.
Everyone in the village sang and danced at the feast except Elder.

When Elder finished working he heard the party and became enraged.
In humble love Father entreated his son but a horrible war was waged.

Like Father, Prodigal and the rest of the village forgave Elder's sin
And devoted their lives to spread the good news of God's love to all men.

Appendix 1

Blessings and Curses From a Father

Blessings	Curses
1. Respects your free choice	Controls you Doesn't care what you do
2. Patient with you Rescues you from personal responsibility	Gives up on you
3. Seeks to love you	Smothers you Neglects you
4. Has compassion for you	Harsh or abusive with you Insensitive to you
5. Forgives your sins	Perfectionistic with you Overlooks your sin

6. Expresses appropriate affection for you

Gives you inappropriate affection
Unaffectionate with you

7. Teaches you right boundaries

Overprotective / too strict
Underprotective / too loose

8. Encourages you

Pressures you to achieve
Discourages you

9. Accepts you as an adult

Pushes you into adulthood
Rejects your emerging adultness

10. Celebrates you

Views you idealistically
Views you pessimistically

11. Teaches you to forgive

Forces you to forgive prematurely
Teaches you to resent

12. Affirms your life purpose

Projects his purpose onto you
Disconfirms your life purpose

Appendix 2

Prodigal and Elder Contrasted

Prodigal in the Far Country	Prodigal in Father's House	Elder in the Fields
1. Ashamed	Humble	Proud
2. Identity in pleasure ("Give me, Father!")	Identity in Father ("I love you, Father")	Identity in work ("Punish them, Father!")
3. Trust in own money	Trust in father	Trust in own abilities
4. Self-debasing	Self-examining	Self-aggrandizing
5. Indulges in sin	Confesses sin	Hiding sin
6. Physical distance from Father	Reconciles with Father	Emotional distance from Father
7. No boundaries; Disregard for law	Right boundaries; Guided by the law	Rigid boundaries; Legalistic/ perfectionistic

8. No accountability	Accountable	Overly accountable
9. Impulsive	Responsible	Compulsive
10. Moody	Celebrates Father's love	Depressed/ repressed rage
11. Envious	Forgiving	Arrogant
12. Purpose to please self	Purpose to share love	Purpose to achieve